Immigrants and Politics

Immigrants and Politics

The Germans of Nebraska, 1880–1900

by

FREDERICK C. LUEBKE

UNIVERSITY OF NEBRASKA PRESS · LINCOLN

Publishers on the Plains

UNP

Manufactured in the United States of America

To the memory of
my father
who lived youthful years
on the plains of Nebraska in the 1890's

Preface

IN THE LATTER PART of the nineteenth century the United States was the beneficiary of the largest mass movement of peoples in the history of the world. Millions of Europeans crossed the Atlantic, hoping to find new homes in the Promised Land of America. This massive transfusion inevitably transformed the United States, just as each immigrant was individually changed by the experience of leaving his native ground and adjusting to life in a strange and sometimes hostile environment.

This study examines a very small part of the mass migration, the Germans who found their way to Nebraska, for a short span of years, the two decades from 1880 to 1900. This group is studied in terms of one aspect of the assimilation process, participation in the political life of their adopted land.

As the research for this project progressed, it became apparent that a study of the role of German immigrants in American politics would involve the use of statistics on a large scale if the pitfalls of filiopietism were to be avoided. It was one thing to discover and delineate the attitudes of Nebraska's Germans toward the political issues of the day; it was quite another to identify actual group voting patterns. Statistics and more statistics had to be accumulated, compared, and interpreted in meaningful ways. Moreover, it became clear that the political attitudes and electoral decisions of immigrants could best be understood in the light shed by sociological research into the process of assimilation and by analyses of modern political behavior. As this study became more interdisciplinary in nature, my intellectual debts to others were correspondingly enlarged.

I must, therefore, express my indebtedness and gratitude to former colleagues at Concordia College—Professor Vance H. Hinrichs in statistics and Professor Harold Kupke in sociology—for their willing assistance in clarifying concepts and improving methods employed in this study. I am also obligated to Professor Samuel P. Hays of the University of Pittsburgh and Professor David F. Trask of the State University of New York at Stony Brook who generously offered valuable suggestions. Special thanks are due Professor James C. Olson, formerly of the University of Nebraska, now

Chancellor of the University of Missouri at Kansas City, whose patient counsel contributed greatly to whatever excellence this study may possess. None of these scholars, of course, bears any responsibility for what appears here.

Invaluable assistance in the preparation of maps was afforded by Professor L. Carl Brandhorst of the Oregon College of Education at Monmouth. Dr. Marvin F. Kivett and the staff of the Nebraska State Historical Society extended many courtesies to me, and I have profited much from a careful reading given the manuscript by Professor Robert D. Fiala, whose sharp criticisms were always tempered by good humor and keen wit.

An expression of gratitude is also due the Danforth Foundation, whose financial aid in the form of a Teacher Grant made most of the research and writing possible. Supplemental research was supported in part by the National Endowment for the Humanities with a summer stipend. Finally, I acknowledge my indebtedness to my wife, Norma Wukasch Luebke, for her help in the tabulation of much of the data and for her efforts to remove infelicities of style, but especially for her patience and understanding.

University of Nebraska   F. C. L.

Contents

A section of illustrations follows p. 150.

Immigrants and Politics

CHAPTER I

Introduction

DR. GEORGE L. MILLER, a prominent leader of the Democratic party in Nebraska and editor of the Omaha *Herald*, wrote in 1882 that "as a rule and probably by force of old habit the great majority of German citizens still follow the fortunes" of the Republican party.[1] His comment was a restatement of a commonly held idea about ethnic politics in America. The affinity of German-born citizens for the party of Abraham Lincoln has frequently been noted ever since those troubled days of the 1850's when Republicanism emerged from the wreckage of the Whig party. Both major parties believed in the existence of such an affinity, and Republican Presidents, especially Lincoln, used their appointive powers to meet their supposed obligations to the Germans.[2] The editors of German-language newspapers, always anxious to place their ethnic group on the side of equality, justice, and reform, customarily asserted that the Germans were solidly aligned with Lincoln's principles. They saw the Great Emancipator as a bulwark in the Republican party against the xenophobia of Know-Nothingism.[3]

This identification of the German ethnic vote with the Republican party was by no means restricted to nineteenth-century opinion. It has been a standard observation of historians and political scientists to the present day.[4]

[1] Omaha *Herald* (weekly edition), August 11, 1882.

[2] Carl Wittke, *The German-Language Press in America* (Lexington: University of Kentucky Press, 1957), p. 147.

[3] See, e.g., *Nebraska Staats Anzeiger* (Lincoln, Nebr.), October 11, 1900; *Nebraska Volksblatt* (West Point, Nebr.), February 13, 1885, February 20, 1885.

[4] See Albert B. Faust's filiopietistic but still valuable *The German Element in the United States* (2 vols.; Boston: Houghton Mifflin Co., 1909), II, 130 f. Faust based his impressions upon the activities of Forty-Eighters like Carl Schurz, Gustav Körner, and others. These cultural nationalists were indeed properly identified with the Republican party. Faust, however, fell into the trap of relying primarily upon evidence from the elite. He and many after him have tended to overrate the influence of the Forty-Eighters on the rank-and-file German immigrants. Among more recent writers who make this sweeping identification of the German voters with the Republican Party is Joseph Roucek, who coupled the Germans with the Scandinavians under the Republican banner. See his "National Minorities in Domestic Politics" in Francis J. Brown and Joseph S. Roucek (eds.), *One America:*

Yet it is probably true that for no sustained period did the majority of citizens of German origin lean more heavily toward the Republican party than did the native American population in whose midst they lived. In fact, considerable evidence exists to suggest that the opposite was the case.

Much research on the political behavior of nineteenth-century Germans in America has centered upon the election of 1860. Perhaps the most significant study was made by Andreas Dorpalen,[5] who intensively analyzed the election records of the states of the Northwest, where the German vote was allegedly decisive. Although he did not examine voting statistics on the precinct level, Dorpalen was able to conclude that Lincoln's victory could not be attributed to the Germans. More important, perhaps, was his effort to demonstrate that, in general, Germans in America tended to be unusually susceptible to environmental pressure and that they voted for Lincoln in 1860 in no greater proportion than did their American-born neighbors. Dorpalen thus suggested that the Germans had no homogeneous voting patterns as a group and that they tended to conform to those of the particular region or community in which they happened to live.[6]

Dorpalen's contribution to the theory and methods of research in ethnic voting behavior is valuable, but probably for reasons other than those intended. While it is true that immigrant voters tended to respond to group pressures and to conform to the prevailing voting patterns of the community, it is also true that the Germans, as well as other immigrant groups, developed voting habits of their own. Dorpalen stresses the former fact at the expense of

---

The History, Contributions, and Present Problems of Racial and National Minorities (New York: Prentice-Hall, 1945), pp. 403, 409. Lawrence Fuchs asserts that the Germans of the Midwest have been one of the most important ethnic groups in the Republican party for one hundred years ("Some Political Aspects of Immigration," *Law and Contemporary Problems*, XXI [Spring, 1956], 272). Clinton Rossiter goes so far as to say that the Germans were to the Republicans what the Irish were to the Democrats (*Parties and Politics in America* [Ithaca: Cornell University Press, 1960], p. 58). Perhaps the most balanced brief account is to be found in John A. Hawgood, *The Tragedy of German-America : The Germans in the United States of America During the Nineteenth Century—and After* (New York: G. P. Putnam's Sons, 1940), pp. 45–50.

[5] Andreas Dorpalen, "The German Element and the Issues of the Civil War," *Mississippi Valley Historical Review*, XXIX (June, 1942), 55–76. Other pertinent studies on this subject include Joseph Schafer, "Who Elected Lincoln?" *American Historical Review*, XLVII (October, 1941), 51–63; George H. Daniels, "Immigrant Vote in the 1860 Election: The Case of Iowa," *Mid-America*, XLIV (July, 1962), 146–162; Paul J. Kleppner, "Lincoln and the Immigrant Vote: A Case of Religious Polarization," *Mid-America*, XLVIII (July, 1966), 176–195.

[6] This point of view has since been strengthened by studies of political scientists and sociologists which reveal the strength of group pressures, especially those of the family, in respect to the persistence of traditional voting patterns. See, e.g., Angus Campbell *et al.*, *The American Voter* (New York: John Wiley and Sons, 1960).

the latter. The response of the individual voter to environmental pressures was by no means always positive, as implied by Dorpalen; just as often the voter responded negatively. His political behavior varied with the psychology of the individual, with the cultural baggage he brought with him to America, and with the salience of the issues involved in a given voting decision. In short, the context of human relationships must be examined if ethnic political behavior is to be understood.

Perhaps the most outspoken advocate of a social orientation in the study of political history is Samuel P. Hays, who has leveled attacks on what has been called the "presidential synthesis" of American history. This view, which has been the prevailing one, has concerned itself primarily with affairs on the national level and has tended to draw heavily upon formal, institutional sources, such as laws and reports, speeches, and press releases. Its guiding spirit, Hays has observed, is the liberal's preoccupation with progress and reform and with the political and economic struggle between "the people" and the business community. The public is understood to be not so much a conglomerate of social and economic groups with divergent goals and interests but a mass, undifferentiated and equalitarian. Progress, according to this view, results from the elimination of group conflict rather than from the victory of one group over another. Conflict is seen as transitory and a prelude to eventual harmony.[7]

Professor Hays has pointed out further that when the assumptions of "presidential" history are ignored and attention is directed to the grass roots and to the network of human relationships on that level, an entirely different conception of party conflict is revealed.[8] People were concerned about the use of foreign languages, governmental control of ethnic religious schools, Sabbatarianism, and, above all, "sumptuary legislation," a term which usually meant the prohibition of alcoholic beverages. National issues such as the tariff, free trade, civil service, government regulation of big business, and the monetary debates were meaningless abstractions to many voters, especially among the immigrants, who understood them imperfectly at best. Social and cultural issues were the topics that filled the pages of the local newspapers and provided subjects for conversation in town on Saturday nights. These were matters that could weaken or strengthen party loyalties or persuade the undecided. With many voters, membership in a particular ethnic or religious group was the decisive factor in party identification.

[7] Samuel P. Hays, "The Social Analysis of American Political History, 1880–1920," *Political Science Quarterly*, LXXX (September, 1965), 373–394. See also Thomas C. Cochrane, "The 'Presidential Synthesis' in American History," *American Historical Review*, LIII (July, 1948), 748–759.

[8] Samuel P. Hays, "History as Human Behavior," *Iowa Journal of History*, LVIII (July, 1960), 196.

To the native American, the ethnopolitical pattern seemed almost incomprehensible. Most Catholics and German Lutherans, bitter opponents in religious matters, agreed that government regulation of their schools had to be vigorously opposed; on the other hand, Scandinavian Lutherans, especially the Swedes, considered the matter to be relatively unimportant. German and Norwegian Lutherans could stand as one in their opposition to woman suffrage, but on the subject of prohibition they generally parted company. Prohibition was an issue that cut across both ethnic and religious lines. It was capable of ranging Bohemian Catholics and German Catholics with German Lutherans against Norwegian Lutherans and German Methodists. The question of the continued operation of the local saloon was able to arouse passions as few other issues could, while the argument over a protective tariff as opposed to a revenue tariff was a pale affair.

The social analysis of history does not, of course, mean that economic matters were absent from political debate on the local level. It means instead that political behavior was more closely connected to the question, for example, of extravagance in the administration of county government, or whether the county should issue bonds for the construction of a railroad, than it was with the issues which are emphasized in typical "presidential syntheses."

The key to the social analysis of history is the examination of sources on the local level. This involves a broadened view of what politics is. Political leadership and participation, if they are based upon cultural and religious elements, necessarily involve more than party leadership or public administration. Educational, religious, and economic leadership in the formation of group norms and attitudes also play an integral role in the decision-making process. Local personages become important, not for what they were or what they did, but for the way in which they may have typified human relationships within the sociopolitical context. Local and county histories and biographies, however deficient they may be in terms of technical standards, sometimes offer insights into the fabric of human affairs that are unobtainable elsewhere. And just as local, small-town newspapers are likely to reveal more valuable data than the big-city dailies, so voting records on the precinct level must be analyzed in preference to those of larger political divisions.

The systematic use of voting data by historians is a relatively recent development.[9] Lee Benson remains the major contributor to the theory and methodology of voting behavior within the context of American history. In a

[9] See the discussion of this topic in William Aydelotte, "Quantification in History," *American Historical Review*, LXXI (April, 1966), 803–825.

monograph entitled "Research Problems in American History,"[10] Benson analyzes the methods historians must use in the study of election statistics. His special emphasis is on the need for interpretation to rest upon detailed comparisons with related data in terms of space, time, and rate of change. While impressionistic evidence has its place and is indispensable for the explanation of phenomena in voting behavior, the systematic use of quantitative data produces factual information on which universal agreement can be achieved. It permits the historian to establish clearly what in fact happened, and it requires him to identify and to express logically hypotheses that are potentially verifiable on the basis of available statistics. In terms of the space dimension, generalizations must be appropriate for the spatial unit under study. The political behavior of German immigrants in Nebraska cannot serve as the sole basis for a hypothesis about German political activity across the nation. In the event it is impossible or impractical to include in the analysis data from all units within a given category, representative samplings from all spatial subdivisions must be used.

In terms of the time dimension, Benson has stressed the systematic use of data from elections both before and after the one under consideration. Data cannot be used without adequate reference to other elections over time. The information must be gathered, organized, and interpreted in a way that permits meaningful comparison. To illustrate, the percentage of Democratic votes cast in Sherman township, Platte County, Nebraska, varied from 52 per cent in 1888 to 89 per cent in 1890 and 47 per cent in 1892; clearly the time dimension reveals that the election of 1890 involved some issue or some circumstance which had extraordinary importance for the voters of Sherman township.

Group voting patterns likewise should not be considered in isolation without comparison to other appropriate economic, ethnic, or religious groups. Platte County, for example, was almost evenly divided between the two major parties in 1880; but what is more important is the fact that the predominantly German Catholic St. Bernard township cast 88 per cent of its votes for the Democratic candidate for President, while the native-American Monroe township, located several miles south, gave 92 per cent of its votes to the Republican candidate.

In his *Concept of Jacksonian Democracy*, Benson has concentrated upon the development of theory for the study of American voting behavior. He offers a classification system for the determinants of voting behavior which is designed to help the historian avoid any one of a variety of monistic interpretations. While extended commentary is not necessary here, it is appropriate

[10] In Mirra Komarovsky (ed.), *Common Frontiers of the Social Sciences* (Glencoe: The Free Press, 1957), pp. 113–183.

to point out that Benson, like Hays, stresses the importance of negative and positive orientation to groups and persons. He also outlines the significance of individual and group fulfillment of political roles, thereby contributing much to the understanding of the persistence of voting patterns long after the political conflict, originally based upon issues, has been resolved or has disappeared.[11]

By drawing upon the concepts, methods, and conclusions of Hays, Benson, and other students of political behavior, this study traces the pattern of politics among the Germans of Nebraska during the two decades from 1880 to 1900. As a background to the political analysis, the history of German immigration into Nebraska is reviewed. Attention is given to the numbers and proportions of the German element, to areas in the state where the German population tended to concentrate, to motivations and methods of immigration to Nebraska, and to the social characteristics of the group as a whole. Since the political behavior of an immigrant group is one phase of the larger process of assimilation into American society, some aspects of the socio-cultural setting are presented. The variables which may influence rates of assimilation and group responses to the stresses of acculturation are examined. This analysis serves as a basis for understanding the relationships of place of birth, occupation, residence, and church and social memberships to political party identification and to political activity. Group patterns of political behavior as contrasted to those of the total voting population are analyzed for successive elections through the use of correlations between census data and precinct election records. The final portion of the study is devoted to the part which the German element played in Nebraska state politics from 1880 to 1900. Extensive use is made of aggregate methods in the study of voting data. For this portion of the study, impressionistic evidence is drawn primarily from local German- and English-language newspapers.

One of the first problems to be met in any study involving German immigrants in America is that of defining what is meant by *German*. For the United States Bureau of the Census the problem was simply and strictly a matter of birth within the political boundaries of what was the German Empire at the time the census was taken. This solution, probably the only sensible one, has created many problems in the use of published census data. How was the Alsatian or the Holsteiner of 1880 to answer the census taker's question regarding place of birth? Unless the problem was clarified for him, the Alsatian German would normally indicate French nativity, since Alsace was French at the time of his birth. In the census of 1880 (as well as in

11 Lee Benson, *The Concept of Jacksonian Democracy : New York as a Test Case* (Princeton: Princeton University Press, 1961), pp. 278–281.

others) an attempt was made to record the state within the German Empire in which the immigrant had been born. The fact that nearly one-third of the German-born in Nebraska failed to specify the state indicates the futility of that effort.[12] The attempt was confounded by the expanding boundaries of the Prussian state before German unification, by the ignorance or lack of cooperation on the part of the census taker, and by the language barrier which sometimes hindered his work.

A further problem arises from the continued existence of German states outside the Hohenzollern empire. Austria, Switzerland, and Luxemburg sent many German immigrants to America. A study made in connection with the census of 1920 revealed that in the United States as a whole, 86 per cent of the Luxemburgers, 82 per cent of the Swiss, and 35 per cent of the Austrians gave German as their mother tongue.[13] According to Bureau of the Census categories these people were not included in the German totals. Yet impressionistic evidence indicates that in Nebraska they normally identified with the German element. They thought of themselves as Swiss or Austrians in much the same way as other Germans thought of themselves as Hanoverians, Saxons, or Hessians. It can be argued, of course, that they brought to America a cultural heritage which differed in several important respects from that of Germans from Germany proper. Yet the Swiss German probably had as much in common with the Württemberger as the Württemberger had with the Holsteiner, if not more; a Luxemburger German shared more, culturally, with a Rhinelander than the Rhinelander shared with a Pomeranian, even though both of the latter were technically Prussians.

Another complication results from the existence of minority ethnic groups within the various European states. Colonies of Germans were not uncommon in Hungary, Rumania, and especially Russia. A few groups wandered as far afield as the Transcaucasian and Siberian provinces of the Russian Empire and even into Iran.[14] Such minorities tended to emigrate much more readily than the dominant ethnic or racial population.[15] In some cases large numbers of these Germans came to the United States. Were they Germans? According to the Bureau of the Census they were not. But when immediate human relationships are taken into account, as they must be in a study of this kind, there can be no doubt about their German-ness. Their years of isolated minority group status, often coupled with a surprising

[12] U.S. Census Office, *Tenth Census of the United States: 1880. Population*, I, 493.

[13] U.S. Bureau of the Census, *Immigrants and Their Children. 1920*, prepared by Niles Carpenter (Washington: Government Printing Office, 1927), p. 341.

[14] Richard Sallet, "Russlanddeutsche Siedlungen in den Vereinigten Staaten von Amerika," *Jahrbuch der Deutsch-Amerikanischen Historischen Gesellschaft von Illinois*, XXXI (1931), 7.

[15] U.S. Bureau of the Census, *Immigrants and Their Children*, p. 341.

measure of political autonomy, made them more conscious of their German cultural heritage than many of their brethren who had emigrated directly from Germany. Despite the fact that Volga Germans had lived in Russia for nearly a century, almost none of them had learned to speak the Russian language. The census statistics of 1920 demonstrate that 14 per cent of the French-born immigrants in the United States indicated German as their mother tongue. The same was true of 19 per cent of the Hungarians and 8 per cent of the Rumanians.[16] While only 8 per cent of the Russians were German-speaking, almost all Russian-born immigrants in Nebraska came from German colonies on the Volga. Smaller numbers came from the Black Sea area.[17]

Emigration from German colonies in other countries was partially compensated for in published census returns by Poles, Jews, Danes, and others who had been subjects of the German Empire before they arrived in America. According to the classification system used by the Bureau of the Census they were counted as Germans. It is unlikely, however, that their total ever approached the number of Germans that were omitted.

When county voting records are studied in relation to proportions of foreign-born inhabitants, one has little choice but to accept the inadequate categories of the Bureau of the Census. For precinct analyses, however, it is possible to base all correlations between voting and census data on totals obtained by direct examination of census manuscripts. This procedure introduces a new set of problems, many of which are the consequence of ineptitude or laziness on the part of the census takers who often omitted information or recorded obviously inaccurate data. The basic challenge for the present study, however, was to decide which Swiss, Austrians, Alsatians, Russians, and Schleswig-Holsteiners were actually Germans. Their names, of course, provided the basic clue. In the great majority of cases no difficulty was encountered.[18] Some German immigrants had translated their names into English equivalents, for example, Schmidt had become Smith,

16 *Ibid.*

17 William H. Werkmeister, "Deutsche Zeitungen in Nebraska" (MS, Werkmeister Collection, Nebraska State Historical Society, Lincoln, Nebr.), p. 12. In an examination of about 125,000 individual names recorded on the census manuscripts of the Nebraska state census of 1885, almost no names were found of persons born in Russia who bore Russian names. Nearly all were German. (*Schedules of theNebraska State Census of 1885* [Washington: National Archives Microfilm Publications, 1961].)

18 August de Belmont Hollingshead, the noted sociologist, was confronted with a similar problem in his study of three Nebraska counties. He classified names on the basis of deed record indices, a source which provides fewer clues than census manuscripts. He conducted a random sample field check which revealed an error of 7.9 per cent. See his "Changes in Land Ownership as an Index of Succession in Rural Communities," *American Journal of Sociology*, XLIII (March, 1938), 768. Merle Curti and his associates, in their exhaustive

Wilhelm Williams, Jaeger Hunter, Schneider Taylor, and Nachtigal had become Nightingale. Others had anglicized the spelling of their names from, for example, Mueller to Miller, Seidel to Sidles, Reiss to Rice. Such names were included in the tabulations of German stock. The line was drawn in cases like that of Alexander Stewart, a farmer of Washington County. His mother was listed as a native of Ireland and his father as German born. Either the gentleman was illegitimate and bore his mother's name or the census taker had been careless in recording the father's place of birth. In either case he would have had very little in common with the Germans.

The use of a few other terms needs to be clarified. *Ethnic group* is ordinarily used to refer loosely to any collectivity based upon race, religion, or national origin. *Ethnic stock* is a technical term. It refers to all first- and second-generation members of a given national origin. Its use is most common in connection with census tabulations and other statistics. Thus, *German stock* includes all German-born plus American-born persons who had one or both parents born in Europe. It excludes third- and fourth-generation descendants of immigrants who may have assimilated very slowly, people who would be included in the broader terms *German ethnic group* or *German element*.

German-American is a term that is somewhat more hazardous to use. Late-nineteenth-century usage ordinarily implied nothing more than the collectivity of German immigrants and their children who had become Americans. In its usual sense it implied American citizenship, although this was not always the case. Its usage in Nebraska increased noticeably toward the end of the century. However, many writers in the twentieth century, particularly since World War I, have used it in the sense of American citizens of German origin who were aggressive exponents of their cultural heritage and who wished to preserve and promulgate it actively. If the term is used in this ethnocentric sense in connection with political behavior, it must refer to citizens of German ethnicity who were politically aware of themselves as Germans and as immigrants, rather than as Germans who in the normal flow of events happened to have become American citizens and who were essentially no different from millions of other new Americans. The use of *German-American* in this narrow sense connotes immigrant political action as a defense of *das Deutschtum* in a hostile environment. The term was indeed used in this sense in Nebraska politics from 1880 to 1900, but the nature of this study requires the broader, less restrictive sense of the term.

study of Trempealeau County, Wisconsin, also classified persons according to national origin by their names (Merle Curti *et al.*, *The Making of an American Community: A Case Study of Democracy in a Frontier County* [Stanford: Stanford University Press, 1959], p. 58).

The political behavior of the ordinary passive citizen is as important as that of the culturally militant latter-day *Acht-und-vierziger*.

Throughout Nebraska's history the German-born have constituted the largest non-English speaking ethnic group. In 1880, when the population of the state was 452,402, the number of German-born citizens totaled 31,125, about one-third of the total number of foreign-born inhabitants in Nebraska. By 1900 the total population had increased to 1,066,300. Of these, 66,810, or 38 per cent of the foreign-born, were German-born. To these must be added the second-generation Germans born in this country. In 1880 this meant an addition of approximately 32,000 to the total; by 1900 the second-generation Germans numbered nearly 125,000.[19] Moreover, none of these figures include Germans who emigrated from countries other than Germany. A reasonable estimate would assign about one-sixth of the state's total population in 1880 to the German element. By 1900 the proportion had risen to one-fifth.

A variety of conditions determined the selection of the two-decade period from 1880 to 1900 for this study. They involved the frontier of settlement, the character of the German immigrant population, the kinds and the availability of census and voting data, newspaper sources, and sources for biographical studies of individual German immigrants. Cutting across all of these considerations were the requirements of the statistical correlations included in the study.

Before there can be any worthwhile estimate of the impact of an immigrant group upon politics, or any consideration of why the group voted as it did, it is necessary first to discover precincts in which the total number of adult males of German stock was high enough to reveal actual voting patterns. The most reliable method of determining concentrations of German stock is through the use of census materials. Unfortunately, however, the Bureau of the Census does not classify its data on place of birth according to civil divisions smaller than the county. Hence, if census data are to be used in preference to other sources, such as tax lists and deed records (which do not yield generational information), the only recourse is to use census manuscripts and to make one's own tabulations. The most recent census which can be used in this way is the special Nebraska census of 1885. The manuscripts of the census of 1890 have been destroyed by fire, and personal information recorded since the census of 1900 has a confidential status by act of Congress.

Other factors make 1885 a propitious year for the purposes of this study. By that time the advancing frontier of settlement had crossed Nebraska. The population in the rural portions of the eastern, agricultural half of the state,

19 *Nebraska's Population: A Preliminary Report* (n.p.: Nebraska State Planning Board, 1937), pp. 16–18.

where most of the Germans lived, had stabilized. This is a most desirable characteristic for the purposes of statistical correlation, since the more stable the population is over a period of time, the more accurate the findings will be. By 1885 the influx of new settlers had nearly ceased in many eastern counties; almost all of the railroad and public lands had been transferred to private ownership. The population of Seward County, for example, was 15,225 in 1885; in 1900 it remained virtually unchanged at 15,690. The population of Otoe County increased from 19,366 to 22, 288 during the same period, with about half of the 4,000 gain occurring in Nebraska City. While Nebraska's total population continued to shoot up from 740,645 in 1885 to about 1,000,000 five years later, much of this increase took place in the western counties and in the larger cities. Many rural townships experienced very little change during the same years.[20]

If 1885 was favorable in terms of stability of population, it was also propitious in terms of the German emigration. In that year the great wave of emigration that had commenced in the 1870's began to subside. One and a half million Germans had left the *Vaterland* for new homes overseas during those years. Ninety-five per cent of them came to the United States. Rising from a trough in 1877, the emigration mounted to a peak in 1881/1882. By 1885 the totals had dropped rapidly to about 50 per cent of the crest. From then to the end of the century, emigration declined steadily.[21] While Germans continued to stream to America and Nebraska, the ecological pattern was fairly well set by 1885. No more virgin lands were available; hence few new concentrations could have been developed in the eastern part of the state after that date. Instead, new arrivals augmented the existing clusters of German stock. Thus, the margin of error that is built into statistical correlations between census data obtained in 1885 and precinct election returns of later years would be in a favorable direction. That is to say, it is likely that the actual coefficients of correlation, if they were obtainable, would tend to be higher than the ones produced by the available data.

The acquisition of precinct voting data also presents problems in connection with the period under study. Since tabulations of precinct returns by the secretary of state of Nebraska have never been required by state law, all

20 *Ibid.*, pp. 86–92; U.S. Census Office, *Twelfth Census of the United States: 1900. Population*, I, *passim*; *Population, Farms, and Industries of Nebraska from the Census Returns of June 1, 1885* (Lincoln: State Journal, State Printers, 1885); August de Belmont Hollingshead, "Trends in Community Development: A Study of Ecological and Institutional Processes in Thirty-four Southeastern Nebraska Communities, 1854–1934" (unpublished Ph.D. dissertation, University of Nebraska, 1935), p. 20; James C. Olson, *History of Nebraska* (Lincoln: University of Nebraska Press, 1955), pp. 208–212.

21 Mack Walker, *Germany and the Emigration, 1816–1885* (Cambridge: Harvard University Press, 1964), pp. 175–181.

data must be obtained from the county clerks. Even though they are required by law to preserve them,[22] some counties have discarded all election records from the nineteenth century. However, most counties in the eastern part of the state have records for most of the elections from 1880 to 1900.

The local newspapers are the only other possible source for precinct election returns. However, the newspapers sometimes recorded minor numerical errors, and, more important, the editors sometimes neglected to include the votes cast for the candidates of minor parties, presumably on the grounds that they were not important enough to record. Yet their omission can seriously distort the percentages of the total vote won by each of the major parties. Thus, correlation of census data and election returns on a precinct basis before 1880 is likely to involve an undesirable number of newspaper sources of voting data.

German-language newspapers are the best source for impressionistic material relating to the political behavior of the German element. Nebraska had a German-language newspaper as early as 1860, when twenty Germans founded the *Nebraska Zeitungs Gesellschaft* in Nebraska City and published a weekly under the editorship of Dr. Frederick Renner.[23] Although three German newspapers were being published in Nebraska by 1872, it was not until the flood of immigration in the early 1880's that there were sufficient readers to support several influential papers. By 1883 the number had increased to five, located in Nebraska City, Omaha, Lincoln, Grand Island, and West Point. Each paper averaged more than a thousand in circulation. Six years later, in 1889, thirteen German-language weeklies were in business. During the 1890's several new papers were started, although some of them were short-lived. By the end of the century, the *Lincoln Freie Presse* claimed a circulation of over 100,000, with copies going to German-Americans throughout the Midwest.[24] Unfortunately, copies of most of these newspapers have not been preserved. There are almost no complete runs for the 1880's, the most complete file being that of the *Nebraska Volksblatt* of West Point. A much greater proportion of the issues of the 1890's are extant, and

[22] *Compiled Statutes of the State of Nebraska, 1881* (3d ed., with amendments to July 1, 1887), Ch. 26, Sec. 46.

[23] Frederick Renner, "Reminiscences of Territorial Days," *Proceedings and Collections of the Nebraska State Historical Society*, V (2d series, 1902), 60.

[24] Karl J. R. Arndt and May E. Olson, *German-American Newspapers and Periodicals, 1732-1955: History and Bibliography* (Heidelberg: Quelle and Meyer, 1961), p. 281; *N. W. Ayer and Son's American Newspaper Annual* (Philadelphia: N. W. Ayer and Son 1883), p. 657; [*Rowell's*] *American Newspaper Directory* [*1889*] (New York: Geo. P. Rowell Co., 1889); Werkmeister, "Deutsche Zeitungen in Nebraska"; [*Rowell's*] *American Newspaper Directory* [*1901*] (March issue; New York: Geo. P. Rowell and Co., 1901), pp. 1330 f.

they may be considered an adequate sampling of German-American editorial opinion in Nebraska during that decade.[25]

The time limitations of 1880 and 1900 are also appropriate for theoretic reasons. In his *Concept of Jacksonian Democracy*, Lee Benson advances a theory of American political behavior which is pertinent to this study. Building upon Richard Hofstadter's emphasis on the common climate of American political opinion and upon Louis Hartz's analysis of America's liberal tradition, Benson had postulated that

the wider the area of agreement on political fundamentals, the more heterogeneous the society (or community), the larger the proportion of its members who have high levels of personal aspirations, and the less centralized the constitutional system, then the greater the number and variety of factors that operate as determinants of voting behavior.[26]

Perhaps during no period in American history was there a greater consensus regarding political fundamentals than during the 1880's. It has frequently been observed that the two major parties differed only on the merits of a protective tariff as opposed to one with rates designed to produce revenue only. The wide area of agreement, superficial though it may have been, was considerably narrowed by the Populist revolt of the 1890's. Thus, if Benson's hypothesis is valid, one should expect a high level of German ethnic political action during the earlier decade and a rapid drop-off after 1889, as the rampant force of Populism focused attention on free silver and reform. As the fever subsided and as the consensus broadened again after 1896, the German element in Nebraska's heterogeneous society, well known for its driving ambition, could be expected to return gradually to the practice of ethnic politics. The evidence uncovered in this study tends to support Benson's theory of American political behavior.

[25] The Nebraska State Historical Society began systematic collection of Nebraska newspapers in 1891. See "Nebraska Newspapers," *Nebraska History Magazine*, XV (April–June, 1934), 67.

[26] Benson, *Concept of Jacksonian Democracy*, p. 276.

CHAPTER II

The Germans Come to Nebraska

GERMAN IMMIGRANTS were among the earliest inhabitants of Nebraska. The first territorial census, taken in November, 1854, reveals that there were seventeen heads of families born in Germany out of a total population of 2,732 persons.[1] At that time the newly created Territory of Nebraska encompassed a vast expanse of prairie, plains, and mountains, stretching from Kansas to the Canadian border and from the Missouri River to the continental divide. Except for the Indian population, the territory was virtually un-inhabited. Although tens of thousands of hardy souls had streamed across Nebraska on their way to the Promised Land in California and Oregon, the only permanent residents of Nebraska were a few squatters along the banks of the Missouri. A few families clustered about Fort Kearny, but the only bona fide settlement was Bellevue, a trading post and Indian mission near the mouth of the Platte River.

After territorial organization had been achieved, the number of German families in Nebraska increased rapidly. Otoe County became an early center of German settlement. Other immigrant communities developed in Douglas, Washington, Dakota, and other counties located on the Missouri River.

Several communities were established through the organized efforts of German immigrants during the 1850's. Fontanelle, a village in the western part of Washington County, became an early center of German population

[1] Mary Ann Jakl, "The Immigration and Population of Nebraska to 1870" (unpublished Master's thesis, Department of History, University of Nebraska, 1936), p. 104. In the century following 1820, Germans constituted the largest single element among the 30,000,000 Europeans who migrated to the United States. German immigration generally corresponded to the larger movement of European people. From a few hundred per year in the 1830's, the numbers of German immigrants steadily increased until a peak of about 215,000 was reached in 1854. Thereafter the numbers dropped sharply and did not resume their former strength until after the Civil War. See U.S. Bureau of the Census, *Historical Statistics of the United States, Colonial Times to 1957* (Washington: Government Printing Office, 1960), p. 57; Carl Wittke, *We Who Built America: The Saga of the Immigrant* (rev. ed.; Cleveland: The Press of Western Reserve University, 1964), p. xv.

under the leadership of Henry Sprick.[2] In 1856 the city of Columbus was founded by a group of Germans and German Swiss, and a lone Irishman. Although Columbus rapidly became polyglot, especially after the arrival of the railroad, Germans continued to dominate the commercial and political establishment for many years.[3] Similarly, Grand Island was established in 1857 by a group of Schleswig-Holsteiners from Davenport, Iowa.[4]

Germans continued to drift into Nebraska Territory during the years before the Civil War. By the time the census of 1860 was taken, Nebraska's total population had grown to 28,841, while the number of German-born residents had increased to 1,742, a figure which does not include their American-born children.[5]

After a decline in numbers during the Civil War, German emigration to the United States assumed flood-like proportions. A few of the several hundred thousand persons who arrived in America at that time found their way to Nebraska. It is not likely, however, that these newcomers exceeded the numbers of prewar immigrants who had lived in Eastern states before they settled in Nebraska.

In the late 1860's the Elkhorn Valley, located in the northeastern part of the state, was opened to settlement by Germans from the Eastern states. West Point at that time was a cluster of about a dozen families, most of them Germans from Watertown, Wisconsin. At about the same time several Catholic German families established themselves in nearby St. Charles Township.[6] Shortly after the Civil War the number of Germans in the valley was swelled by a colony from Ixonia, Wisconsin. This group had originally emigrated from Brandenburg in 1843, largely for religious reasons. Moving up the Elkhorn Valley beyond West Point, the colony founded Norfolk in 1867. From there some members of the group spread north into Pierce County and northeast into Stanton and Wayne counties.[7] Mean-

[2] Verne C. Fuhlrodt, "The Pioneer History of Fontenelle [sic], Nebraska" (unpublished Master's thesis, University of Nebraska, 1930), pp. 137-144. Henry Sprick subsequently served several terms as a member of the Nebraska state legislature and was a prominent Republican leader.

[3] Margaret Curry, The History of Platte County, Nebraska (Culver City, Calif.: Murray and Gee, 1950), pp. 26-35.

[4] Esther A. Bienhoff, "The Original German Settlement at Grand Island, Nebraska (1857-1866)" (unpublished Master's thesis, University of Nebraska, 1929).

[5] Jakl, "Immigration and Population of Nebraska," p. 115.

[6] J. R. Buchanan, "The Great Railroad Migration into Northern Nebraska," Proceedings and Collections of the Nebraska State Historical Society, XV (2d series, X, 1907), 27; Henry W. Casper, History of the Catholic Church in Nebraska: The Church on the Northern Plains, 1838-1874 (Milwaukee: Bruce Press, 1960), pp. 171-190.

[7] William H. Werkmeister, "Die Deutschen Gruenden Norfolk" (MS, Werkmeister Collection, Nebraska State Historical Society), pp. 56 f.; "Geschichte des Nebraska-

while another group of nearly twenty German families settled along Rock Creek in Cuming County while a dozen others established themselves near Stanton in Stanton County.[8]

Many other German settlements were founded during the first years after the Civil War had come to a close. Omaha had had a large German colony since its earliest days. St. Helena, a landing place on the Missouri River in Cedar County, became another focal point for the settlement of Catholic Germans. Additional clusters of German immigrants also developed in Lancaster, Seward, York, and other counties before 1870.[9]

The emerging geographic pattern of the German *Einwanderung* into Nebraska was revealed by the census of 1870, which showed that the numerical strength of the German element was concentrated in the old, more populous counties along the Missouri River. Nearly one-third of all the German-born inhabitants of the state lived in Douglas and Otoe counties (see Appendix I, Table A-1), but the counties with the highest percentage of Germans in the population were those along the frontier of settlement, which at that time followed an irregular line from the Kansas border near Fairbury to the Platte River near Columbus. From there the line shifted westward to Grand Island and then northward through sparsely populated territory to the junction of the Niobrara and Missouri rivers.[10] The counties with the highest percentages of Germans were located on or near this line and included Hall, Pierce, and Cedar counties (see Appendix I, Table A-1).

During the next decade the same pattern of immigration continued. New German settlements, like Friedensau in Thayer County, were established on the fringe of settlement. Others appeared in pockets of less desirable, unoccupied land that had been by-passed by earlier settlers.[11] It has been estimated that by 1872 there were as many as 55,000 German-speaking persons in the state.[12]

Distrikts," *Ev.-Luth. Gemeinde-Blatt*, LXI (Organ der Allgemeinen Evang.-Luth. Synode von Wisconsin und anderen Staaten, August 15, 1926), 260.

[8] E. Eckhardt, *Geschichte des Nebraskadistriktes* (Battle Creek, Nebr.: E. Eckhardt, n.d.), p. 8; Meroe J. Outhouse, *A History of Stanton County, Nebraska* (published Master's thesis, Colorado State Teachers College, 1944), p. 50.

[9] Hildegard Binder Johnson, "The Location of German Immigrants in the Middle West," *Annals of the Association of American Geographers*, XLI (March, 1951), 24–28.

[10] Lloyd B. Sellin, "The Settlement of Nebraska to 1880" (unpublished Master's thesis, University of Southern California, 1940), p. 194.

[11] Wilfried W. Wegener, "A Historical Study of the Parochial Schools of Trinity, Immanuel, St. Peter's and St. Mark's Lutheran Churches of the Missouri Synod in Thayer County, Nebraska" (unpublished Bachelor's thesis, Concordia Teachers College, 1941), p. 6.

[12] Karl J. R. Arndt and May E. Olson, *German-American Newspapers and Periodicals, 1732–1955: History and Bibliography* (Heidelberg: Quelle and Meyer, 1961), p. 281.

In 1873 large numbers of Germans from Russia began to enter Nebraska. Coming from the vicinity of Saratov on the Volga River, these people emigrated chiefly to escape a program of Russification inaugurated by the Russian government.[13] Sutton in Clay County was the early goal of this migration. From there many of the *Volgadeutsch*, as they were often called, spread to other communities, especially in the southern part of the state.[14]

The census of 1880 was taken just as the greatest wave in the history of the German *Auswanderung* was getting under way. Hence the 1880 census data reflect the ebb years of the 1870's, when the number of Germans entering the United States averaged only about 30,000 per year.[15] While Nebraska's total population increased by 268 per cent (from 122,993 in 1870 to 452,402 in 1880), the number of German-born grew only 184 per cent (from 10,944 to 31,125), and the percentage of German-born inhabitants dropped from 8.9 per cent to 6.9 per cent. If a more inclusive definition of *das Deutschtum* is used, however, the rate of growth was comparable to that of the total population.[16]

Few changes in the numerical concentrations of German-born inhabitants are revealed by the census of 1880. The areas with the highest proportion of German-born likewise continued to be found in the lightly populated counties of the northeastern part of the state (see Appendix I, Table A-2). The geographical distribution of the German-born population as a percentage of the total number of inhabitants in each county is shown in Map 1. In addition to their heavy concentration in the northeast, German-born residents were to be found in moderate numbers almost everywhere else in the state.

During the early 1880's the German *Einwanderung* attained unprecedented proportions, enabling the German-born portion of the population to keep pace with the total growth of the state. While Nebraska increased from 452,402 inhabitants in 1880 to 1,062,656 in 1890—an increase of 135 per cent —the increase of German-born was almost as great (131 per cent—from

[13] Adolph Schock, *In Quest of Free Land* (San Jose, Calif.: San Jose State College, 1964), pp. 92–97.

[14] Richard Sallet, "Russlanddeutsche Siedlungen in den Vereinigten Staaten von Amerika," *Jahrbuch der Deutsch-Amerikanischen Historischen Gesellschaft von Illinois*, XXXI (1931), 108; Theodore Schmidt, "The Mennonites of Nebraska" (unpublished Master's thesis, University of Nebraska, 1933); John D. Unruh, Jr., "The Burlington and Missouri River Railroad Brings the Mennonites to Nebraska, 1873–1878," *Nebraska History* (March and June, 1964), 3–30 and 177–206; George J. Eisenach, *A History of the German Congregational Churches in the United States* (Yankton, S.D.: The Pioneer Press, 1938).

[15] U.S. Bureau of the Census, *Historical Statistics*, p. 57.

[16] *Nebraska's Population: A Preliminary Report* (n.p.: Nebraska State Planning Board, 1937), pp. 16–18.

NEBRASKA

0 – 1.9

2 – 3.9

4 – 5.9

6 – 7.9

8 – 9.9

Over 10

Map 1. Distribution of German-born inhabitants in Nebraska in 1880, by percentage in each county. For precise data, see Appendix I, Table A-2. The German-born were most numerous in Douglas County, where they numbered 3,616 out of a population of 37,645. They were proportionately strongest in Pierce County, where they accounted for 24 per cent of the total population.

31,125 to 72,000).[17] The German immigrants who arrived in Nebraska during this decade tended to settle in established German communities. Since most of the land in the agriculturally attractive areas had been taken by that time, only in the Sandhills and in the Panhandle was it possible to establish new communities.[18]

By 1900 the peak of German immigration to Nebraska had passed. Largely as a consequence of the rapid industrial development in Germany that alleviated the population problems of earlier decades, the *Auswanderung* declined steadily until 1898, when a mere 17,111 German-born entered the United States, the lowest annual figure since 1843.[19] As the source of new recruits dried up, the number of European-born in the Nebraska *Deutschtum* decreased, while the second generation increased. The percentage of all foreign-born in the state dropped from 19 per cent of the total population in 1890 to 16.6 per cent in 1900. At the same time the percentage of native-born whites of foreign and mixed parentage climbed from 23.6 per cent to 30.4 per cent. An indeterminate number of the remainder were third-generation descendants of immigrants. In many of the more isolated communities, especially in rural areas, grandchildren of *Einwanderer* often learned to speak German or another foreign language before they learned English. By 1900 the great majority of the German element in Nebraska was bilingual.[20]

Quantitative patterns of German immigration to Nebraska provide a framework for inquiry into motivational factors. If we are to provide a basis for understanding the political behavior of the German immigrants, we must first establish in a general way why they emigrated and why they chose Nebraska as their new home. We must determine their socioeconomic status, religious preferences, occupations, and aspirations. Both the push of Germany and the pull of America must be considered.

A variety of circumstances in nineteenth-century Germany fostered emigration. During the earlier period of the *Auswanderung*, that is, from about 1830 to the beginning of the American Civil War, economic and social dislocations associated with overpopulation seem to have been basic causes, especially in southwestern Germany, where, because inherited lands could be subdivided, the size of the average agricultural holding was diminishing. Moreover, improved farming techniques had not yet sufficiently increased

[17] *Nebraska's Population*, pp. 16–18.

[18] The work of "Old Jules" Sandoz, a French Swiss, in locating Germans and Swiss Germans in the upper Niobrara Valley has been made unforgettable by his daughter Mari in her biography *Old Jules* (Boston: Little, Brown, and Co., 1935).

[19] U.S. Bureau of the Census, *Historical Statistics*, pp. 56 f.

[20] U.S. Census Office, *Compendium of the Eleventh Census: 1890. Part II. Population*, p. 285. For the percentage distribution of German-born inhabitants in Nebraska in 1900, see Map 2.

Map 2. Distribution of German-born inhabitants in Nebraska in 1900, by percentage in each county. For precise data, see Appendix I, Table A-4. In 1900 the German-born accounted for 8,373 out of a population of 140,590 in Douglas County. Cuming County had the highest percentage of German-born inhabitants (17.6 per cent).

production to levels that could satisfy the new demands. Conditions became critical in Baden, Württemberg, the Rhineland, and the Hesses. Thousands of small landowners were threatened by starvation.

At the same time these circumstances had forced up the price of land. By selling his property at a dear price, many a German peasant gained the means for a new start in America. It appears, therefore, that the typical German emigrant of the pre-Civil War period was neither rich nor destitute, but of the lower middle class. He was not an agricultural proletarian—he emigrated in order to avoid becoming one.[21]

Many other conditions spurred emigration from Germany. Marcus Lee Hansen has vividly described the role of the potato blight.[22] Improved means of transportation, the destruction of the old customs barriers by the *Zollverein*, and high taxes were also important. Some emigrants fled from a cholera epidemic. Others were moved to leave by revolutions, political unrest, and rumors of war. Religious motivations were basic in some instances. The so-called Old Lutherans, for example, protested against the forced union of Lutheran and Reformed congregations that had taken place under rationalist leadership in several German states, beginning with Prussia in 1817. The Saxon emigration to Missouri in 1838 under the leadership of Martin Stephan stemmed largely from a desire to escape religious oppression. One group of Prussians settled in Buffalo, New York, for similar reasons, while another group, whose members later founded Norfolk in Nebraska's Elkhorn Valley, settled in Wisconsin.

The center of the early emigration was in the southwestern German states of Baden and Württemberg. By 1845 the fever moved rapidly north into Hesse-Kassel, Hanover, and Oldenburg, and in an easterly direction into Saxony, Schleswig-Holstein, Pomerania, and especially Mecklenburg. As more emigrants came from these northern areas the social composition of the *Auswanderung* began to change. Most of the emigrants continued to be small landowners, artisans, and shopkeepers, but a larger proportion were coming from the lower socioeconomic classes. Northeastern Germany was a region of vast estates. Hence there were more day laborers, apprentices, and the like among the emigrants than formerly.[23]

The great wave of German emigration that followed the American Civil War did not differ greatly from that of the 1850's. Overpopulation ceased

21 Oscar Handlin, *The Uprooted: The Epic Story of the Great Migrations that Made the American People* (New York: Grosset and Dunlap, 1951), pp. 7–36; Marcus Lee Hansen, *The Atlantic Migration, 1607–1860* (New York: Harper Torchbooks, [1940] 1961), pp. 211–214; Mack Walker, *Germany and the Emigration, 1816–1885* (Cambridge: Harvard University Press, 1964), pp. 47–49.

22 Hansen, *Atlantic Migration*, pp. 213, 220, 242–253.

23 Walker, *Germany and the Emigration*, pp. 33, 55, 157–165.

to be the factor that it had been earlier, while escape from military conscription became more important. Bismarck's *Kulturkampf* is often cited
as a cause during this period, especially by Catholic writers.[24] That ten-
year onslaught on the Roman church was undeniably oppressive. Yet it is
possible that its impact has been overestimated since the *Auswanderung*
began its great downward swing in the mid-1870's, when the *Kulturkampf*
was most intense.[25]

The pull of America was often as strong as the push of the old country.
The numbers of immigrants rose and fell in a pattern which generally
paralleled the rise and fall of American prosperity. But other factors were
not without significance. The decrease in immigration during the late
1850's, for example, was not due merely to the Panic of 1857, but also to
restrictions imposed on emigration by sensitive German governments in
response to the mounting passions of nativism during the Know-Nothing
era.[26]

Because land loomed large in the minds of the *Einwanderer*, the Homestead Act of 1862 was of paramount importance to Nebraska's Germans.
Dozens of them reported in the biographical sketches printed in county and
regional histories that news of free land under the Homestead Act had
spurred them to come to Nebraska, where large tracts of tillable land
remained for the taking, and where it was comparatively easy for an immigrant to become the owner of a farm—to be his own boss—to be "somebody."
In the more rigid social structure of Germany, group norms required that
respect and honor be paid to landowners and to all in authority (and in the
experience of many North Germans the two were indistinguishable). Thus
Nebraska, with its easily acquired land, offered a chance for the poor
Pomeranian day laborer to acquire both land and status at a single stroke.
Moreover, land ownership compensated for the intense feelings of confusion,
anxiety, and rootlessness with which many immigrants struggled as they tried
to adjust to life in what seemed to them an alien and hostile environment.
Nor was this yearning, this lust for land, felt only by erstwhile German

[24] See, e.g., Colman J. Barry, "The German Catholic Immigrant," in Thomas T.
McAvoy (ed.), *Roman Catholicism and the American Way of Life* (Notre Dame, Ind.:
University of Notre Dame Press, 1960), p. 190.

[25] U.S. Bureau of the Census, *Historical Statistics*, p. 57. Nevertheless, the movement was
not without significance for Nebraska. In the wake of Bismarck's directives against religious
orders, a group of refugee Franciscan fathers fled Westphalia to Nebraska, where they
helped to establish a center of German Catholicism in Columbus and the north central
part of Platte County. See Eugene Hagedorn, *The Franciscans in Nebraska* (Humphrey and
Norfolk, Nebr.: Humphrey Democrat, Norfolk Daily News, 1931); Sister M. Aquinata
Martin, *The Catholic Church on the Nebraska Frontier, 1854–1885* (Washington: Catholic
University of America, 1937), pp. 158–159.

[26] Walker, *Germany and the Emigration*, pp. 171–173.

peasants. Most other European immigrants shared it fully, though not all of them had the same opportunities for its fulfillment.[27]

Time and again prosperous German farmers directed their biographers to convey these sentiments in the few paragraphs that were to be devoted to them in local histories.[28] Other biographical sketches reveal that many immigrant craftsmen and artisans abandoned their trades as soon as they acquired the means to establish themselves as landowners and farmers.

Many Germans in Nebraska had been farmers in states farther east before they came to Nebraska. Frequently they had been landowners. Because those states were older and more densely populated, the land could command high prices. Thus, when a German farmer living in the eastern United States wished to provide his sons with land in the neighborhood, as most dreamed of being able to do, he often found that prices were prohibitive. By selling out in Ohio, Illinois, or Missouri, he was able to reestablish the larger family group on Nebraska's more plentiful, cheaper land.[29]

Nebraska was also attractive because of its low taxes, or so they seemed to many immigrants, from eastern states and foreign lands alike. Since Nebraska had not been a state during the Civil War, it had not incurred heavy war and bounty debts, and the prospect of a lightened tax burden appealed to settlers taking their chances in the new state of Nebraska.[30]

The good news of land in Nebraska reached prospective German immigrants in a variety of ways, formal and informal. Railroads, colonization companies, state and local agencies, churches, private individuals—all

[27] The novelist Sophus K. Winther describes this reverence for land ownership in Peter Grimsen, a Dane who settled in eastern Nebraska near the end of the nineteenth century. See his *Mortgage Your Heart* (New York: Macmillan Co., 1937). Craftsmen and artisans also felt these emotions. Many of the immigrant farmers described by Willa Cather in her *O Pioneers!* (Boston: Houghton Mifflin Co., 1913) had been *Handwerker* in Europe. In *Giants in the Earth: A Saga of the Prairie* (New York: Harper and Brothers, 1929), Ole Rölvaag's Norwegians had been Lofoten Island fishermen before they began their struggle with the Dakota sod.

[28] For a notable example, see the biography of Thomas Knoell in C. H. Scoville (compiler), *History of the Elkhorn Valley, Nebraska* (Chicago: National Publishing Co., 1892), p. 546.

[29] Louis Siekmann, "The German Element and Its Part in the Early Development of Otoe County, Nebraska" (unpublished Master's thesis, University of Nebraska, 1930), p. 18. An example of such a resettlement may be seen in the experiences of the present writer's grandfather, who was a farmer in Washington County, Illinois, in the midst of a heavily German district. Anticipating no prospect of providing farms for his five sons in Illinois, he sold out in the early 1890's and relocated on the high plains of Perkins County, Nebraska. His adult sons acquired contiguous property. The times were such that they lost everything within a few years. Together they subsequently made a new start in the more agriculturally attractive Merrick County two hundred miles to the east.

[30] Nebraska City *News*, Feb. 12, 1868.

participated in the efforts to attract others to the veritable Eden that many claimed Nebraska to be.

The railroads conducted what was probably the most systematic and sustained effort to attract settlers. Thanks to the largess of the United States Congress, the Union Pacific and the Burlington railroad companies had hundreds of thousands of acres for sale. Operating what was in effect a vast real estate enterprise, the railroads disposed of most of their lands to native Americans. Yet the foreign-born got their share. Hollingshead records that between 1870 and 1885 the Burlington sold 77 per cent of its land in Seward County to native Americans, while 23 per cent went to foreign-born buyers. This division matched almost perfectly the proportion of native-born to foreign-born in the state in 1880.[31]

A variety of sales methods were used by the railroads. One of the most effective was the distribution of propaganda extolling the remarkable opportunities which Nebraska presumably offered. Circulars were prepared in English, German, and other languages and were spread wherever there was a prospect of attracting settlers, both at home and abroad. The Burlington, for example, acquired the services of Professor Samuel Aughey of the University of Nebraska, a former Lutheran clergyman with German-American connections, to prepare a description of Nebraska's soil and climate entitled "Das Südliche Nebraska."[32]

Another method used by the railroads was to send agents to Europe to encourage and organize groups of emigrants to locate on railroad lands in Nebraska and elsewhere. The idea was to establish small colonies of immigrants, varying in size from ten to a hundred families. Considerable assistance would be given to get the project started. The railroads knew that if the colony was successful its population would subsequently be swelled by friends and relatives who would come later of their own accord. Agents of the Union Pacific were active in Germany for a twelve-year period from 1870 to 1882. As a result, several colonies were established on Union Pacific lands along the Platte River.[33]

The Burlington railroad was also successful in locating colonies of Germans on its Nebraska lands, mostly in the southern part of the state. Its

[31] August de Belmont Hollingshead, "Changes in Land Ownership as an Index of Succession in Rural Communities," *American Journal of Sociology*, XLIII (March, 1938), 767; *Nebraska's Population*, p. 17.

[32] Richard C. Overton, *Burlington West: A Colonization History of the Burlington Railroad* (Cambridge: Harvard University Press, 1941). Aughey's circular is duplicated on p. 443.

[33] Frederick Hedde, a leader of the company of Germans which founded Grand Island, was one of the earliest of the Union Pacific's agents. Morris N. Spencer, "The Union Pacific's Utilization of Its Land Grant with Emphasis on Its Colonization Program" (unpublished Ph.D. dissertation, University of Nebraska, 1950), pp. 198–228, 256–278.

best efforts were achieved with German Mennonites from the Volga region of Russia. This group of immigrants, under the leadership of Peter Jansen, selected a large tract of 20,000 acres in Jefferson County in 1874. In the same year another group of Mennonites purchased lands in York and Hamilton counties near Henderson.[34]

Platte County was the scene of another successful venture in German colonization by the Burlington. In 1877 the railroad reserved 30,000 acres in northern Platte County and in the southern part of neighboring Madison County for the purpose of founding a colony of German Catholics. The venture was widely advertised in both the United States and Germany. German Catholics flocked to St. Bernard's, as the colony was called. Most of the new settlers came from states of the Old Northwest.[35]

Not all of the colonization efforts were connected with railroads. Some of the earliest German settlements in Nebraska may be traced to the organized efforts of German Catholics. St. Benedict's, a German Catholic parish in Nebraska City, was the result of such a project undertaken in 1857. The same year a group of German Catholics in Buffalo, New York, founded a society which led to the establishment of Arago, a now defunct community in Richardson County.[36] Some of the earliest Germans to settle in Cuming County arrived in 1857 under the auspices of the Nebraska Settlement Association, an organization founded by a number of Germans from Omaha.[37]

The state government of Nebraska also participated in the campaign to populate the state. A Board of Immigration, established in 1866, distributed pamphlets and hired a part-time agent in New York City who could speak both English and German. In general, this effort was not effective because of constant reorganization, personnel changes, and inadequate appropriations. Although several governors continued to request appropriations for this work, the grasshopper plague of 1874 wrought devastation in state finances, with the result that the government virtually stopped all immigration promotion after that date.[38]

[34] Unruh, "The Burlington Brings the Mennonites," pp. 21–23, 188–194.

[35] Hagedorn, *Franciscans in Nebraska*, p. 357.

[36] Francis A. Murphy, "The Foundation and Expansion of the Catholic Church in Nebraska, 1850–1900" (unpublished Master's thesis, University of Nebraska, 1933), p. 89; Casper, *History of the Catholic Church in Nebraska*, p. 145.

[37] William H. Werkmeister, "Weitere deutsche Siedlungen" (MS, Werkmeister Collection, Nebraska State Historial Society).

[38] Helen M. Anderson, "The Influence of Railway Advertising upon the Settlement of Nebraska" (unpublished Master's thesis, University of Nebraska, 1926), pp. 47–50; Kieve Stubenhaus, "Origins and Growth of the Nebraska Population, 1870–1900" (unpublished Master's thesis, University of Nebraska, 1935), p. 6.

It is difficult to overestimate the importance of the churches in the settlement of Germans in Nebraska. Those denominations which had their immediate roots in Germany—Lutherans, Catholics, Evangelicals, Mennonites—had to depend for support upon gatherings of immigrants in a given area, unlike American denominations such as Methodists, Baptists, and Presbyterians. Hence, the immigrant churches had an institutional interest in maintaining a steady flow of new arrivals from Germany into their communities.[39]

The efforts of the clergy to induce immigration were ordinarily unsystematic and informal. They were most effective at the point of emigration, either in Germany or in America. The migrant would be exhorted to settle in a place where a congregation of his faith had already been established. He would be given information which would enable him to find fellow believers and fellow countrymen with ease. In this way Nebraska churches frequently served as nuclei for ethnoreligious settlements.

This function of the church was not assumed merely in its own self-interest. The immigrants themselves found that in a strange environment they needed the assurances gained through social intercourse with others who shared their language, customs, and beliefs. Few could stand up alone under the pressure. More often than not, they were anxious to get whatever information and assistance their church could provide.[40]

When small groups of immigrants moved beyond the territory served by their church, they would often write to the pastor in their former home or petition church officials to send a pastor to them. Sometimes they would send for a pastor directly and undertake his support. In this way dozens of Lutheran congregations got their start. Once on the scene, these pastors worked tirelessly to organize congregations wherever they could find clusters of co-religionists. Karl T. Gruber, for example, was called to serve two small congregations in Seward County in 1870. During the next several years he organized a string of congregations from Emerald in Lancaster County to Hampton in Hamilton County. These parishes served as the backbone for a strong German Lutheran immigration into that area during the 1870's and 1880's.[41]

The German conferences of the Methodist, Baptist, and Presbyterian churches seem to have functioned in much the same way. During the 1850's, German Methodist circuit riders made occasional trips east to urge

[39] August de Belmont Hollingshead, "The Life Cycle of Nebraska Rural Churches," *Rural Sociology*, II (June, 1937), 182.

[40] On this subject, as with other aspects of the acculturation process of rural immigrants on the plains, a reading of Rölvaag's *Giants in the Earth* is profitable. See also Handlin, *The Uprooted*, pp. 117–143.

[41] [A. F. Wegener], *A Brief History of the Southern Nebraska District of the Lutheran Church—Missouri Synod, 1922–1947* (n.p.: Southern Nebraska District, 1947), pp. 11 f.

their people to settle in Nebraska so that they might not only advance the cause of German Methodism but also save the Nebraska territory from the evils of slavery.[42]

Mennonite settlements were colonized more systematically. Among these people, theological considerations were paramount. By pursuing deliberate policies of separation and cultural isolation, the Mennonites created tightly knit, exclusive communities. They set themselves apart from what they perceived to be a sinful world, hoping thereby to preserve the purity of their faith. When an established Mennonite community attained a full measure of growth, it frequently established new, highly organized daughter colonies in new territory. Over the years, all available farmland in the new location would be bought up and homogeneous Mennonite neighborhoods created. In this fashion a large colony of Amish Mennonites from Ohio was organized in 1876 in Seward County west of the town of Milford.[43]

It is likely that no medium was more effective than private letters in transmitting the attraction of America and Nebraska to prospective German immigrants. Theodore Blegen, the distinguished historian of Norwegian immigration, has stated that the "America letters," more than any other factor, brought discontent into focus among the relatives and friends in the Old Country and precipitated decisions to partake of the land and opportunity and hope offered by America.[44]

Whatever the forces and attractions were that convinced the immigrants to begin a new life in the New World, they combined to bring large numbers of Germans to the new, raw, frontier state of Nebraska. Perhaps the most widely held conception regarding the German immigrant and his relationship to the settlement process and to the land is that he commonly displayed a marked tendency to remain in or near the community in which he or his parents originally settled. Characterized as ill-suited for the rigors of pioneer life and addicted to the amenities of civilization, the Germans (as well as other ethnic groups) are often described as having moved into a given area after the land had been subdued by British and native American stock.[45]

[42] Siekmann, "German Element in Otoe County," p. 47.

[43] Peter F. Bargen, "Mennonite Land Settlement Policies," *Mennonite Life*, XV (October 1960), 187; W. W. Cox, *History of Seward County, Nebraska* (Lincoln: State Journal Co., 1888), pp. 189 f.

[44] Theodore C. Blegen (ed.), *Land of Their Choice: The Immigrants Write Home* (Minneapolis: University of Minnesota Press, 1955), p. 7. Unfortunately there is no comparable collection of letters on the German emigration such as those that have been edited and translated by Blegen from Norwegian sources.

[45] For a classic statement of this conception see John A. Hawgood, *The Tragedy of German-America: The Germans in the United States of America During the Nineteenth Century—and After* (New York: G. P. Putnam's Sons, 1949), p. 23.

According to the tradition, they purchased the land and subsequently improved it through a combination of superior farming methods and a stubborn, unyielding determination to succeed. The "Yankees" cleared the trees and broke the sod; the Germans came later and made the land productive.

Like all myths, this one contains much truth. Like most myths, it has been seriously questioned. Census data demonstrate that in Nebraska German immigrants were just as numerous on the frontier as native Americans. Moreover, Merle Curti shows in his elaborate study of Trempealeau County in Wisconsin that German-born settlers moved on almost as frequently as the "Yankees." Other ethnic groups, especially Poles and Norwegians, were even more mobile. Curti explains the phenomenon in terms of the immigrants' inability to cope with such difficulties as excessive interest charges and freight rates, falling prices, drought, disease, and grasshoppers. [46]

In Hollingshead's intensive study of the problem of succession in land ownership in Nebraska are data which suggest that the situation is best understood, not in terms of the original settlers or their mobility, but in terms of the replacement population, that is, those who purchased the land from the original settlers when it became available. Drawing his data from deed records in Cass, Saline, and Seward counties, Hollingshead discovered that in 94 per cent of four hundred cases of sales by Americans, the land was purchased by members of non-English speaking immigrant groups. In foreclosure sales of mortgaged farms during the depression-ridden 1890's, 82 per cent of the lands were purchased by foreigners.[47]

Hollingshead explains the phenomenon in terms of attitudes toward the family and the land. The typical native American family, he points out, viewed itself as an autonomous unit. A man married the woman of his choice and settled wherever he willed. When he left his father's house to establish his own family, the responsibility of his parents toward him ceased. He and his bride pre-empted or homesteaded a farm, built a cabin, and made a slight impression on the soil. When increased population forced up the value of the land, they often sold out at a profit and started over again farther west. It was a kind of experimental land ownership. There was little sentimental

---

[46] Merle Curti et al., *The Making of an American Community : A Case Study of Democracy in a Frontier County* (Stanford: Stanford University Press, 1959), pp. 65–72.

[47] Hollingshead, "Changes in Land Ownership," pp. 773 f. In his analysis of persistence among nativity groups in Kansas, James C. Malin demonstrated that the number and character of the replacement population was the key issue, because the proportion of farmers who left their land remained almost constant through periods of both prosperity and depression until 1915 (James C. Malin, *The Grasslands of North America* [Lawrence, Kansas: published by the author, 1961], pp. 281–283).

attachment to the soil. The native American might abuse it, exploit it, and leave it without regret.[48]

The German settler, like most European immigrants, had attitudes which differed from those of the native American in several important respects. He valued the solidarity of the larger patriarchal family; he married the bride his parents chose for him; and he lived in close association with his parents long after he had established a family of his own. The father aimed to provide his sons with nearby land and to arrange the marriage of his daughters to the sons of other German landholders in the vicinity. As less prosperous families moved away from the community, an increasing proportion of the land passed into the hands of a few interrelated German-stock families.[49]

To summarize, the census data demonstrate that German immigrants had been a significant segment of Nebraska's population ever since its territorial organization. Although many Germans came to Nebraska directly from Europe, others worked as farmers, craftsmen, or laborers in eastern states before they moved west. Many arrived in America during the great wave of German emigration which preceded the American Civil War. Coming from overpopulated rural areas, they were predominantly lower-middle-class farmers, craftsmen, and shopkeepers. Like most Europeans, the Germans valued land ownership highly. Even though the factors which prompted emigration varied greatly among individuals, it was largely the quantity and quality of the land which attracted them to Nebraska. Hence the German-born, who constituted from 6 to 9 per cent of the total population of the state during the nineteenth century, tended to concentrate in rural and frontier counties, where land was cheap and easily acquired. Many were located in Nebraska through the influence of railroad companies and colonization societies, but it is likely that the majority arrived as a consequence of the less formal efforts of churches and private persons who, in their letters, urged their relatives and friends to join them in Nebraska. The great *Auswanderung*, which occurred after the Civil War, reached its peak just as the last remaining portions of public and railroad lands in the eastern part of the state were passing into private ownership. As a result, the later immigrants, among whom North German Lutheran farmers were most numerous, tended to swell the population of German settlements that had been established by

[48] August de Belmont Hollingshead, "Trends in Community Development: A Study of Ecological and Institutional Processes in Thirty-four Southeastern Nebraska Communities, 1854–1934" (unpublished Ph.D. dissertation, University of Nebraska, 1935), p. 294. See also Robert Diller, *Farm Ownership, Tenancy, and Land Use in a Nebraska Community* (Chicago: University of Chicago Press, 1941), p. 22.

[49] Hollingshead, "Changes in Land Ownership," pp. 771 f.

the pioneers. Like many native Americans, Germans were also among those who moved on, but on the whole, they showed a high level of persistence, due primarily to Old World attitudes toward land ownership and the family and to the environmental pressures of immigrant status in American society.

CHAPTER III

Nebraska's Germans and the Process of Assimilation

SHORTLY AFTER the *Volgadeutsch* Mennonites settled in Jefferson County, one of their number purchased a yoke of oxen from an American. When the time came to put the animals to work, the newcomer discovered that the oxen refused to respond to his commands. After some prodding the animals began to run and the immigrant found it impossible to stop them. Eventually they halted of their own accord and were once again stolid and immovable. The poor man remained helpless until two Americans happened to pass by. They immediately recognized the difficulty and employed effective, profane English on the beasts.[1]

It is not likely that many immigrants were able to anticipate this kind of difficulty as they contemplated emigration. The typical *Einwanderer* knew that he was going to have certain difficulties with language. But he expected to experience them with respect to people, not oxen. He realized, for example, that new units of weights and measurements would have to be learned, that climatic conditions would force some yet unknown modifications in farming methods, and that American political practices would be unfamiliar. Rational men could forsee such difficulties. But there was nothing in the typical immigrant's experience to prepare him for the myriad frustrations, disillusionments, and negative encounters with American people and American customs, the sum total of which we call cultural shock.

To his dismay and confusion, the immigrant found that the marks of his self-respect in Europe, which granted him status in his Old World community, counted for nothing in America. His clothes, his mannerisms, and his speech often became objects of derision and contempt. Old standards of conduct seemed to malfunction in the new environment. He had been uprooted, socially and psychologically, and for this he was unprepared.[2]

[1] Melvin Gingerich, "Russian Mennonites React to Their Environment," *Mennonite Life*, XV (October, 1960), 178.

[2] The cultural shock of the immigrant is a much discussed topic in the historical and sociological literature of the *Einwanderung*. See especially Oscar Handlin, *The Uprooted:*

The immigrant discovered that, if he intended to achieve the goals which motivated his decision to emigrate, he had to accommodate his behavior to the dominant American pattern. Thus he quickly abandoned European dress; he modified his mannerisms to the extent that they no longer evoked ridicule; and he learned whatever English was necessary to get along. In short, circumstances forced the immigrant to adapt his external behavior patterns to whatever extent his community demanded. Many newcomers speedily learned to participate freely and fully on many levels in American society, especially in economic matters. They often became American citizens, voted regularly, and sometimes even held political offices.

In his heart, however, the acculturating immigrant often remained a German, an Italian, or a Swede. His accommodation usually did not involve his family relationships, his circle of close friends, or his church. The typical German immigrant continued to speak German in his home and among his friends. He continued to read German-language publications, to worship his German God in his German church, and to send his children to a German school. He had his reservations about American ways, but usually he was discreet enough to voice them only in his family circle or among his close friends. His self-image was that of a German in America, a German-American, a hyphenate. He thought of himself as an American, just as good but not the same as that other hyphenate, the Anglo-American, who lived down the street, and who by chance had inherited the dominant culture of American society.

In a general way, this level of acculturation is descriptive of what Milton Gordon has called *behavioral assimilation*. It may be distinguished from a second, more thoroughgoing phase which he has labeled *structural assimilation*. The latter level was not attained until immigrant groups had achieved large-scale admission into the cliques, clubs, and institutions of native American society. With it came close, personal relationships with members of the "establishment." In other words, the immigrant had at last gained entrance into the structure of the social and institutional life of the host society.[3]

The Epic Story of the Great Migrations That Made the American People (New York: Grosset and Dunlap, 1951); Robert E. Park and Herbert Miller, *Old World Traits Transplanted* (New York: Harper and Brothers, 1921), pp. 1–66; William C. Smith, *Americans in the Making* (New York: Appleton-Century-Crofts, 1939), pp. 61–84.

[3] An excellent introduction to Milton Gordon's theories of assimilation is his "Assimilation in America: Theory and Reality," *Daedalus*, XC (Spring, 1962), 263–285. His ideas are fully developed in his *Assimilation in American Life* (New York: Oxford University Press, 1964). Sociologists are by no means in agreement regarding the process and the terms used to define it. S. N. Eisenstadt, who emphasizes the pluralist character of the receiving society, prefers to speak of the "absorption" of immigrants rather than of their "assimilation." See his *The Absorption of Immigrants* (Glencoe: The Free Press, 1955), or his briefer "The Place of Elites and Primary Groups in the Absorption of New Immigrants in Israel," *American Journal of Sociology*, LVII (November, 1951), 222–231.

In Nebraska, as elsewhere, the response of the individual German immigrant to the stress of cultural disorganization and subsequent acculturation was dependent upon a wide range of variables. One of the most important of these was place of residence. The majority of Nebraska's Germans lived in rural areas where physical isolation greatly restricted the number and quality of interpersonal contacts with native Americans. Days could pass without the immigrant communicating with anyone outside his own family. Moreover, nearby farmers were frequently of the same ethnic stock. Small-town merchants often hired bilingual clerks; professional people who could speak German sometimes advertised the fact in the local newspapers. Occasionally political campaigns for such posts as county clerk or sheriff were based upon promises to select German-speaking deputies for the convenience of the more recent arrivals. In general, it seems that immigrant institutions operative in the rural and small-town environment were fairly successful in easing the process whereby the newcomer was assimilated, mostly, perhaps, by slowing it down.

On the other hand, residents of a polyglot community tended to assimilate more quickly than those who lived in distinctively German communities. In mixed situations, less nativist opposition was aroused. Lack of uniformity in language and customs hastened the adoption of dominant American patterns. Father Philip Erlach, a pioneer Catholic priest in Columbus, noted the presence of German, Bohemian, Irish, and French Catholics in his parish and the consequent use of English as the language most common to all.[4] If the mixed immigrant community was small, establishing social and religious institutions on an ethnic basis was difficult. Unless the German was a resident of a ghetto, he was forced to mingle with the dominant native American stock, which greatly increased the tendency to conform to majority standards.[5]

Another variable which had a bearing upon an immigrant's rate of assimilation was his economic status. Prosperity was normally accompanied by a more rapid assimilation. As the immigrant moved up the ladder of success, he tended to shift his loyalties from his ethnic group to his new economic class. Not only was his life filled with more contacts with native Americans, but his ethnic bonds often were impediments to economic success.[6]

[4] Eugene Hagedorn, *The Franciscans in Nebraska* (Humphrey and Norfolk, Nebr.: Humphrey *Democrat*, Norfolk *Daily News*, 1931), p. 204.

[5] Joseph H. Fichter, "The Americanization of Catholicism," in Thomas T. McAvoy (ed.), *Roman Catholicism and the American Way of Life* (Notre Dame, Ind.: University of Notre Dame Press, 1960), p. 120.

[6] John A. Hawgood, *The Tragedy of German-America: The Germans in the United States of America During the Nineteenth Century—and After* (New York: G. P. Putnam's Sons, 1940), pp. 289 f.; Smith, *Americans in the Making*, pp. 168–170; James W. Vander Zanden, *American Minority Relations* (New York: Ronald Press, 1963), p. 278.

The rate of immigration into a given area was also important. If a large number of immigrants entered a community within a short period of time, the likelihood of exciting nativist fears was enhanced. If an immigrant drifted into Nebraska alone, his rate of assimilation was likely to be rapid.[7] Certainly the more mobile an immigrant was, the more rapid was his accommodation to American standards. Many of Nebraska's Germans, such as the founders of Grand Island and Norfolk, had been residents of Eastern states before they moved to the plains.

Even though the tempo of assimilation was usually slower in the rural areas than in the cities, naturalization rates were higher among the farmers. There are several explanations for this phenomenon. The cities were the distributing centers for the dispersion of immigrants to rural areas. They were the temporary homes of laborers and craftsmen who hoped to establish themselves on the land as soon as they could afford it. Moreover, in order to acquire land under the terms of the Homestead Act, the immigrant had to declare his intention of becoming a citizen, that is, he had to take out his first naturalization papers. This was also a prerequisite of voting in Nebraska and several other midwestern states prior to World War I.[8] Thus thousands of German immigrant farmers in Nebraska, Kansas, and the Dakotas were eligible to vote before they had a functioning English vocabulary.

Each immigrant, as he faced the problems of adjustment to life in America, was influenced both by his particular character traits and by his psychological needs. For one person the consolations of orthodox religion were paramount; for another economic security was the primary consideration. Basically there were two types of immigrants: those whose psychological orientation was American and those whose cultural bonds continued to be with the land that gave them birth.

The attitude of the first type was characterized by a resolve to break with the past and to make a satisfactory adjustment to the new environment. Whatever it was that prompted the original decision to emigrate—economic hardship, political upheaval, personal disgrace, or flight from justice—this type of immigrant had a minimal attachment to his ethnic group and sought interpersonal contacts with Americans in order to discover the new norms and standards to which he was expected to conform. He learned English rapidly, discarded membership in immigrant social, religious, and economic

---

[7] The population schedules of the Nebraska State Census of 1885 reveal large numbers of single adult males who were born in Germany. Residents of rooming houses and hotels, they were frequently found in railroad towns such as Nebraska City, Columbus, and Grand Island.

[8] Edmund de S. Brunner, *Immigrant Farmers and Their Children* (Garden City, N.Y.: Doubleday, Doran and Co., 1929), pp. 18 f. *United States Statutes at Large*, XII, 392 f.; *Compiled Statutes of the State of Nebraska, 1881* (1887), Ch. 26, Sec. 3.

institutions as quickly as possible, and was admitted into the structure of the host society to whatever degree circumstances permitted. In short, he thought of himself as an American.[9]

By contrast, fond memories of home reigned unchallenged in the mind of the European-oriented immigrant. He regretted that conditions had made it necessary for him to emigrate. He regarded European values as superior and was anxious to preserve or recreate institutions based upon them. The mother tongue was nurtured, and identification with the ethnic group was cultivated. For such a person emigration exacted a sentimental loss that could never be replaced.[10]

Ole E. Rölvaag has vividly described these prototypes of immigrant psychology in his novel, *Giants in the Earth*. Per Hansa, the hero-figure of the story, gloried in the opportunities offered by the Dakota prairie. The struggle for life was by no means easy for him, yet his vision and self-confidence fired his energies and made him a source of strength, resourcefulness, and leadership for his Norwegian community. Almost pathetic in his eagerness to conquer the wilderness, Per Hansa was so different from his wife that they were virtually estranged.[11]

In her own way, Per's wife, Beret Holm, was also successful. After her husband's death she managed very well with the help of her sons. But she was driven by anxiety to recreate her Norwegian heritage in her sod house. Cultural isolation intensified her loyalties to her God, her parents, and her Norway. To speak English in preference to Norwegian was almost sacrilegious. Emigration had been an act of betrayal for her, and she never overcame her feelings of guilt. She was convinced that God was punishing her for her disloyalty. As the privations of pioneer existence passed, she was tormented by the manifestations of assimilation which she saw in her family and in the Norwegian community in which she lived.[12]

Rölvaag's figures are archetypal. In actuality there were few immigrants who consistently matched the characteristics that he portrayed. Per Hansa

---

[9] Park and Miller, *Old World Traits Transplanted*, pp. 83–92.

[10] *Ibid.*, pp. 92–96.

[11] Ole Rölvaag, *Giants in the Earth: A Saga of the Prairie* (New York: Harper and Brothers, 1929). This classic contrast has been pointed out by Percy Boynton, *The Rediscovery of the Frontier* (Chicago: University of Chicago Press, 1931), pp. 126–134. See also John T. Flanagan, "The Immigrant in Western Fiction," in Henry Steele Commager (ed.), *Immigration and American History* (Minneapolis: University of Minnesota Press, 1961), p. 86.

[12] Rölvaag's sequel to *Giants in the Earth* is *Peder Victorious* (New York: Harper and Brothers, 1929). This book focuses on the conflict between the first and second generation immigrants. For the purposes of this study, it offers as many insights as the earlier, more famous book.

and his wife represented extremes. Yet the Per Hansa-Beret Holm antithesis is useful as an aid to understanding the political behavior of Nebraska's Germans. Ideally, the Per Hansa type stood for rapid assimilation, economic success, urban or small-town residence, urban-type occupations, and associational activity in American institutions. He desired to learn English and showed a preference for public school education and affiliation with Anglo-American Protestant denominations. He was active in the political arena, displayed higher rates of naturalization, voting, and political activity, and tended to identify himself with the Republican party.

The Beret Holm type, by contrast, symbolized slower assimilation, rural isolation, and the preservation of Old World heritages through support for immigrant institutions, including German newspapers, churches, and schools. This type was characterized by a wariness of native American institutions and activities, by lower rates of naturalization, voting, and political activity, identification with the Democratic party, and the playing of ethnic politics.[13]

It is likely that the Beret Holm type was the more numerous among the German immigrants of Nebraska. However, the Per Hansa type was less noticeable because of his psychological orientation. He was moving with greater speed toward absorption and therefore tended to play down his obviously German characteristics. Thus there is a danger of underestimating the number of rapid assimilators. On the other hand, persons with capacity for leadership were more frequent among the Per Hansas. More likely to enter politics in the first place, this type often espoused policies which reflected their determination to accommodate the German element to prevailing American attitudes. Both Henry Sprick of Washington County and Peter Jansen of Jefferson County, to cite two examples, were staunch prohibitionists.[14] Other German leaders gave considerable support to the reform movement within the Republican party. Paul Schminke of Nebraska City, for example, was a political lieutenant of Charles H. Van Wyck, the leader of the antimonopolists in Nebraska for many years.

Perhaps the dichotomy is best illustrated by the public behavior of two

[13] Cf. Joshua A. Fishman *et al.*, *Language Loyalty in the United States: The Maintenance and Perpetuation of Non-English Mother Tongues by American Ethnic and Religious Groups* (The Hague: Mouton and Co., 1966). See especially Ch. 9, "German-American Language Maintenance Efforts," by Heinz Kloss. The pathological behavior that Beret Holm displayed as a fictional character should not be transferred to the typology. As a symbol, Beret Holm was also typical of a successful acculturation. The point is that this type required, for psychological reasons, a much slower assimilation if pathological behavior was to be avoided.

[14] Blair *Courier*, October 15, 1892. Jansen's prohibitionism was rooted in his Mennonite faith. Sprick, however, was a Lutheran. For a study of the role of leaders in the assimilation process. see Eisenstadt, "The Place of Elites and Primary Groups."

German-born newspaper publishers and editors who lived in Grand Island. During the weeks preceding the election of 1886, these two gentlemen raged at each other on their editorial pages. One of them, Fred Hedde, was clearly an "Americanizer." Born in Germany in 1818, he had been trained as a lawyer. At the age of thirty-six he came to the United States and settled in Davenport, Iowa. Subsequently he joined William Stolley and the company of Germans who established Grand Island in 1857. Sometime after his temporary return to Germany as a Union Pacific agent, Hedde purchased the Grand Island *Independent*, an English-language newspaper. Like many educated German immigrants, he was strongly attracted to the Republican party by its reformist element. His church affiliation was Lutheran. It is significant, however, that he was a member of an *English* Lutheran congregation.[15]

Much less is known about his antagonist, Henry Garn, who at that time was the militantly Democratic editor of Grand Island's *Der Herold*, a German language newspaper.[16] To Garn the fundamental issue in the election of 1886 was prohibition. In response to vigorous efforts by its temperance wing, the Republican party had endorsed the proposal to submit an amendment to the voters of the state which would prohibit the liquor traffic.[17] To Garn the proposal was nothing less than a massive assault by puritanical fanatics upon the personal liberties and rights of liberal-minded immigrants. He assumed the role of the sturdy defender of *das Deutschtum* in Hall County. He rejected native American standards, defended the European tradition of moderate, convivial consumption of beer and wine, and strongly urged support for the Democratic party, which, in its platform, had denounced prohibition as "dangerous to the liberty of the citizen and hostile to the interests of the people."[18] Garn was not opposed to reformist legislation designed to curb the monopolistic practices of the railroads, yet he was exceedingly suspicious of it, claiming that the antimonopolist reform wing of the Republican party included many of the same people who supported prohibition.[19]

[15] A. F. Buechler, R. J. Barr, and Dale P. Stough, *History of Hall County, Nebraska* (Lincoln: Western Publishing and Engraving Co., 1920), p. 562.

[16] For several years Garn also published an English-language weekly called the Grand Island *Herald*. While its political position was the same as his German newspaper, its content appealed to a broad readership.

[17] Addison E. Sheldon, *Nebraska: The Land and the People* (3 vols.; Chicago: Lewis Publishing Co., 1931), I, 648 f.

[18] [U.S. Work Projects Administration, Nebraska], *Nebraska Party Platforms* (Sponsored by the University of Nebraska, 1940), p. 121.

[19] *Der Herold* (Grand Island), October 6, 1886; October 14, 1886; Grand Island *Herald*, October 1, 1886; October 22, 1886.

Fred Hedde's handling of the issues of 1886 illustrates the contrast in attitude and thought patterns between the two types. Although Hedde was regularly denounced as a prohibitionist by his rival, the charge was not true. He also opposed prohibition but for entirely different reasons. His pro-assimilationist orientation would not permit him to fight prohibition for ethnic-based reasons, as did Garn. He condemned such efforts as sick attempts "to stir up the 'nationality' strife . . . in a worn out dodge that disgusts the better class of German-Americans. It is an insult to all voters of German descent."[20] To Hedde the central issue was reform. He saw the Republican party as the only potential vehicle for antimonopolist legislation, even though it was, at the moment, in control of the antireformist, stalwart wing. His opposition to prohibition was based upon the fantasy that it was just another monopolistic game, that is, another phase of big business domination of Nebraska's political and economic structure.[21]

Both journalists used the same kind of argument. Garn viewed the antimonopolists as mere variations of the prohibitionist reformers who were seeking to impose a Puritan ethic upon an unwilling citizenry by legislative means; Hedde insisted that prohibition was simply a device of the robber barons to divert attention away from the real issue of whether the monopolies or the people should rule. Neither Garn nor Hedde was right, but the argument affords an unusual insight into the minds of German-American leaders in Nebraska politics.

For the second-generation immigrant the conflict between the native and the immigrant cultures was especially intense. Nurtured in the warmth of ethnic family life, the children of the immigrants learned to speak their parents' native tongue before they learned English. They shared the ethnic life of their parents. Yet it was impossible for them to share it completely because their experiences were also American. Though their love and loyalty for their parents were genuine, many were also keenly aware that their ethnic status was a source of deprivation and humiliation.

The second-generation immigrants were thus caught between two worlds of culture. They responded to the conflict in several ways.[22] One type

---

[20] Grand Island *Independent*, October 2, 1886.

[21] *Ibid*. See also October 9, 1886.

[22] The typology which follows is taken from Irvin L. Child's *Italian or American? The Second Generation Conflict* (New Haven: Yale University Press, 1943). See also the discussion of the generational aspect of ethnic identification by Vladimir C. Nahirny and Joshua A. Fishman in their essay, "Ukrainian Language Maintenance Efforts in the United States" in Fishman *et al.*, *Language Loyalty in the United States*, pp. 343–356. Oscar Handlin provides a historical background for the problem of the second generation immigrant in his introduction to *Children of the Uprooted* (New York: George Braziller, 1966). He suggests that the marginality of the second generation has often been overstated, that it was largely

tended to identify strongly with the parental group and to embrace the ethnic culture. Since this response often involved a denial of his American heritage, the member of this group sometimes compensated for his consequent feelings of insecurity with a militantly defensive posture. Indeed, he occasionally became a caricature of the European system with which he identified. Defenders of a cultural complex that had only limited reality for them, such men often became pitifully conservative, sometimes more extreme in their views than their fathers had been.

Another second generational response was that of the "rebel." Resentful of the disabilities imposed upon him by his ethnic inheritance, he sought to divest himself as thoroughly as possible of all immigrant symbols. It was relatively easy for the German newcomer, for example, to anglicize his name, or to shed membership in his ethnic church and join a denomination favored by native Americans.

Efforts to minimize the marks of ethnic group membership and gain entrée into the native American social structure were no doubt less common in regions where the German-stock population was heavy, and where the sting of social disapprobation would be keenly felt. *Die Beatrice Post*, for example, roundly condemned those Germans who wanted to pass as being completely "Yankeefied" once they were able to speak a sentence in broken English.[23] To want to be assimilated was one thing, but to be willing to reject one's heritage in the process was another, and it evoked bitter reactions from the faithful. The Republican gubernatorial candidate in 1900, Charles H. Dietrich, a second generation German, had a reputation as a "rebel." As such, he was unacceptable to many German voters of the Beret Holm psychology. Some of them deeply resented Dietrich's refusal to support their efforts to maintain the German language and German cultural institutions. A German from Hastings, Nebraska, Dietrich's home town, vented his ire in a letter, which he released to the press during the campaign of 1900:

Charles Dietrich thought he was too good for the Germans until this fall. . . . During all the time he has lived here he refused to identify himself with the Germans, or to associate with them except where he had to. We organized a German Knights of Pythias lodge and asked Mr. Dietrich to join, but he refused. We organized a German society—a sort of turnverein, and Mr. Dietrich would neither join nor help support it. Not only that but he has been rude and brusque in his manner toward our people. A little thing happened to me, several years ago, when I could not talk English as well as I can now, that I will never forget. I talked to him in German as it was hard for me to use English. He figited around for

a phenomenon of the period 1840 to 1920, and that the second generation encompassed a much wider variety of types than earlier scholarship had assumed.

[23] *Die Beatrice Post*, July 16, 1896.

a while, and then brought his fist down on the table with a bang and said, with an oath: "I wish you'd talk United States, and not your d——d Dutch." That's the kind of German he was before he began to run for office.[24]

The third type of response made by the children of immigrants to cultural clash was that of apathy. Sensitive to the counterpulls of the two cultures, this type often sought to evade the problem by avoiding all situations in which ethnic origins might have a part. Such a German-American, for example, would turn his back on German churches, schools, *Turnvereine*, *Sängerbünde*, and other immigrant-oriented organizations. At the same time, however, he was afraid to participate in native American institutional life for fear his ethnic background would be a source of embarrassment.

The reaction of the individual immigrant or his children to the stresses and strains of the assimilation process was determined in part by the kind of reception he experienced in the host society. Merle Curti has pointed out that there was no basic cleavage in the value systems of the native-born and the immigrants and that generally the reception accorded the newcomers was favorable. Edmund Brunner also found that the intergroup relations were marked by friendliness. He observed that this good will was based on profitable economic relationships and noted that in the absence of an economic bond the attitude of the native Americans was more likely to be one of indifference. In any case, however, social recognition lagged far behind and entrée into the social structure of the community came only after an immigrant had achieved economic success. Moreover, in the realm of practice governed by law, native Americans expected the foreign-born to conform immediately and completely. In other matters they were much more permissive.[25]

As a general rule, if the reception accorded the immigrant was friendly, the rate of assimilation was stimulated. But if it was marked by strong prejudice and discrimination, the effects were ambivalent. For some newcomers the desires to escape were heightened; for others the pressures evoked stronger tendencies toward group identification and group solidarity.[26]

Historically there have been three general attitudes among native Americans regarding the manner in which immigrant peoples were assimilated.

[24] Nebraska City *News*, November 2, 1900. Originally elicited by a correspondent of the Omaha *World Herald*, the letter was widely reprinted in Nebraska papers, both German and English, during the last few days before the election. Though the letter must be judged as political propaganda, it retains validity as a document that reflects immigrant attitudes.

[25] Merle Curti *et al.*, *The Making of an American Community: A Case Study of Democracy in a Frontier County* (Stanford: Stanford University Press, 1959), pp. 137 f.; Brunner, *Immigrant Farmers*, pp. 96–98.

[26] J. Milton Yinger, "Social Forces Involved in Group Identification or Withdrawal," *Daedalus*, XC (Spring, 1961), 253.

These have involved (1) Anglo-conformity, (2) the concept of the "melting pot," and (3) cultural pluralism. The first of these assumed the desirability of maintaining English institutions and culture as the standard in American life. Immigrants from any source were welcome in moderate numbers so long as they were willing to conform to the dominant pattern within a reasonable period of time. The melting pot theory, based on the contrasting view that the American nationality was a composite of many ethnic strains, is related to Frederick Jackson Turner's belief that the frontier functioned as a crucible that fused a mixed race—not English but something new and distinctively American. More recently the notion of cultural pluralism has gained currency. Based on the assumption that American society is permanently heterogeneous, it accepts membership in diverse, unassimilated cultural minority groups as desirable. Its sole qualification is loyalty to the American political and economic systems.[27]

The first of these attitudes—Anglo-conformity—prevailed in Nebraska in the latter part of the nineteenth century. The Lincoln *Daily Call*, for example, stated in 1890 that it was happy to welcome foreigners and "to see them absorbed into the whole body politic of our nation and see the last vestige of nationality wiped away."[28] Yet many who were pouring into the country at that time held divergent views on temperance and Sabbatarianism and hence aroused anxiety over the ability of the nation to absorb them. The *Call* was severely critical of those Germans in the state who seemed to think that Americans were all cranks and fanatics. Anglo-conformist views like those of the *Call* were not in themselves racist, nativist, or restrictionist. It is clear, however, that they helped create a climate in which anti-Catholicism, exclusionist legislation, and notions of Nordic superiority could thrive, as they did in the 1890's.

In the early part of the nineteenth century, problems of assimilation had not loomed large or complex. As the volume of immigration expanded, however, native Americans were increasingly reluctant to admit immigrants or their children into their primary group relationships. By 1900 the Protestant Anglo-Saxon leadership of American society had effectively excluded foreign-born stock of the Catholic and Jewish faiths from their associational activities.[29] Moreover, the nativist efforts of those days, as

[27] Gordon, "Assimilation in America," pp. 265–279; Smith, *Americans in the Making*, pp. 114–119; Oscar Handlin, "Immigration in American Life: A Reappraisal," in Commager (ed.), *Immigration in American History*, p. 11.

[28] Lincoln *Daily Call*, October 15, 1890. See also Omaha *Weekly Herald*, August 1, 1888, for an editorial which opposed free immigration of "the swarthy and ignorant hordes of Southern Europe."

[29] E. Digby Baltzell, *The Protestant Establishment: Aristocracy and Caste in America* (New York: Random House, 1964), p. 74.

Oscar Handlin has pointed out, were more than a struggle of "Americans" against immigrants. They were attempts of a particular ethnic group to retain its dominance over American society and culture.[30] Thus, the ethnocentric Omaha *American*, the organ of the American Protective Association in Nebraska, asserted that the "impure effusions" of foreign authors like Boccaccio and Rabelais ought never to find a place in American homes.[31]

Exclusionist attitudes and practices were also observable in rural and small-town Nebraska. There, as elsewhere, no genuine invitation was extended to immigrants and their children to become structurally assimilated. For example, when a women's literary group, called the Fin de Siècle Club, was formed in Seward in 1897, its membership consisted exclusively of Anglo-Saxon Protestants. Although several wealthy and thoroughly acculturated German women of the second generation were residents of the town at that time, their names were not among the list of officers and charter members.[32] Local newspapers displayed similar characteristics. Seward's *Nebraska Reporter*, a Republican weekly, was attractive to the Anglo-Saxon Protestant "in-group." Members of the large German population in the community were only infrequently mentioned in the gossip columns of this paper. On the other hand, references to German residents tended to be more frequent in the Seward *Independent-Democrat*, a publication which seems to have drawn support from political and social out-groups. Admission to economically based organizations like the Seward Board of Trade, however, was easy for both Lutheran and Catholic Germans. German merchants were prominent among its officers and directors.[33]

The individual immigrant discovered shortly after his arrival in America that there were others whose assimilational experiences and problems matched his own. Members of various ethnic groups inevitably were drawn together. They spoke the same language, literally and figuratively. In Europe, language rarely functions as a checkpoint for the comparisons and contrasts which a person uses to locate himself in society. An immigrant ordinarily thought of himself as a *Bayer*, a *Pommer*, or a *Sachse*, not as a German, but in the alien American environment he discovered that the old distinctions had lost much of their meaning. In America, nationality was considered a unique attribute, and language was its primary distinguishing feature. Moreover, as the immigrant group became increasingly aware of itself as a cultural minority, it discovered that ethnic group action could be

[30] Oscar Handlin, "Historical Perspectives on the American Ethnic Group," *Daedalus*, XC (Spring, 1961), 231.

[31] *The American* (Omaha), September 21, 1894.

[32] Seward *Independent-Democrat*, September 22, 1897.

[33] *Blue Valley Blade* (Seward), October 17, 1883.

surprisingly effective in the new environment. As isolated groups of Hesse-Darmstadters or Westphalians they could not accomplish much, but as Germans their numbers were adequate for successful ethnic enterprises.

Consequently each immigrant group went about building a society of its own within American society. In this effort the newcomers were motivated not only by their own psychological inability to participate in the associational affairs of the host society but also by the exclusionist policies of native Americans. The strength of the ethnic enclaves was directly proportional to the number and effectiveness of the institutions, both formal and informal, that the immigrants created.

In the larger cities of Nebraska the Germans established a variety of social, cultural, religious, economic, and political organizations. Such institutions were most successful in Omaha where the German community was large and powerful, but they were to be found in the smaller cities as well. Hastings had its German-American bank, Seward its German-American insurance company, and Grand Island's Liederkranz Hall was a cultural center of the community. In Nebraska, however, the success of such formal institutions was limited by the sparseness of the population. Nebraska City, for example, had several singing societies, but none of them survived for long.[34]

Informal ties, especially in economic affairs, were common among Nebraska's Germans. Almost every small town that served a German rural community had at least one clothing store, grocery, hardware store, or saloon operated by a German. A blacksmith, a shoemaker, or a harness maker could almost always be found who was also a *Landsmann*. Staplehurst, for example, had a German-born auctioneer who advertised his ability to "cry sales" in both languages and Dr. A. K. Seip of Milford advertised in English-language newspapers that "hier wird Deutsch gesprochen."[35]

In rural areas the churches were by far the most important immigrant institutions, serving as nuclei around which the newcomers could organize their lives in America. They had the best potential for maintaining the unity of the group and for symbolizing the sentiments and values that had suffered erosion through transfer to the new world. As the immigrant struggled to preserve something of the old familiar ways, he frequently rediscovered religion. Under these circumstances the church tended to assume an importance that it had not had for him in Europe.[36]

[34] Louis Siekmann, "The German Element and Its Part in the Early Development of Otoe County, Nebraska" (unpublished Master's thesis, University of Nebraska, 1930), pp. 65–71.

[35] *Blue Valley Blade* (Seward), October, 21, 1891; *Milford Nebraskan*, October 13, 1886.

[36] H. Richard Niebuhr, *The Social Sources of Denominationalism* (New York: Meridian Books, [1929] 1960), pp. 222 f. and *passim;* Brunner, *Immigrant Farmers*, pp. 142 f.; A. B. Lentz *et al.*, *Story of the Midwest Synod, ULCA, 1890–1950* (n.p.: n.d.), pp. 40 f.

This is not to say, of course, that all immigrants were religious. Some bore a long-standing resentment toward the church and all that it stood for. Others became hostile when they realized the full implications of separation of church and state in America. Still others opposed church membership because of the financial support it implied. Forced by circumstances to be frugal, many immigrants found giving to the church a painful experience. They found it easier to denounce the pastor as a grasping, domineering rascal who lived off the labor of others. Certainly the rapid assimilators were prone to keep the immigrant church at arm's length. For them the Anglo-American denominations were a stronger attraction. Moreover, many members of the second generation did not feel the same psychological need for the church that their parents had.

Contrariwise, the Beret Holms among the German immigrants realized that if their cherished European values were to endure in America, the preservation of the mother tongue was indispensable. Speaking German in the home was hardly enough to counter the effects of the many interpersonal contacts which their children were experiencing with the American-born, especially in the schools. As a rule American public schools took no account of the cultural background of the children. Their special needs and capacities were ordinarily ignored. Old world customs, dances, music and folklore were denigrated, often unwittingly, by teachers who were anxious to instill a love of America in their charges. The children, eager to please, readily joined in the rituals of the American secular religion. The songs were sung, the recitations learned; the symbols were revered, and the secular saints venerated. Inevitably the gulf between the parents and their children widened.[37] To the church-minded immigrant there was no better solution to these problems than the parish school.

Among the German Catholics and German Lutherans of Nebraska, parish schools were common. More often than not, the typical Roman Catholic congregation was polyglot, and English was necessarily the medium of instruction. The schools of such parishes may actually have hastened rather than retarded the process of assimilation. In the purely German Catholic parishes, the German language was usually used in the schools, but gradually English-language instruction increased, so that by 1900 German was commonly used only in religion classes.[38]

[37] W. Lloyd Warner and Leo Srole, *Social Systems of American Ethnic Groups* (New Haven: Yale University Press, 1945), pp. 220–253; Brunner, *Immigrant Farmers*, p. 106; Walter H. Beck, *Lutheran Elementary Schools in the United States: A History of the Development of Parochial Schools and Synodical Educational Policies and Programs* (St. Louis: Concordia Publishing House, 1939), p. 153. Rölvaag, as usual, describes the conflict vividly. See *Peder Victorious*, pp. 83–95, 119–122.

[38] Sister M. Aquinata Martin, *The Catholic Church on the Nebraska Frontier, 1854–1885* (Washington: Catholic University of America, 1937), p. 100; J. A. Burns, *The Growth and*

The role played by the parochial school in preserving the immigrants' cultural heritage was much more apparent among the German Lutherans than among the Catholics. Their churches were exclusively German in composition. They were most common in the small towns and in the country-side where social isolation was almost complete. These Lutherans came from the lower classes in German society and were frequently lacking both in education and in worldly riches. Moreover, many of them tended to be cultural nationalists, especially after the unification of Germany in 1871. Unlike his Catholic counterpart, the typical Lutheran pastor, upon his arrival in a Nebraska community, almost always established a school of some kind with himself as teacher.[39]

Attitudes toward parish schools varied among the several German Lutheran synods. The archly conservative Missouri Synod considered schools to be essential parts of the parish program. In 1885, for example, there were fifty-seven Missouri Synod schools in Nebraska, enrolling 2,084 children, whereas the twenty-two Catholic schools in the state enrolled a total of only 1,911 children, not all of whom were of German stock.[40] Other Lutheran synods had similar policies, although none were as large nor as solid in its support of parochial school education as the Missourians. The Iowa Synod, which was particularly strong in Otoe County, established schools on the same pattern. The Wisconsin Synod also operated schools, particularly in the Norfolk area. Even the German Nebraska Synod, which often opposed whatever the Missouri Synod favored, seems to have main-tained a few schools.[41]

Development of the Catholic School System in the United States (New York: Benziger Brothers, 1912), pp. 299–302. See also William H. Werkmeister, "Deutschen Katholiken in Nebraska" (MS, Werkmeister Collection, Nebraska State Historical Society), pp. 9 f.

[39] Carl S. Meyer (ed.), *Moving Frontiers : Readings in the History of the Lutheran Church —Missouri Synod* (St. Louis: Concordia Publishing House, 1964), pp. 353 f.; [Lutheran Church—Missouri Synod. Nebraska District], *Erster Synodal-Bericht des Nebraska Distrikts der deutschen evang.-luth. Synode von Missouri, Ohio und anderen Staaten. 1882* (St. Louis: Lutherischen Concordia-Verlag, 1882), pp. 54 f.; [Lutheran Church—Missouri Synod], *Statistisches Jahrbuch der deutschen evang.-lutherischen Synode von Missouri, Ohio, und anderen Staaten für das Jahr 1900* (St. Louis: Concordia Publishing House, 1901), pp. 75–80, 113.

[40] [Lutheran Church—Missouri Synod], *Statistisches Jahrbuch der deutschen evang.-lutherischen Synode von Missouri, Ohio und anderen Staaten für das Jahr 1885* (St. Louis: Lutherischen Concordia-Verlag, 1886), pp. 45 f.; Patrick F. McCarthy, "Catholic Church in Omaha and Nebraska" and Michael A. Shine, "South Platte Catholicism and the Lincoln Diocese," in J. Sterling Morton and Albert Watkins, *Illustrated History of Nebraska* (Lincoln: Jacob North and Co., 1907), II, 441, 464.

[41] Johannes Deindoerfer, *Geschichte der Evangel.-Luth. Synode von Iowa und anderen Staaten* (Chicago: Wartburg Publishing House, 1897), pp. 245–286; *Eine Kurze Geschichte der Ev.-Luth. St. Pauls-Gemeinde zu Norfolk, Nebraska* (50th anniversary pamphlet, 1866–1916); Lentz *et al.*, *Midwest Synod*, p. 17.

The fact that many persons identified with the German element spoke English did not necessarily mean that they had achieved any significant measure of structural assimilation. They had accommodated their behavior to American standards, but their subsociety was capable of continuing for generations. In this, the churches and schools were most important, not merely as preservers of language and culture, but as promoters of endogamy, that is, marriage within the group. While there had always been marriages which crossed group lines, especially among the rapid assimilators, partners were normally sought within the ethnoreligious group, a practice which was strongly encouraged by the churches and by social pressure.[42] Exogamy, or intermarriage with other groups, has always been the most effective means of breaking down such barriers.[43]

Cultural isolation among German religious groups was also fostered by theology. Both the Lutheran and Catholic churches were authoritarian. Rome has her Pope; Lutherans have their doctrine of scriptural inerrancy. Rome has insisted that there is no salvation outside her embrace; Lutherans, especially the Missouri Synod, have claimed that they represent the True Visible Church on earth and that all other bodies are shot through with error. If Lutheran doctrinal purity was to be maintained there could be no fellowship with heresy. General movements toward church union were rejected, higher criticism and evolutionary theories were ridiculed, and the Social Gospel was branded as a perversion of the church's mission. Every theological weapon was wielded in the battle to preserve the religious identity of the church. All these factors, combined with the heightened sense of self produced by denominational competition, served to produce a conservative orientation and cultural isolation among the Lutherans which was exceeded only by that of the Mennonites.[44]

[42] Cf. Ruby Jo Reeves Kennedy, "Single or Triple Melting Pot? Intermarriage Trends in New Haven, 1870–1940," *American Journal of Sociology*, XLIX (January, 1944), 331–339. Census statistics are misleading in this respect because they do not record the ethnic origins of marriage partners among the native-born. Examination of Nebraska population schedules shows that in the overwhelming majority of marriages between immigrants and native-born persons, the partners were of the same ethnic origin.

[43] Handlin, "Historical Perspectives," pp. 230 f.; Gordon, "Assimilation in America," p. 273. August de Belmont Hollingshead has pointed out that the surplus of males to females in typical immigrant populations made exogamy inescapable and therefore hastened the assimilation process. See his "Trends in Community Development: A Study of Ecological and Institutional Processes in Thirty-four Southeastern Nebraska Communities, 1854–1934" (unpublished Ph.D. dissertation, University of Nebraska, 1935), pp. 22–24.

[44] This line of thought is developed further in Frederick C. Luebke, "The Immigrant Condition as a Factor Contributing to the Conservatism of the Lutheran Church—Missouri Synod," *Concordia Historical Institute Quarterly*, XXXVIII (April, 1965), 19–28. See also Meyer (ed.), *Moving Frontiers*, pp. 362–365.

Knowing whom or what the German immigrants opposed reveals as much as knowing whom or what they favored. The immigrant's perception of the native American was especially significant. Rarely did the newcomer distinguish the New Englander from the Southerner or other native types. All were Yankees. Bewildered and confused by so many contacts, the immigrant usually lumped them all into a distorted, composite image—that of a grasping, rootless, materialistic snob, always ready to take advantage of an unsuspecting newcomer. The Yankee frequently appeared to the German as a fanatic and a bigot, eager to use his highly developed sense of politics to impose by legislative means his superficial, pharisaical moral code on unwilling immigrant peoples. The Yankee was industrious enough, the German thought, but his energies were frequently misdirected; he was frugal enough, yet he was remarkably wasteful of his agricultural resources.[45]

Some of these sentiments are reflected in the following impressions, penned by a German-born resident of Saunders County, who had observed native Americans as they moved to Nebraska and took up land:

One hears much about the hardship of the people that came west in the covered wagen . . . many of people in South an East rigged up a team of some Kind, Mules and oxen as a rule but some had horses or one hor[s]e and Stir or Cow. I have seen 10 to 20 Wagens in a Croup and two to 3 troup pase in one day . . . but the[y] Cheerfully past on and I know by there own words the[y] enjoyed the life, roamen and all, better then anything els The[y] generaly didn't travel very far a day, stoping at every town about two hours trading horses, Kidds traded Jack Knifes, the way the[y] made there expenses always get a little to bood so the[y] could buy there Bacen, Cornmeal and Tabak. There living was very simple. when the[y] got near a creek ore some green spot near a spring the[y] unheatched to let there stock feed and mad fire for the cooking. many times the[y] would not make more than 3 miles and 10 miles wuse about the most. Ther living condition where about the poorest possible and must of them grossly ileterate very few ware able to write ther name and body vermence were consideret a singe of good health After locating on pics of land the[y] would not very often mak expensiv emprovement or develope ther land, the[y] would go to every town meeting, campmeeting and convention, Know all about polatics and have the Bible by harde, the yung folks go to the horse race and play cards, generaly the[y] borowed as much money as the[y] could get on the land and when som Foreign Emegrant came along and offered more as the[y] thought ther land wuse worth the[y] sold out and moved on. only a very small persent stayed and emproved the land to make a permanend home.[46]

45 Philip D. Jordan, "The Stranger Looks at the Yankee," in Commager (ed.), *Immigration and American History*, pp. 55–78.

46 [August Widmann], handwritten MS, Werkmeister Collection, Nebraska State Historical Society.

The importance of group standards for the individual person varied with the context of issues. Some issues commanded a significant measure of uniformity. Most Germans in Nebraska were united in their opposition to woman suffrage and prohibition. In the language of the political scientist, these issues had a high level of salience for the Germans. On other matters, such as bimetallism and imperialism, salience decreased and voting decisions by immigrants were likely to be made on the basis of standards derived from other than immigrant groups. The transmission of group standards was also of importance, that is, the effectiveness with which the standards of the German element in Nebraska were conveyed to its individual members.[47] No doubt German-language newspapers were a basic means. In 1880 their number in the state was small. One may therefore assume that the transmission of group standards was less effective at that time than in the 1890's, when German-language publications were more numerous and influential.

The positive and negative relationships of subgroups within the Nebraska *Deutschtum* were also significant. The Germans, like American society itself, were heterogeneous, and there is much evidence to suggest that smaller groups, especially ethnically based churches, attracted a loyalty stronger than that accorded the German element in general.[48]

A few examples follow. In 1867 a German-born farmer homesteaded in the midst of a German Catholic settlement in Cuming County. When his compatriots discovered that he was an Evangelical and not a Catholic they ceased all relationships with him to the point of refusing to sell him the grain he needed to commence farming.[49] In 1883 several Catholic families from the German colonies on the Volga settled in Sutton. The religious affiliation of this *Volgadeutsch* settlement was overwhelmingly Protestant, chiefly German Reformed and Congregational. The reception accorded the Catholics was so cool that a short time later they moved on to Albion, the Boone County seat, where many Catholics but no Volga Germans were to be found.[50]

Similarly, the German Methodists were anathema to German Lutherans. The Lutherans were repelled by the Methodists' emphasis on temperance,

47 Angus Campbell, *et al.*, *The American Voter* (abridged ed.; New York: John Wiley and Sons, 1960), pp. 161–183.

48 In contrast to these findings, Milton M. Gordon indicates that, in general, ethnic loyalties take precedence over religious bonds. See his *Assimilation in American Life*, especially Ch. 2, "The Subsociety and the Subculture," pp. 19–59.

49 C. H. Scoville (compiler), *History of the Elkhorn Valley, Nebraska* (Chicago: National Publishing Co., 1892), p. 509.

50 Richard Sallet, "Russlanddeutsche Siedlungen in den Vereinigten Staaten von Amerika," *Jahrbuch der Deutsch-Amerikanischen Historischen Gesellschaft von Illinois*, XXXI (1931), 24.

Sabbatarianism, and other reformist notions, all of which seemed to reduce religion to a mere matter of right living. Moreover, German Lutherans found the emotionalism of the Methodist revival techniques repugnant. Vitriolic editorials denouncing the work-righteousness of Methodism, as well as its unionistic tendencies, were frequently printed in Lutheran church periodicals. The Methodists and others who shared their views returned the scorn. To them, the formalism and intellectualism of German Lutheranism seemed to rob religion of all vitality. They dismissed the Lutherans as "memory Christians" or "Catechism Christians."[51]

Catholics, Mennonites, and many Lutherans were opposed to lodges and secret societies. While these churches unquestionably opposed the lodges for theological reasons, they also recognized them as competitors for the loyalty of the German element.[52] The antipathy that the Missouri Synod Lutherans felt for the lodges was a basis for much bitter strife between the Missouri Synod and the German Nebraska Synod, which was much more relaxed in its attitude toward secret societies.[53]

It is readily apparent that there was no issue or group goal that had the potential of uniting all the component groups which made up the whole of the German element. The heterogeneity of the Germans was unusual compared to other ethnic groups. German editors sometimes castigated their readers for failing to unite as the Irish always seemed to do.[54] But the comparison was hardly fair. Long before their arrival in America, the Catholic Irish had been models of cohesiveness compared to the Germans. Their unity had been forged by four centuries of opposition to protestant English rule. The Germans, by contrast, had a 400-year heritage of *Kleinstaaterei*, of religious wars, and of religious dissension. Now, suddenly, in America the Germans were told that they were all one, a cultural minority that must close ranks and fight together. But they could rarely agree on what they were fighting for, much less on when and how to fight, or whom to follow.

[51] Meyer (ed.), *Moving Frontiers*, p. 238; Lentz *et al.*, *Midwest Synod*, p. 38. In their studies of the social impact of church membership in America, sociologists have generally demonstrated a lack of appreciation of the doctrinal differences that have separated protestant denominations. Hence, they have ordinarily lumped all protestants together in a single category and contrasted them with Catholics and Jews, thereby failing to measure an important dimension of the problem.

[52] Melvin Gingerich, *The Mennonites of Iowa* (Iowa City: State Historical Society of Iowa, 1939), p. 165; Deindoerfer, *Geschichte der Iowa Synode*, pp. 287, 302; Meyer (ed.), *Moving Frontiers*, p. 383; O. Fritiof Ander, "The Immigrant Church and the Patrons of Husbandry," *Agricultural History*, VIII (October, 1934), 166–168.

[53] Lentz *et al.*, *Midwest Synod*, pp. 9, 19.

[54] Max O. Gentzke, the publisher of the West Point *Nebraska Volksblatt*, harped on this theme for years. See e.g., August 3, 1894; also *Nebraska Biene* (Columbus), September 23, 1898.

Thus, if we are to analyze the political behavior of the Germans in Nebraska, it is useless to ask how and why the Germans voted unless we first attempt to discover in what ways the first-generation immigrant differed in his political behavior from the second; how the German farmer differed from his compatriot in the towns; what influence church membership had on the Catholic, Lutheran, or other Protestant voter as compared to the influence exerted by lack of affiliation with any church at all; if lodge membership made a difference in the political behavior of the Germans; and finally we must attempt to discover the importance of the regional factor, that is, how closely the German immigrant conformed to the pattern of the community or region in which he resided.

CHAPTER IV

The Germans of Nebraska : A Collective Portrait

ONE AVENUE to an understanding of immigrant political behavior is the employment of research techniques that permit analyses and comparisons of group characteristics. By tabulating information drawn from the biographies of representatives of the group under study, systematic data may be acquired which reveal relationships between political behavior and a variety of social, economic, and cultural variables.

A collective approach is especially appropriate for research in immigration history. Group problems, group developments, group responses, and group characteristics are often more important than are the individual records of prominent members of the group.[1] Indeed, one of the most serious hazards connected with research in immigration history is the attribution of evidence drawn from the leaders to the rank-and-file members of the group. Excessive reliance on such elite-type evidence may easily distort perceptions of group attitudes and behavior.

In many instances the findings of the collective biography technique substantiate traditionally held views based upon impressionistic evidence. In such cases our understanding of the past is strengthened by empirical

[1] The collective biography approach is similar to the panel technique employed by political scientists. Through extensive interviewing of a panel of representative voters during an election year, they have repeatedly demonstrated the importance of socioeconomic status, religion, and identification of urban or rural residence. See Paul F. Lazarsfeld, Bernard Berelson, and Hazel Gaudet, *The People's Choice* (New York: Columbia University Press, 1948), p. 174; Peter H. Rossi, "Four Landmarks in Voting Research," in Eugene Burdick and Arthur J. Brodbeck (eds.), *American Voting Behavior* (Glencoe: The Free Press, 1959), p. 18. While the use of the panel technique is obviously denied the historian, the collective biographical approach resembles it in some respects. One of the first and best-known studies of this kind was conducted by C. Wright Mills. By using data extracted from the *Dictionary of American Biography*, he offered new insights into the origins, education, church affiliation, etc., of American business leaders in the late nineteenth century. See his "The American Business Elite: A Collective Portrait," *Journal of Economic History*, V (Supplemental issue, 1945), 20–44.

data. Sometimes, however, the results suggest that our views have been out of focus, that they have lacked proper proportions, or that they have been in error. In any case, statistics must be used cautiously, for the proof they offer is frequently more apparent than real. Moreover, as Theodore Blegen has warned, historians must realize that "immigrants are people, not nicely tabulated statistics, and that to understand people . . . sources as varied and far-reaching as their interests and activities, their minds and emotions, their work and ambitions" must be used.[2]

Fortunately, biographical sketches of many German immigrants in Nebraska are available for the period 1880 to 1900. During those years and well into the twentieth century, several publishing companies produced massive histories of counties or regions. These compilations were largely financed through subscriptions. If a person agreed in advance to purchase a copy of the forthcoming book, he would be assured of a place for his personal history in the biographical section reserved for representative residents of the area. Standard information was then compiled regarding the subject's birth, education, occupation, family, church affiliation, political activity, land ownership, and so on. Though poorly written, these brief sketches provide more readily accessible information about more ordinary persons than any other source.

Certain limitations regarding the use of these biographies need to be observed. The first of these concerns socioeconomic status. Since most of the subjects were middle-class persons, a balanced cross section of the population is not offered. Successful farmers dominate the pages, but their hired hands are absent. Small town merchants and bankers are listed, but their clerks are not. Professional people and craftsmen appear, but not their assistants.

Another limitation results from the withholding of information. A local merchant, for example, may not have wanted his Republican customers to know that he was a Democrat. Clergymen in particular did not often divulge their political preferences. No doubt many half-truths also slipped in. A person may have wanted it recorded for posterity that he was religious, even though the local pastor might have disputed his alleged status as a church-goer. Obviously, tabulated percentages should be accepted with a measure of skepticism. They reveal trends and tendencies but not with precision.

For the purposes of this study, data were drawn from the personal histories of 653 first- and second-generation Germans of Nebraska. Place of birth, occupation, church affiliation, lodge membership, political party identification, and levels of political activity were recorded for each. The

2 Theodore C. Blegen, "The Saga of the Immigrant," in Henry S. Commager (ed.), *Immigration and American History* (Minneapolis: University of Minnesota Press, 1961), p. 140.

subjects of the study constituted all of the members of the German ethnic group who happened to be included in four county and regional histories.[3] The earliest group includes 124 German residents living in 1889 in Otoe County, located on the Missouri River in the oldest section of the state. The second group consists of 230 persons who inhabited the Elkhorn River Valley in 1892 (chiefly in Dodge, Cuming, and Stanton counties), a region with a heavy concentration of German immigrants. The third group consists of 108 persons, living in 1899 in five contiguous counties south of the Platte River, mostly in Seward and York counties. The fourth sampling includes 191 persons who lived in heavily Catholic Platte County in 1915. Since the data for the final group were gathered more than a decade after the others, potential distortions were compensated for by eliminating from the study all biographies of persons born after 1875. Thus all the persons in the Platte County group could have voted in 1896 and in subsequent elections.

In the tables which follow, percentages are recorded separately for each group rather than for all subjects combined. This is done so that regional differences within the state may be revealed, thereby testing the contention that the Germans had a tendency to adopt the political habits of the host community. Since Otoe County had a tradition of Republican allegiance, the number of German Republicans in that county could be expected to be greater than in Platte County, where the Democratic party tended to dominate. In the same way the traditionally Republican Seward-York area could be compared to the Democratic Elkhorn Valley. Platte County was especially desirable as a test case because of its heavy Catholic element and because its total population was unusually heterogeneous.

In order to make the categories employed in the tables meaningful, some explanation is necessary. Generational data were tabulated in accordance with the definition of *ethnic stock*, that is, on the basis of European birth of the subject or of one or both parents. All sorts of occupations were recorded. Farmers usually accounted for more than two-thirds of all subjects. It was discovered that the numbers of other occupations were to small for meaningful tabulations. Hence all persons engaged in urban or small-town occupations are lumped together under the heading *business and professional*. Blacksmiths, harnessmakers, shoemakers, and other craftsmen were included in this category because their activity was also commercially oriented.

3 *Portrait and Biographical Album of Otoe and Cass Counties Nebraska* (Chicago: Chapman Brothers, 1889); C. H. Scoville (compiler), *History of the Elkhorn Valley, Nebraska* (Chicago: National Publishing Co., 1892); *Memorial and Biographical Record and Illustrated Compendium of Biography of Butler, Polk, Seward, York and Fillmore Counties, Nebraska* (Chicago: George A. Ogle and Co., 1899); and G. W. Phillips (ed.), *Past and Present of Platte County, Nebraska* (2 vols.; Chicago: S. J. Clarke Publishing Co., 1915).

Although this broad definition lumps together such antipathetic occupations as pastor and saloonkeeper, it offers the advantage of separating the subjects on an urban-rural basis.

All varieties of church affiliation were discovered among the German immigrants. Lutherans were most numerous, then Catholics. The numbers of non-Lutheran Protestants were usually so small that they had to be grouped in one category. This created a problem in that ideally a distinction should be made between immigrant and American churches. It was found, however, that the subjects of the biographies did not consistently distinguish between the English-speaking and the German versions of those Protestant denominations which had German conferences, notably the Methodists, Congregationalists, and Baptists. These churches functioned as immigrant institutions in the same way as the Catholic, Lutheran, and Mennonite denominations. The category of *other Protestant* may nevertheless be justified for the reason that the German conferences were almost indistinguishable from their English-speaking equivalents in their theological orientation. The German Methodist, for example, differed from the mainstream of American Protestantism chiefly in language. The German Lutheran by contrast differed in language and ritual, as well as in theological heritage. Thus a prohibitionist could be found as readily in a German Methodist congregation as in an American one. If no church affiliation was indicated in the biography, the subject was recorded in the *not stated* category. No doubt most persons in this classification were unaffiliated, although the grouping necessarily includes those who did not wish to reveal their church connections.

Some attempt was made to record the evidences of activity in social organizations. This was done on the assumption that memberships in formal groups increased the number of interpersonal contacts and therefore resulted in an increased rate of assimilation into American society. This in turn implies a higher level of political activity.[4] It was found that the only kind of social activity that was consistent enough or frequent enough to warrant tabulation was lodge membership. Membership in German or religious lodges or their equivalents, such as the Sons of Herman or the Knights of Columbus, was not included in the tabulation. Some lodges, like the Modern Woodmen of America and the Ancient Order of United Workmen, used the structure or format of the secret society for fraternal insurance programs. Membership in these organizations were tabulated. Perhaps the most important lodges in terms of impact on the assimilation process were the Masonic orders, the Independent Order of Odd Fellows, and the Knights of Pythias, although the latter sometimes chartered local lodges organized on an ethnic basis. The strong opposition which the secret

4 Lazarsfeld *et al., The People's Choice*, p. 146.

societies encountered from the Catholic, Lutheran, and Mennonite churches lends added significance to lodge membership as an index to rates of assimilation.[5]

About 75 per cent of the subjects revealed that they adhered to either the Republican or the Democratic parties. The remainder were classified as members of several minor parties, as independent voters, or as *not stated*. The final category included the politically apathetic as well as those subjects who chose to reveal nothing about their political preferences.

Persons classified as *politically active* were distinguished from the inactive by having held some kind of governmental or partisan office at some time in their lives. The positions ranged from high office in state government to such local posts as township road supervisor or member of the school district board. The *politically active* also included a few subjects who noted that they had been defeated as candidates for higher offices, especially in state government. Postmasters were included because they normally held office as a reward for political services. It should also be noted that there were subjects who indicated that they were politically active but chose not to reveal their party connections.

Table 1 reveals the general characteristics of the 653 adult males of German ethnic stock who were included in the tabulations. Approximately 75 per cent were born in Europe. The occupational data show that an average of two-thirds of the members of all four groups were farmers. Although only about half of Nebraska's total population held church memberships at that time,[6] approximately four-fifths of the Germans included in the survey claimed to be affiliated with some church. About 15 per cent were Catholic, 40 per cent were Lutheran, and 20 per cent were members of other Protestant churches.[7] The lodges attracted an average of one out of every six Germans in the study.

The political identification data provide support for the contention that German immigrants tended to conform to established patterns of political

[5] Thus it may be assumed that if a German immigrant held memberships in both the Catholic church and a Masonic order, he was a rapid assimilator and that, theoretically at least, he should also have been highly accultured politically.

[6] U.S. Bureau of the Census, *Religious Bodies: 1906* (2 vols.; Washington: Government Printing Office, 1910), I, 335–337. The tables record communicant members only. The figures must be augmented by the numbers of children thereby excluded.

[7] The actual Catholic percentage for Otoe County probably was higher than 6.4; there were no less than three predominantly German Catholic parishes in the county. The high percentage of Catholics in Platte County (36.1 per cent) is accounted for by the strong Catholic settlement in the north central part of the county and in the city of Columbus, the county seat. The *other protestant* category is remarkably uniform except for the 7.8 per cent recorded for the Elkhorn Valley group. This divergence may be partially explained by the relatively high percentage of first generation Germans in the region.

TABLE 1

Percentage Distribution of Characteristics of 653 German-American Adult Males in Nebraska

	1889 *Otoe* *County*	*1892* *Elkhorn* *Valley*	*1899* *Seward-York* *Area*	*1915* *Platte* *County*
No. of subjects:	(124)	(230)	(108)	(191)
Place of Birth				
Europe	75.8	83.0	77.8	67.0
America	24.2	17.0	22.2	33.0
Occupation				
Farmer	62.9	70.0	80.6	60.2
Business and professional	37.1	30.0	19.4	39.8
Church Affiliation				
Catholic	6.4	16.5	13.9	36.1
Lutheran	49.2	38.3	45.4	35.6
Other protestant	22.6	7.8	22.2	19.9
Not stated	21.8	37.4	18.5	8.4
Lodge Membership Indicated				
Yes	14.7	15.2	17.6	24.1
No	85.3	84.8	82.4	75.9
Political Party Identification				
Republican	58.1	21.3	33.3	21.5
Democratic	25.8	56.1	28.7	53.4
Populist	—	7.0	8.3	—
Prohibition	2.4	.4	—	.5
Socialist	—	—	.9	—
Independent	3.2	2.6	6.5	9.9
Not stated	10.5	12.6	22.2	14.7
Political Activity				
Active	37.9	27.4	37.0	38.7
Inactive	62.1	72.6	63.0	61.3

NOTE: In Tables 1–9 percentages may not add to 100.0 per cent in every case, due to rounding.

behavior. In the Republican counties south of the Platte River the Germans clearly preferred the GOP. In Otoe County, for example, the ratio was two German Republicans for each German Democrat. But the relationship was exactly reversed in the Democratic territory north of the Platte. There the number of German Democrats was more than double that of the Republicans. Moreover, the data also demonstrate that the Germans were not attracted by the Populist party.[8] Since they tended to associate nativism, prohibition,

[8] This finding runs counter to one of the main points made in Walter T. K. Nugent's excellent study, *The Tolerant Populists: Kansas Populism and Nativism* (Chicago: University of Chicago Press, 1963). Although significant exceptions may be found, Nebraska voting statistics show that generally German voters were less inclined toward the Populist ticket than the total voting population. See below, Chapters VII and VIII.

and Sabbatarianism with the Populists as well as with reformist Republicans, it is likely that the small Populist identification came from formerly Republican Germans who were inclined to assimilate rapidly. In any case, the figures of 7.0 and 8.3 per cent for the Populist party are remarkably low, considering the fact that in 1892 the Populist share of the total vote for president in the state was 42.3 per cent.[9] The proportion of the subjects who indicated political activity shows an unusually consistent figure, close to 37 per cent; the lower figure recorded for the Elkhorn Valley Germans may be explained in terms of the heavier percentage of first-generation immigrants.

How much validity Table 1 has for the total German population of the state must remain problematic. No doubt most of the German adult males in Nebraska belonged in this middle-class grouping of independent farmers and businessmen. There is no way of knowing what proportion of wealthy and influential Germans were omitted in the four groups. It is not likely, however, that there were many, nor would their inclusion seriously affect the results of the survey. The poor were of course much more numerous. Yet it can be argued that their lower socioeconomic status precluded the likelihood of their having much political significance.

The data of Table 1 do not reveal the comparative influence of place of birth, occupation, religion, or lodge membership on political party identification or on levels of political activity. The figures merely describe quantitatively what the sample of the German population was like at the time. Not until the four groups of immigrants are classified and compared on a percentage scale can the relative effect of these variables be estimated.

Table 2 shows the relationship between place of birth and political party identification. It assesses important similarities as well as differences between the first and second generations of German immigrants. In the first place, it appears that the European-born were remarkably active in politics.[10] Between 80 and 90 per cent revealed some sort of political identification, a proportion which is nearly the same as that of the American-born. This fact is not in accord with the traditional view of the immigrant. Presumably he arrived on the American scene confused and disorganized by cultural shock, and only gradually did he accommodate his behavior to American norms and become assimilated into American society. The supposition was that the

---

9 *Nebraska Blue Book for 1901 and 1902* (Lincoln: The State Journal Co., 1901), p. 177.

10 This high rate of participation in politics among immigrants is in sharp contrast to the customary view. Cf. Oscar Handlin, *The Uprooted: The Epic Story of the Great Migrations that Made the American People* (New York: Grosset and Dunlap, 1951), p. 202, or William I. Thomas and Florian Znaniecki, *The Polish Peasant in Europe and America* (Boston: Richard G. Badger, 1918), I, 141.

TABLE 2

Percentage Distribution of Political Party Identification of 653 German-American
Adult Males, as Related to Place of Birth

	1889 Otoe County	1892 Elkhorn Valley	1899 Seward-York Area	1915 Platte County
Born in Europe				
No. of subjects	(94)	(191)	(84)	(128)
Republican	58.5	18.3	35.7	25.8
Democratic	24.5	56.0	27.4	47.7
Populist	—	8.4	8.3	—
Prohibition	2.1	—	—	—
Socialist	—	—	—	—
Independent	4.3	3.1	7.1	9.4
Not stated	10.6	14.1	21.4	17.2
Born in America				
No. of subjects	(30)	(39)	(24)	(63)
Republican	56.7	35.9	25.0	12.7
Democratic	30.0	56.4	33.3	65.1
Populist	—	—	8.3	—
Prohibition	3.3	2.6	—	1.6
Socialist	—	—	4.2	—
Independent	—	—	4.2	11.1
Not stated	10.0	5.1	25.0	9.5

lowest rates of political involvement occurred among the most recent arrivals,
that the longer the immigrant lived in America the greater was his political
acculturation, and that the second generation made noteworthy progress
over the first. The data of Table 2, however, support more recent assimilation theory, which assumes that immigrants may have participated extensively
in political affairs shortly after their arrival in America and that they may
have voted regularly and even held minor political offices, even though their
comprehension of American political practice and of the English language
may have been low. In short, there may have been extensive political acculturation without significant movement in the direction of structural assimilation.[11]

In the second place, the data demonstrate that there were significant
differences in party identification between the two generations. In general,
the American-born displayed a slight tendency to abandon the party of their
fathers and to embrace its rival. In three or four instances, the party which
was less attractive to the fathers experienced an increase in the proportion of
the adherents it won among the sons. In Otoe County, preference for the

[11] Milton Gordon, "Assimilation in America: Theory and Reality," *Daedalus*, XC
(Spring, 1962), 280.

Democratic party increased from 24.5 per cent among the first generation to 30.0 per cent among the second. In the Elkhorn Valley, preference for the Republican party increased from 18.3 per cent among the European-born to 35.9 per cent among the American-born. In the Seward-York area, Democratic party followers increased from 27.4 per cent to 33.3 per cent while preference for the Republican party dropped from 35.7 per cent to 25.0 per cent. The figures seem to support Irvin L. Child's study of the second-generation conflict.[12] As *marginal men* or as victims of sharp cultural conflict, many of the American-born Germans could be expected to rebel against first generation norms regarding political behavior. One might also expect an increase among the politically apathetic of the second generation, as measured by the proportion who indicated no political identification. In this case, however, traditional theory is upheld, since the *not stated* category decreased in the Elkhorn Valley from 14.1 per cent among the European-born to 5.1 per cent among the American born. Similarly, the percentages in Platte County dropped from 17.2 per cent to 9.5 per cent.

A third distinction revealed by Table 2 in the partisan identification of German immigrants is that it was the Democratic party which benefited from the changes in the two generations. In Otoe County, the Democrats experienced a 5.5 per cent increase among the American-born. In the Seward-York area, the Democratic gain was 5.9 per cent. In strongly Catholic Platte County, the Democratic percentage climbed 17.4 points to 65.1 per cent. Among the members of the Elkhorn Valley group, the Democratic proportion remained constant at about 56 per cent.

It is likely that the Democratic trend in party identification is related to the immigrant's perception of the two major parties in America. Upon his arrival in the United States the German immigrant often identified with the Republican party because of its reputation as the opponent of slavery and preserver of the Union. This image was strengthened by the examples of well-known German-American politicians, notably Carl Schurz and the editors of certain widely distributed German-American publications. Gradually, however, as the German immigrant acquired sophistication in political affairs, he began to perceive that the Democratic party was the friend of the immigrant. It was a conservative party of states' rights and strict construction. It was a liberal party of free trade and the largest measure of personal liberty consistent with law and order. By contrast the German immigrant tended to see the Republican party as progressive and aggressive, the party of nativism and Puritan virtues, of exploitation by big business and

[12] *Italian or American? The Second Generation Conflict* (New Haven: Yale University Press, 1943).

of the centralization of power.[13] Moreover, the immigrant sensed an aristo-
cratic quality about the Republican party, a certain lack of compassion. It
seemed money-centered rather than man-centered.[14] The Republican party
was attractive to the ambitious, self-assertive Per Hansa types for whom a
successful adjustment to American life was paramount. For the more
numerous Beret Holms, however, the Democratic party made more sense. It
often seemed to ease the burden imposed by the inexorable process of
assimilation.

Table 3 indicates the relationship between place of birth and levels of
political activity. The tendency for members of the second generation to be
more active politically than the first generation is clearly revealed by the
data. In Otoe County the percentage of the politically active persons increased from 35.1 per cent among the European-born to 46.7 per cent
among the American-born. The data for Platte County are almost the same.
The figure for the Elkhorn Valley Germans nearly doubled from 23.6 per
cent to 46.2 per cent. Only in the Seward-York area did the proportion of
politically active persons drop among the second generation. This may be
explained by the fact that the Germans were least numerous in this area,
particularly among the residents of the county seats, the communities which
normally provide a disproportionate share of the political leaders. In other

TABLE 3

Percentage Distribution of Levels of Political Activity of 653 German-American
Adult Males, as Related to Place of Birth

	1889 Otoe County	1892 Elkhorn Valley	1899 Seward-York Area	1915 Platte County
Born in Europe				
No. of subjects	(94)	(191)	(84)	(128)
Politically active	35.1	23.6	39.3	33.6
Politically inactive	64.9	76.4	70.8	66.4
Born in America				
No. of subjects	(30)	(39)	(24)	(63)
Politically active	46.7	46.2	29.2	49.2
Politically inactive	53.3	53.8	70.8	50.8

[13] For a recent study of the relationship between immigrant attitudes and the so-called
progressive reforms of the era, see Alan P. Grimes, *The Puritan Ethic and Woman Suffrage*
(New York: Oxford University Press, 1967).

[14] For sample editorials which reveal popular images of the parties in Nebraska during
the 1880's and 1890's, see *Omaha Herald* (weekly edition), October 13, 1882; Nebraska
City *News*, October 28, 1882, and October 10, 1890; *Blue Valley Blade* (Seward, Nebr.)
October 29, 1884; Blair *Courier*, July 13, 1889; Lincoln *Weekly Herald*, October 11, 1890;
Lincoln Freie Presse, October 11, 1894.

words, German-American residents of these counties were probably more likely than members of the other three groups to experience generational conflicts capable of manifesting themselves in political apathy.[15]

Table 4 shows the relative importance of occupation and/or urban-rural residence in association with political party identification. Theoretically the Republican party should have been proportionally stronger than the Democratic party among the commercially minded German residents of the cities and towns. The urban setting likewise provided many more interpersonal contacts, which are assumed to speed behavioral assimilation. By contrast, the rural townships should have harbored a greater proportion of slow assimilators—that is, potentially Democratic voters.

TABLE 4

Percentage Distribution of Political Party Identification of 653 German-American Adult Males, as Related to Occupation

	1889 Otoe County	1892 Elkhorn Valley	1899 Seward-York Area	1915 Platte County
Farmers				
No. of subjects	(78)	(161)	(87)	(115)
Republican	59.0	18.6	33.3	20.0
Democratic	25.6	59.6	29.9	52.2
Populist	—	9.3	8.0	—
Prohibition	2.6	.6	—	—
Socialist	—	—	1.1	—
Independent	5.1	1.9	6.9	10.4
Not stated	7.7	9.9	20.7	17.4
Business and Professional				
No. of subjects	(46)	(69)	(21)	(76)
Republican	56.5	27.5	33.3	23.7
Democratic	26.1	47.8	23.8	55.3
Populist	—	1.4	9.5	—
Prohibition	2.2	—	—	1.3
Socialist	—	—	—	—
Independent	—	4.3	4.8	9.2
Not stated	15.2	18.8	28.6	10.5

The data show that in three of the four groups occupation and/or urban-rural residence was a variable of almost no importance. To illustrate, the Republican party attracted 59.0 per cent of the German farmers in the Otoe

[15] This response conforms to recent studies which have noted the increase in nonvoting among persons caught in various cross-pressures. See Henry W. Riecken, "Primary Groups and Political Party Choice," in Burdick and Brodbeck (eds.), *American Voting Behavior*, p. 178; Seymour Martin Lipset, *Political Man: The Social Bases of Politics* (Garden City, N.Y.: Anchor Books, 1963), pp. 211–226. Cf. also Marcus Lee Hansen, *The Immigrant in American History* (New York: Harper Torchbooks, 1964), p. 93.

County sample and 56.5 per cent of the business and professional persons. In the Seward-York region, the Republican party attracted exactly one-third of both groups. In Platte County 20.0 per cent of the farmers claimed to be Republicans compared to 23.7 per cent of the urbanites. The data conform to theoretic expectations only among the Elkhorn Valley Germans. In this instance the Republican proportion was 18.6 per cent for the country people while the figure for the city dwellers was notably higher at 25.7 per cent. Conversely, the Democratic party attracted 59.6 per cent of the German voters in the rural precincts but only 47.8 per cent in the cities and towns.

Urban or rural residence seems to have been a factor of importance, however, when associated with the *not stated* group. In both Otoe County and the Elkhorn Valley the incidence of partisan identification was twice as common among the city people as among farmers. As businessmen and professional persons they were likely to have felt more keenly the conflict of attitudes and goals between their ethnic group and native Americans. Many resolved the problem by avoiding politics altogether. Only in Platte County, where the proportion of urbanites was high, was the trend reversed.

The relationship between political activity and urban or rural occupation is revealed by Table 5. Since residents of cities and towns had both the

TABLE 5

Percentage Distribution of Politically Active Persons among 653 German-American Adult Males, as Related to Occupation

	1889 Otoe County	1892 Elkhorn Valley	1899 Seward-York Area	1915 Platte County
Farmers				
No. of subjects	(78)	(161)	(87)	(115)
Politically active	30.8	20.5	36.8	31.3
Politically inactive	69.2	79.5	63.2	68.7
Business and Professional				
No. of subjects	(46)	(69)	(21)	(76)
Politically active	50.0	43.5	38.1	51.7
Politically inactive	50.0	56.5	61.9	61.3

contacts and opportunities requisite for higher rates of political activity, they could be expected to provide proportionately many more persons who held some kind of political position. Rural areas dominated by the German immigrant population would provide exceptions. In such cases nearly all public and party officials came from immigrant ranks. The data of Table 5 indicate that the business and professional persons were decidedly more active in politics than the country folk. Nevertheless, place of residence was not a significant variable among the Germans of the Seward-York group.

This variation in the pattern may be explained by the predominantly rural character of the German population in that area.[16]

The relationship of church membership to political party identification is shown in Table 6. The religious factor clearly appears to have been a variable of greater importance than either place of birth or occupation. Catholic

TABLE 6

Percentage Distribution of Political Party Identification of 653 German-American Adult Males, as Related to Church Affiliation

	1889 Otoe County	1892 Elkhorn Valley	1899 Seward-York Area	1915 Platte County
Catholics				
No. of subjects	(8)[a]	(38)	(15)	(69)
Republican		5.3	—	7.2
Democratic		76.3	40.0	78.3
Populist		2.6	6.7	—
Prohibition		—	—	—
Independent		2.6	13.3	5.8
Not stated		13.2	40.0	8.7
Lutherans				
No. of subjects	(61)	(88)	(49)	(68)
Republican	59.0	18.2	42.9	17.6
Democratic	27.9	71.6	24.5	50.0
Populist	—	5.7	10.2	—
Prohibition	1.6	—	—	—
Independent	3.3	3.4	6.1	19.1
Not stated	8.2	1.1	16.3	13.2
Other Protestants				
No. of subjects	(28)	(18)	(24)[b]	(38)
Republican	71.4	38.9	33.3	47.4
Democratic	14.3	44.4	33.3	26.3
Populist	—	11.1	8.3	—
Prohibition	7.1	—	—	2.6
Independent	3.6	—	4.2	7.9
Not stated	3.6	5.6	16.7	15.8
No Church Membership				
No. of subjects	(27)	(86)	(20)	(16)
Republican	48.1	27.9	35.0	37.5
Democratic	25.8	33.7	25.0	25.0
Populist	—	9.3	5.0	—
Prohibition	—	1.2	—	—
Independent	—	2.3	5.0	18.8
Not stated	25.9	25.6	30.0	18.8

[a] The number of subjects is too small for meaningful distribution on a percentage scale.
[b] Percentages add to 95.8 rather than 100.0 per cent; a member of the Socialist party has been omitted.

[16] See above, Table 1. The Seward-York group was 80.6 per cent rural.

Germans consistently and overwhelmingly considered themselves to be Democrats. In Platte County, for example, 78.3 per cent of the German Catholics included in the sample were Democrats while a mere 7.2 per cent identified with the Republicans. Among the Elkhorn Valley group the contrast was even more dramatic with a ratio of 76.3 per cent to 5.3 per cent.

Wide variations in partisan identification, however, existed among the Lutherans. They tended to follow patterns of local or regional political behavior. Lutheran association with the GOP ranged from 59.0 per cent in Otoe County to 17.6 per cent in Platte County while loyalty to the Democrats ranged from 71.6 per cent among the Elkhorn Valley Germans to 24.5 per cent among those of the Seward-York region. Like the Catholics, many Lutherans perceived that the Democratic party was in harmony with immigrant goals and concerns. The Republican party, on the other hand, seemed to pose a threat to their values and attitudes. Yet the Lutheran Germans were decidedly more Republican than the Catholics and more Democratic than other protestants.

Attachment to the Republican party was most common among the German Baptists, Methodists, Congregationalists, Mennonites, and Evangelicals. With certain exceptions, these denominations openly sympathized with the prohibition, Sabbatarian, and woman suffrage movements.[17] These measures in turn regularly received strong though not always official support from Republicans in Nebraska during the 1880's and 1890's. Inevitably German adherents of these non-Lutheran protestant denominations were drawn to the Republican party. In Otoe County 71.4 per cent of their number were Republican as compared to 59.0 per cent of the Lutherans. In Platte County 47.4 per cent were Republican compared to 17.6 per cent of the Lutherans and 7.2 per cent of the Catholics. Even when the Democratic non-Lutheran protestants outnumbered the Republicans, as they did among the Elkhorn Valley Germans, the really important statistic is that the Republican tendency was twice as strong among them (38.9 per cent) as among the Lutherans (18.2 per cent) and seven times stronger than among the Catholics (5.3 per cent). Non-Lutheran protestants, moreover, were more frequently residents of the cities and towns than the members of the other religious subgroups.[18] Hence, they were more likely to have felt the pressures of the established Anglo-Saxon protestant norms. In politics this usually meant voting the Republican ticket.

17 Immigrant churches like the Mennonite bodies and the Evangelical Synod did not share this enthusiasm for woman suffrage. These groups deemed it destructive of their concept of the home and family.

18 Frederick C. Luebke, "German Immigrants and the Churches in Nebraska, 1889–1915," *Mid-America*, L (April, 1968), 116–130.

Partisan identification among those who revealed no church membership closely resembles that of non-Lutheran protestants. Frequently urban dwellers, they also were attracted to the Republican party. Presumably the unaffiliated included large numbers of rapid assimilators whose need for the immigrant church as an ameliorative institution was not great. It is significant also that the members of no church were usually the most numerous among those who indicated no political party ties. Apathy in one area of life seems to have carried over into another.

The religious factor is related to political activity in Table 7. The data readily demonstrate that Lutheran and Catholic Germans were less likely

TABLE 7

Percentage Distribution of Politically Active Persons among 653 German-American Adult Males, as Related to Church Affiliation

	1889 Otoe County	1892 Elkhorn Valley	1899 Seward-York Area	1915 Platte County
Catholics				
No. of subjects	(8)[a]	(38)	(15)	(69)
Politically active		21.1	40.0	39.1
Politically inactive		78.9	60.0	60.9
Lutherans				
No. of subjects	(61)	(88)	(49)	(68)
Politically active	29.5	25.0	36.7	27.9
Politically inactive	70.5	75.0	63.3	72.1
Other Protestants				
No. of subjects	(28)	(18)	(24)	(38)
Politically active	50.0	33.3	37.5	50.0
Politically inactive	50.0	66.7	62.5	50.0
No Church Membership				
No. of subjects	(27)	(86)	(20)	(16)
Politically active	48.1	31.4	35.0	56.3
Politically inactive	51.9	68.6	65.0	43.7

[a] The number of subjects is too small for meaningful distribution on a percentage scale.

to engage in political activity than were members of non-Lutheran protestant denominations or the unaffiliated. Church affiliation as related to levels of political activity was also an aspect of urban or rural residence, since these groups were also proportionately more numerous in the cities and towns. Conversely, German residents of the Seward-York area, for whom the data indicate no relationship between the two variables, were the most rural of the four samplings.

Table 8 relates lodge membership to political party identification. In a general way the data show that high levels of social interaction with native

TABLE 8

Percentage Distribution of Political Party Identification of 653 German-American
Adult Males, as Related to Lodge Membership

	1889 Otoe County	1892 Elkhorn Valley	1899 Seward-York Area	1915 Platte County
Lodge Members				
No. of subjects	(18)	(35)	(19)	(46)
Republican	50.0	25.7	42.1	36.9
Democratic	38.9	62.9	15.8	41.3
Populist	—	2.8	15.8	—
Prohibition	—	—	—	2.2
Socialist	—	—	—	—
Independent	—	—	10.5	10.9
Not stated	11.1	8.6	15.8	8.7
Lodge Membership Not Indicated				
No. of subjects	(106)	(195)	(89)	(145)
Republican	59.4	20.5	31.5	16.5
Democratic	23.6	54.9	31.5	57.2
Populist	—	7.7	6.7	—
Prohibition	2.8	.5	—	—
Socialist	—	—	1.1	—
Independent	3.8	3.1	5.6	9.7
Not stated	10.4	13.3	23.6	16.5

Americans, as manifested by membership in secret fraternal organizations, was associated with Republican party attachments. This relationship was strongest in Platte County, where Republicans were twice as common among the lodge members (36.9 per cent) as among nonlodge members (16.5 per cent). The reverse pattern may be observed among the Democrats. Whereas 41.3 per cent of the Platte County lodge members were Democrats, a significantly larger proportion (57.2 per cent) of the nonlodge members affiliated with the Democrats. Lack of political involvement is also related to nonmembership in secret societies. In three of the four groups, the proportion who indicated no political party ties was larger among the nonmembers than among the members. In Platte County, for example, the percentage of the former was 16.5 while the latter registered 8.7 per cent.

The relationship of lodge membership to the holding of public or party office among the Germans of Nebraska is shown in Table 9. The data uniformly indicate that membership in secret fraternal societies was associated with higher levels of political activity. This was most clearly the case in Otoe County, where 72.2 per cent of the lodge members were politically active, while only 32.1 per cent of the nonmembers were. The same relationship, though less dramatic, may be observed in each of the other groups. Of course both lodge membership and political activity are necessarily associated

TABLE 9

Percentage Distribution of Politically Active Persons among 653 German-American
Adult Males, as Related to Lodge Membership

	1899 Otoe County	1892 Elkhorn Valley	1899 Seward-York Area	1915 Platte County
Lodge Members				
No. of subjects	(18)	(35)	(19)	(46)
Politically active	72.2	42.9	42.1	58.7
Politically inactive	27.8	57.1	57.9	41.3
Lodge Membership Not Indicated				
No. of subjects	(106)	(195)	(89)	(145)
Politically active	32.1	24.6	36.0	32.4
Politically inactive	67.9	75.4	64.0	67.6

with urban residence. Yet lodge membership seems to have exerted an independent influence because the proportions of politically active lodge members were usually higher than the proportion of politically active urban dwellers. In Platte County, for example, 58.7 per cent of the lodge members held public or party office compared to 51.7 per cent of the business and professional persons resident in the cities and towns.[19]

By way of summary it may be said that church membership is clearly the best guide to the political behavior of the four groups of German residents of Nebraska. Catholic tendencies toward the Democratic party were always strong. While Lutherans may have had a large proportion of Republicans, as in Otoe County, they normally were less inclined to identify with that party than were the members of other Protestant denominations. Republican tendencies were also strong among those who revealed no church connections. Political activity was regularly highest among non-Lutheran Protestants and least common among Catholics, except when they constituted a large part of the population, as they did in Platte County.

Generally, occupation and/or urban-rural residence was the least reliable index to party identification. In three of the four groups, however, political apathy (defined as the failure to reveal partisan preference) was proportionately greater among the Germans in the business and professional category.

The data connected with place of birth substantiate the theory that the second generation tended to abandon the political party of the first generation and to embrace its rival. Some evidence of this trend could be detected in each of the four groups. The attraction of the Democratic party was somewhat stronger for the American-born than it was for the European-born, although the pattern of the Platte County Germans did not conform to this

[19] Cf. Table 9 with Table 5.

generalization. The second generation regularly showed higher levels of political activity except in the case of the strongly rural Seward-York region.

. In general, place of birth, occupation, and church affiliation proved to be better indices of levels of political activity than of political party identification. The most active German was likely to be an American-born urbanite of Republican sentiments and a member of a lodge and a non-Lutheran Protestant church.

The data lead to the conclusion that slow assimilators, usually loyal to immigrant churches and more frequently residents of rural than urban areas, tended to find the Democratic party compatible with their group goals and interests. Their levels of party identification were high while their involvement in partisan activity was low. On the other hand, the more rapid assimilators were more likely to be found among the craftsmen and the business and professional persons of the towns and cities. The urbanites were more frequently members of nonimmigrant churches and of secret societies and therefore tended to conform to nativist norms of political behavior, as manifested by Republican party identification and by higher levels of political activity.[20]

[20] At those points in this analysis where the statistics do not conform to theoretic models, it does not necessarily follow that the theories are to be discarded. Only a few variables have been examined. Others were at work which are not subject to quantification. Moreover, one action or tendency may have been balanced by another working in the opposite direction so that neither appears statistically. Because of individual psychological differences a variable of importance for one person may seem irrelevant for another. Hence, it is remarkable how well and how often the data substantiate assimilation theory as it impinges upon political behavior.

CHAPTER V

Political Trends and Party Preferences, *1880–1900*

WHILE IT IS TRUE that German immigrants tended to conform to the dominant voting patterns of the community or district in which they lived, it does not follow that they were without distinctive political preferences of their own. They also displayed a unity which varied in strength according to the issues they perceived as impinging upon their collective interest. The existence of such bloc-voting may be discovered by comparing the party preferences of the German ethnic group with those of the total population.

Perhaps the best way to uncover distinctive voting patterns involves the use of mathematical formulas that produce coefficients of correlation between two variables. By relating (1) the numbers of German voters, expressed as a percentage of the total adult male population within the several precincts of a given county, to (2) the numbers of votes cast for a given candidate, expressed as a percentage of the total number of votes cast in the same precincts, indices of the degree of association between the two variables may be produced. A special value of this method is that it places no significance upon the outcome of a particular election, that is, on whichever party or candidate happened to win. Instead, it focuses upon voting tendencies, in this case, the tendency of Germans to vote for one of the parties, compared to the voting tendency of the rest of the voting public. Coefficients of correlation may reveal, for example, that the German voters in a given county had a greater tendency to vote Democratic even though every precinct in the county, including those with heavy German populations, may have cast a majority of its ballots for Republican candidates. Traditionally, historians could be expected to cite the majority vote in the German precincts as proof that Germans were voting Republican and thereby obscure the more significant fact that there was a stronger Democratic tendency among the German voters than among the total population.

The mathematical tool employed in this study for purposes of correlation is Charles Spearman's rank-difference formula in which the coefficient of

correlation is symbolized by the Greek letter rho.[1] The proportions of males
of German stock of voting age were obtained from the population schedules
of the Nebraska state census of 1885. Precinct voting data were acquired
from the records maintained in the offices of county clerks and from newspaper sources. The results from the elections of governor and President
were used on the assumption that these elections normally excited the most
interest.[2] In most instances the percentages won by the Democratic party
were used in the calculations because samples demonstrated that coefficients
of correlation were more likely to be positive than negative when associated
with the numbers of potential voters of German stock.

The selection of appropriate counties to be included in the analysis
presented certain problems. While it is neither possible nor necessary to
calculate correlations for every county in the state, certain conditions had to
be met by a county if it was to serve satisfactorily for correlation purposes.

The first consideration was the existence of a significantly large German
population within the county. Without this, there would be little to correlate.
Thus, nearly all of the counties selected were among those with the highest
concentrations of German stock as determined by the decennial censuses
from 1880 to 1900. Moreover, most counties chosen had a wide range of
concentration of German population. In Platte County, for example, the
range extended from a high of 95 per cent German-American adult males (in
Sherman township) to a low of 2 per cent (in Walker township).

A second prerequisite was the availability of voting data. If the county
clerk had failed to retain election records, newspapers had to be available to
supply the lack. In many instances neither source could produce the required
data.

Congruence of voting precincts with census districts was also vital.
Normally the census district coincided with township and ward boundaries.
A county could not be used, however, if it changed the boundaries of its
subdivisions shortly after the census. In a few cases the reorganization of
township boundaries consisted of nothing more than subdividing precincts

[1] The formula is

$$\rho = 1 - \frac{6 \sum D^2}{N(N^2 - 1)},$$

in which D is the difference in rank orders of the two variables and N is the number of
units being ranked. For a discussion of the use of correlational formulas in connection with
voting data, see Appendix II.

[2] As a general rule, the party vote was very strict during the 1880's. Hence little variation
occurred between the total number of votes won by a given party's candidate for governor
and, for example, state auditor. With the advent of the Australian ballot in 1891, however,
the amount of "scratching" increased greatly. The result is that significant differences may
be found in the precinct totals won by the several candidates of the same party after that
date.

as they existed in 1885, so that data could be made to conform to the original boundaries by grouping subsequent precinct voting data.

Regional location was also a consideration in the selection of counties to be analyzed. It was desirable to choose them from both the North and South Platte territories, from the Missouri River counties, and from farther west. No really satisfactory county could be found to represent the western half of the state. These lands were still too close to the frontier to be suitable for correlation purposes. Township or precinct boundaries, as well as county lines, were not stable. In 1880 the Sandhills territory was unorganized; by 1900 eleven counties had been created out of it. What was Cheyenne County in 1880 was five counties by 1900. Moreover, a number of the counties in the southwestern part of the state did not preserve election records before 1900. Others had a population so low as to make correlational analysis meaningless. Ultimately Hitchcock County was chosen because its election records were available and because one of its four 1885 townships had a sizable German and German-Russian population.

Thus few counties could be found which possessed all the desired qualities for the full twenty-year period. In addition to Hitchcock County, the following were finally selected: Otoe and Washington counties for the Missouri River area; Seward, Jefferson, and Thayer counties for the South Platte country farther west; Cuming and Madison counties for the Elkhorn Valley; and Platte and Hall counties for the Platte River Valley (see Map 3).

An analysis of each county follows. Brief references will be made to the geography and settlement of each, with special notice given to the centers of German population. Coefficients of correlation between German adult male population and the votes cast for Democratic candidates for President and governor from 1880 to 1900 will then be presented and analyzed.[3]

Otoe County

Otoe County (Map 4) embraces a hilly region in the southeastern part of Nebraska. Because of its location along the Missouri River, it was one of the earliest counties in the state to be settled. Its county seat, Nebraska City, was prominent as one of the state's leading cities and as a transportation center, not only for river traffic but also for the overland freight route to Kearney and later for railroads.

Germans were among the first settlers of the county. Three centers had been established by 1860. The first was located in the north central part of the county, with Berlin township serving as its nucleus. A second community

[3] The necessity for basing voting statistics on potential voting population rather than on total population has been stressed by George A. Boeck. See his "A Historical Note on the Uses of Census Returns," *Mid-America*, XLIV (January, 1962), 46–50.

74

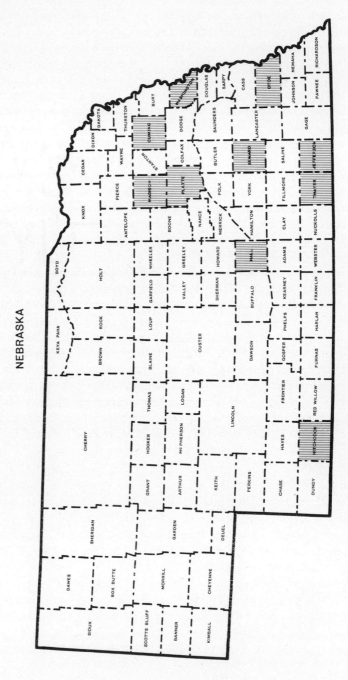

NEBRASKA

Map 3. Counties selected for correlational analysis.

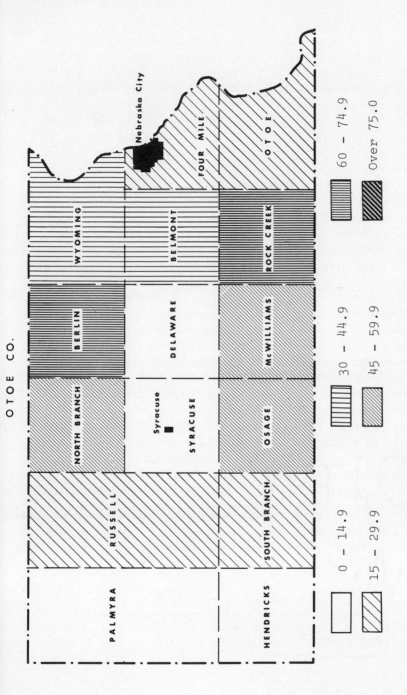

Map 4. Distribution of German–American adult males by townships in Otoe County, Nebraska, in 1885, by percentage of the total adult male population.

developed in Nebraska City. Throughout the early history of the town
members of the German colony were prominent in commercial and political
affairs. A third settlement of Germans was started in 1859 in the southern
part of the county in Rock Creek and McWilliams townships by immigrants
who had first settled in Illinois.[4] Gradually these centers of German population expanded into neighboring districts. By 1885 Germans constituted
about one-fourth of the potential voting population of Nebraska City and
of the county as a whole. In the two rural settlements the domination was
more complete, reaching nearly 75 per cent in Rock Creek precinct.

Approximately 10 per cent of the German element in Otoe County came
from Alsace, Austria, and Switzerland. There were few representatives of
other ethnic groups in the county. The precincts in the western part were
strongholds of native American population.

In voting behavior, the two rural German settlements were strikingly
different. While Rock Creek was usually among the most Democratic
precincts, Berlin was regularly more Republican than the county as a whole.
The explanation for this seems to lie in church affiliations. Berlin precinct
was the home of the mother church of German Methodism in Nebraska.[5]
It also had a congregation of the German Nebraska Lutheran Synod.[6] Of
the several German Lutheran synods, its spirit was the most closely allied to
American protestantism. By contrast, Democratic Rock Creek precinct had
a large Lutheran congregation of the conservative Iowa Synod. Its pastor
taught a parish school. A large Catholic parish was located near the center of
the precinct.[7] The party preferences of the two colonies thus parallel the
political predilections of the dominant religious groups of the two townships.

Figure 1 shows the coefficients of correlation that were obtained in Otoe
County for the election from 1880 to 1900. The range of possible coefficients
extends from +1.00 to −1.00. If a calculation produced a coefficient of
+1.00, it would mean that the order of precincts, ranked from most-German

[4] Louis Siekmann, "The German Element and Its Part in the Early Development of
Otoe County, Nebraska" (unpublished Master's thesis, University of Nebraska 1930),
pp. 13–17.

[5] Otto Kriege, Gustav Becker, Matthäus Herrmann, and C. L. Körner, *Souvenir der
West Deutschen Konferenz der Bischöflichen Methodistenkirche* (Cincinnati: Jennings and
Graham, 1906), pp. 138 f.

[6] A. B. Lentz et al., *Story of the Midwest Synod, ULCA, 1890–1950* (n.p.: n.d.),
p. 354.

[7] Michael A. Shine, "South Platte Catholicism and the Lincoln Diocese," in J. Sterling
Morton and Albert Watkins, *Illustrated History of Nebraska* (Lincoln: Jacob North and
Co., 1907), II, 460 n.; *Portrait and Biographical Album of Otoe and Cass Counties Nebraska*
(Chicago: Chapman Brothers, 1889), p. 153; Johannes Deindoerfer, *Geschichte der Evangel.-
Luth. Synode von Iowa und anderen Staaten* (Chicago: Wartburg Publishing House, 1897),
p. 354.

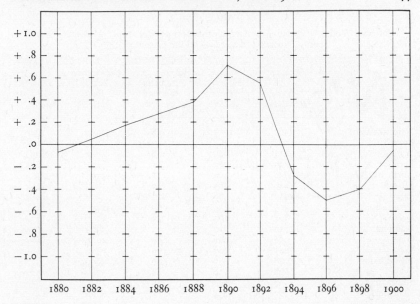

FIGURE 1. Coefficients of correlation between percentages of potential German voters according to the census of 1885 and the percentages of votes cast for Democratic candidates for President and governor in Otoe County, Nebraska, 1880–1900. Data for the elections of 1882 and 1886 are incomplete, making it impossible to calculate coefficients of correlations for those elections.

to least-German as indicated by Table 10 is identical to the order of the precincts, when ranked according to the percentages of votes given to Democratic candidates. If a coefficient of −1.00 was obtained, it would mean that the rank order is exactly reversed. It does not necessarily follow that a German proclivity for the Republican party would in that case be demonstrated because some votes normally went also to the Populist, Prohibition, and other minor parties in existence at that time.

The significance of a coefficient is customarily estimated by its square. Theoretically such a figure refers to the proportion of changes between the variables that can be accounted for by the correlation. To illustrate, there were many influences which impinged upon a typical German voter's decision in 1890 to vote Democratic. One of them may have been the fact that he was a member of the German ethnic minority group. Since the coefficient of correlation between the percentages of potential German voters and the percentages of votes cast for the Democratic candidate for governor in 1890 is +.71, about 50 per cent of all the variables bearing upon the decision theoretically could be accounted for by the fact of membership in the German group.

TABLE 10

Potential Voting Population among German-American Adult Males of Otoe County, Nebraska, According to the Census of 1885

Precinct	Total Population	Total Adult Males[a]	Potential German Voters[b]	Per Cent of Total Adult Males	Rank
Nebraska City	5597	1655	388	23.4	9
Four Mile	734	205	47	22.9	10
Wyoming	811	229	88	38.4	6
Berlin	735	202	131	64.9	2
North Branch	728	201	111	55.2	3
Russell	1326	368	60	16.3	12
Palmyra	1710	468	27	5.8	16
Syracuse	1505	459	65	14.2	13
Delaware	804	260	35	13.5	14
Belmont	736	217	72	33.2	7
Otoe	1058	290	58	20.0	11
Rock Creek	827	227	169	74.4	1
McWilliams	1048	296	146	49.3	5
Osage	668	158	85	53.8	4
South Branch	517	144	40	27.8	8
Hendricks	562	154	12	7.8	15
County	19,366	5533	1534	27.7	

[a] Adult males are defined as those persons twenty years of age and above. Twenty is used instead of twenty-one because of the tendency of people to use round numbers when replying to census takers' questions. See Merle Curti *et al.*, *The Making of an American Community : A Case Study of Democracy in a Frontier County* (Stanford: Stanford University Press, 1959), p. 457.

[b] Includes all males twenty years of age and above who were born in Europe or who had one or both parents born in Europe.

A coefficient of .00 means that there is no statistical relationship between the variables. For example, the coefficient for the election of 1880 in Otoe County is −.07. This may mean that German ethnicity had nothing to do with the voting decision made by an individual German voter. He may have cast his ballot as a merchant, or as a Lutheran, or as a lodge member, but not as a German. It is possible that, to use the language of the political behaviorist, the distinctiveness of the German group behavior was low, the probable explanation being that the transmission of group standards was weak. Few German language newspapers were published in the state in 1880 and a lack of unity characterized the German churches, which were among the few well-organized immigrant institutions in the state at that time. While group pressures to conform to certain standards of voting behavior undoubtedly existed among the Germans, it is unlikely that they extended much beyond the confines of the local community.

For the election of 1900 the coefficient of correlation for Otoe County is −.06, almost identical with the figure for the election of 1880. It is likely, however, that an entirely different circumstance prevailed. By 1900 there was no dearth of German-language publications and other German-American institutions were flourishing in addition to the churches. In this instance the transmission of group norms may be said to have lacked clarity, that is, conflicting standards of political behavior were being conveyed by the normal channels of communication within the group. Indeed, some German newspapers in 1900 fiercely condemned Republican imperialism and urged their readers to vote for William Jennings Bryan, while others were equally insistent that the unorthodox monetary policies endorsed by Bryan and the Democrats would ruin the prosperity that the Republicans had achieved under the leadership of William McKinley. No doubt hundreds of German voters of both parties marched to the polls in 1900 convinced of the righteousness of their party's position. Thus one German voter, disturbed by the prospect of imperialism and potential military conscription, could have his ballot cancelled out statistically by the choice of another German whose heritage of frugality was affronted by Populist fiscal doctrines. Both persons could have voted as Germans, even though the coefficient fails to indicate it.

What of the elections between 1880 and 1900? As Fig. 1 shows, a distinct pattern emerges when the coefficients are graphed over time. The affinity of the Germans for the Democratic party steadily increased through the 1880's as advocates of temperance and woman suffrage gained strength in the Republican party. The trend was climaxed by the extraordinary campaign of 1890, in which the chief issue as far as the Germans were concerned was the proposed prohibition amendment to the state constitution. The indentification of the Republican party with prohibition and related issues was devastatingly complete. The coefficient for the election of that year attains the remarkable level of +.71. When the potential German voters are associated with the percentages of votes cast against the prohibition amendment, the coefficient climbs still higher—to +.78.

The greatest shift of all in the voting behavior of the Germans of Otoe County occurred in 1894. From the relatively high figure of +.54, recorded for the election of 1892, the coefficient plunges to −.28. Apparently this dramatic change was the consequence of the fusion between the Democratic and Populist parties that had been engineered by Bryan in that year. Coefficients calculated between the German voters and the percentages of votes won by the Populist candidates demonstrate how unacceptable that new party of radical agrarianism was to the German ethnic group. For 1890, the first year in which the Populists offered a slate of candidates, the coefficient is −.52. For the election of 1892 it is still decidedly negative at −.31. Later, after the fears of Populism had been dissolved by the responsible gubernatorial administrations of Silas Holcomb and William Poynter, many

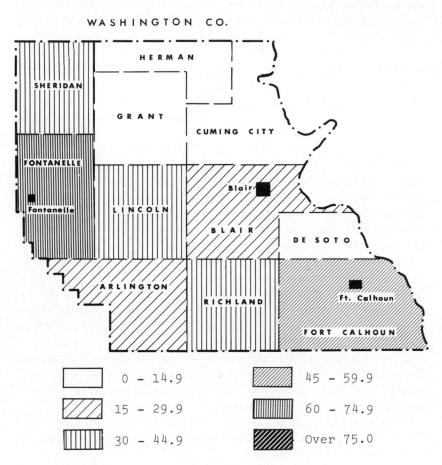

Map. 5. Distribution of German-American adult males by townships in Washington County, Nebraska, in 1885, by percentage of the total adult male population.

Germans of Otoe County drifted back to their old Democratic loyalties, especially under the impetus of Republican imperialism in 1898 and 1900. Yet the majority of the German voters of the county remained in the Republican fold after 1894.

Washington County

Washington County (Map 5), located about forty miles north of Otoe County, occupies a region between the Missouri River on the east and the Elkhorn River on the west. Among the earliest settlers in the county were German immigrants who developed two separate German communities by 1860. One was centered in Fort Calhoun township in the southeastern part of the county and the other in the northwestern townships of Fontanelle and Sheridan. The latter colony was overwhelmingly Lutheran in its religious beliefs, while the former was distinguished by a lack of rural churches of any denomination.[8] By 1885 (Table 11) Germans constituted about half the potential voting population of Fort Calhoun and Sheridan townships and nearly three-fourths of the voters of Fontanelle. For the county as a whole the figure was 25.3 per cent. One contemporary account estimated

TABLE 11

Potential Voting Population among German-American Adult Males of Washington County, Nebraska, According to the Census of 1885

Precinct	Total Population	Total Adult Males	Potential German Voters	Per Cent of Total Adult Males	Rank
Cuming City	770	211	11	5.2	12
Herman	767	124	9	7.3	10
Sheridan	681	154	69	44.8	3
Fontanelle	790	199	139	69.8	1
Arlington	1080	333	77	23.1	6
Lincoln	817	201	62	30.8	5
Grant	940	251	37	14.7	8
Richland	978	229	78	34.1	4
Fort Calhoun	1149	350	159	45.4	2
DeSoto	240	69	4	5.8	11
Blair	1511	359	61	17.0	7
City of Blair	2132	586	70	11.9	9
County	11,855	3066	776	25.3	

[8] William H. Buss and Thomas T. Osterman (eds.), *History of Dodge and Washington Counties, Nebraska, and Their People* (Chicago: American Historical Society, 1921), I, 370 ff.; Forrest B. Shrader, *A History of Washington County, Nebraska* (n.p.: 1937), pp. 180–185; Henry Rohwer, untitled MS, Werkmeister Collection, Nebraska State Historical Society.

that by the end of the century Germans accounted for more than 95 per cent of the population of both Fontanelle and Sheridan townships.[9] While the Germans of the western settlement were of diverse origins, the majority of the others in the county came from Holstein. Danish immigrants dominated the central part of the county while native Americans were strongest in the northeastern townships.

Unfortunately, the election records of Washington County for the nineteenth century have not been preserved. Hence voting data had to be gathered from newspaper sources. These proved to be inadequate for the elections from 1882 to 1888, as Fig. 2 indicates.

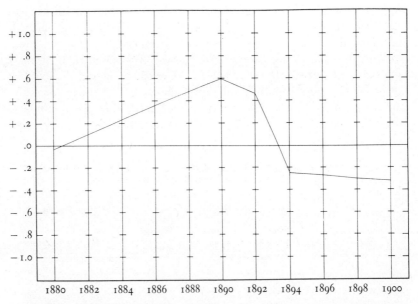

FIGURE 2. Coefficients of correlation between percentages of potential German voters according to the census of 1885 and the percentages of votes cast for Democratic candidates for President and governor in Washington County, Nebraska, 1880–1900. Data for the elections from 1882–88 are not available.

The pattern created by the graphing of coefficients of correlation for Washington County bears a distinct resemblance to that established for Otoe County. Both were Missouri River counties, both were settled at about the same time, and both were characteristically Republican with about one-fourth of the potential electorate of German stock. Both counties built up to a climax of Democratic strength among the Germans in 1890. This was

[9] Daniel N. Carr (ed.), *Men and Women of Nebraska. A Book of Portraits. Washington County Edition* (Fremont, Nebr.: Progress Publishing Co., 1903), p. 63.

followed by a sharp drop-off in 1894 with continued Republican loyalties thereafter.

The coefficient of correlation between German voters and ballots cast for the Democratic candidate for president in 1880 was −.04. In that election Washington County gave 69.9 per cent of its votes to the Republican party and 28.5 per cent to the Democrats. The heavily German precincts deviated little from this division. Fontanelle, for example, was slightly more Democratic than the county as a whole, while Fort Calhoun matched the county almost perfectly. The conclusion is unavoidable that in 1880 the fact of German ethnic origin had little influence upon the individual German voter's electoral decision in Washington County.

By 1890 a vital change had occurred. While the county as a whole gave 44.7 per cent of its ballots to the Democratic candidate, Fort Calhoun township gave him 72.3 per cent and Fontanelle 63.6 per cent. The coefficient for the election of that year is +.60.[10] When the German voters are associated with the percentages of votes cast against the prohibition amendment of that year, an almost identical coefficient of +.59 is obtained, thereby lending statistical support to the impressionistic evidence attributing the bloc voting to temperance agitation.

As in Otoe County, the Germans of Washington County made a spectacular switch in party allegiance in 1894 as they fled from Democratic-Populist fusion and embraced Republicanism once more. In that year the county voted 44.9 per cent Republican. Fontanelle, however, was the banner Republican precinct with 71.2 per cent. During the remainder of the decade the Germans of Washington County retained Republican tendencies and responded not at all to the Democratic alarms against imperialism in 1898 and 1900.

Seward County

Seward County (Map 6) is located in an agriculturally rich portion of the South Platte territory west of the state capital at Lincoln. While most of the county lies in the central loess plain, the eastern quarter is less attractive agriculturally than the high, flat prairies to the west. No important cities were to be found in Seward County, although nearly a dozen small towns and villages dotted the countryside.

The heaviest concentrations of Germans were in two rural areas. In H precinct nearly 60 per cent of the potential voters were Germans in 1885 (Table 12). This colony extended southward into I precinct. The other

---

[10] The coefficient would have been noticeably higher had it not been for the fact that tiny DeSoto precinct, which had many foreign-born citizens but few Germans, shared German fears and also voted strongly Democratic.

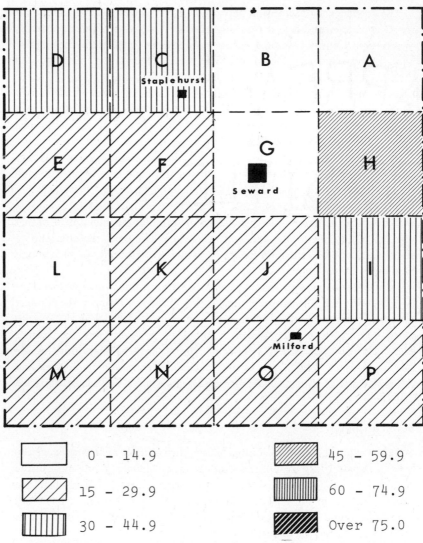

Map 6. Distribution of German-American adult males by townships in Seward County, Nebraska, in 1885, by percentage of the total adult male population.

TABLE 12

Potential Voting Population among German-American Adult Males of Seward
County, Nebraska, According to the Census of 1885

Precinct	Total Population	Total Adult Males	Potential German Voters	Per Cent of Total Adult Males	Rank
A	394	105	8	7.6	15
B	571	158	7	4.4	17
C	1076	311	98	31.5	4
D	777	202	78	38.6	3
E	1225	348	69	19.8	10
F	882	264	43	16.3	11
G	746	200	27	13.5	13
City of Seward	1982	589	77	13.1	14
H	1095	235	139	59.5	1
I	690	174	72	41.4	2
J	776	204	50	24.5	6
K	672	192	48	25.0	5
L	843	216	13	6.0	16
M	750	209	48	23.0	8
N	748	211	32	15.2	12
O	1462	396	81	20.5	9
P	536	148	35	23.7	7
County	15,225	4162	925	22.2	

center was located in the northwestern part of the county along Lincoln
Creek, primarily in C and D precincts. Germans were also scattered throughout the southern parts of the county but not often in solid clusters. By 1885,
22 per cent of the adult male population was of German stock. The Seward
Independent-Democrat [11] estimated in 1897 that about one-half of the county's
population was German. Few other ethnic groups were represented by
significant numbers in Seward County. Irish were not uncommon, especially
in C township. Danes were present in small numbers in C and M townships.
Although Bohemians later dominated A and B townships, these lands were
occupied almost exlusively by persons of Anglo-American origins in 1885.

The church affiliations of the Germans of Seward County were strongly
Lutheran. A string of seven Missouri Synod congregations was established
across the northern half of the county and every one of them maintained a
parish school. Before the end of the century three more congregations were
founded by the Missouri Synod in the southern part. Besides these, there
was an Iowa Synod congregation in I precinct and a Wisconsin Synod
church in D precinct. There were no German Catholic parishes. What few
German Catholics there were constituted minorities in three predominantly
Irish parishes. Other protestant denominations, especially Evangelicals and

[11] October 28, 1897.

Mennonities, were represented in the county. The western half of O precinct was the seat of a very strong Amish Mennonite settlement which traced its roots back through Ohio to the Pennsylvania Amish. Even though these people remained a German cultural island generation after generation, most were not classified as German stock. Their numbers, however, were supplemented by a few European-born Germans, especially from Alsace.[12]

Seward County, like Otoe and Washington, had a traditional attachment for the Republican party. The Germans of the county were, however, consistently more inclined toward the Democrats throughout the 1880's, as Fig. 3 demonstrates. The coefficient for the election of 1880 is +.32, a figure high enough to indicate leanings toward the Democrats. It is the more

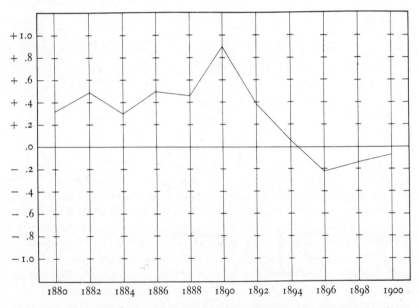

FIGURE 3. Coefficients of correlation between percentages of potential German voters according to the census of 1885 and the percentages of votes cast for Democratic candidates for President and governor in Seward County, Nebraska, 1880–1900. Voting data for the elections of 1880 and 1882 are correlated with census data from the federal census of 1880. Data from the state census of 1885 were used for all other elections.

12 [The Lutheran Church–Missouri Synod], *Statistisches Jahrbuch für das Jahr 1900*, pp. 77–81; W. W. Cox, *History of Seward County, Nebraska* (2nd ed.; University Place, Nebr.: Jason L. Claflin, 1905), pp. 416–422; "Geschichte des Nebraska-Distrikts," *Ev.-Luth. Gemeinde-Blatt*, LXI (August 15, 1926), p. 261; Theodore Schmidt, "The Mennonites of Nebraska" (unpublished Master's thesis, University of Nebraska, 1933), pp. 74–78; August de Belmont Hollingshead, "Trends in Community Development: A Study of Ecological and Institutional Processes in Thirty-four Southeastern Nebraska Communities, 1854–1934" (unpublished Ph.D. dissertation, University of Nebraska, 1935), p. 188.

noteworthy because I precinct, the third heaviest German township in 1880, gave 81.5 per cent of its votes to the Republicans, compared to 59.5 per cent for the county as a whole. In 1882 a woman suffrage amendment found a place on the ballot, largely under the sponsorship of the Republican party. The foreign-born instinctively reacted against it as a nativist threat to their conception of the family. Others identified the proposal as a preliminary step toward prohibition. In any case, the Germans were against it and they tended to associate it with the Republican party. The coefficient for the election of 1882 in Seward County is +.48, indicating a marked improvement in the fortunes of the Democrats among the Germans, despite the continued status of I township as the leading Republican precinct.[13]

As in other counties, the German attachment for the Democratic party in Seward County reached its climax in the election of 1890, for which the coefficient of correlation is a remarkable +.89. This loyalty, forged by the prohibition issue, was quickly dissolved during the next several elections until a low point was reached in 1896. The figure for that contest is − .23. A slight trend back to the Democrats may be noted in 1898 and 1900, but generally the Germans were divided according to community tendencies. Thus, while the county as a whole was almost evenly divided between the two parties in 1900, I township was 68.6 per cent Republican and equally German D township was 59.2 per cent Democratic.

Jefferson County

Jefferson County (Map 7) is located about twenty-five miles south of Seward County. Its German population, which constituted 17.6 per cent of the adult male population in 1885, was centered in three distinct communities (Table 13). The best known was the Russian-German colony founded in Cub Creek township by Peter Jansen in 1874. While Germans made up 76 per cent of the potential voting population more than half of these were *Volgadeutsch*. Mennonite churches predominated in the Cub Creek area, but small congregations of German Methodists and Evangelicals had also been established there by 1890.[14] Directly north of the Mennonite colony lay another German settlement of a rather different character. Located in

13 While I precinct went 76.1 per cent Republican, only 16.9 per cent of its votes were in favor of the woman suffrage amendment. Obviously the call to conform to group norms was loud and clear in this precinct. The coefficient of correlation between German voters and votes cast against the amendment in Seward County was +.77.

14 D. Paul Miller, "The Story of the Jansen Churches," *Mennonite Life*, X (January, 1955), 38–40; D. Paul Miller, "Jansen, Nebraska: A Story of Community Adjustment," *Nebraska History*, XXXV (June, 1954), pp. 129 f.; Kriege *et al.*, *Souvenir*, p. 103. See also *Plat Book of Jefferson County, Nebraska* (n.p.: Northwestern Publishing Co., 1900).

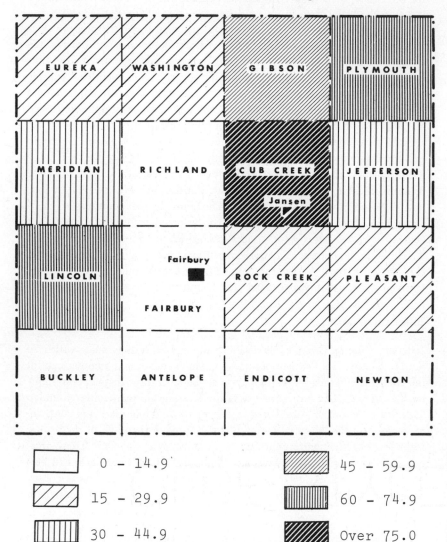

Map. 7 Distribution of German-American adult males by townships in
Jefferson County, Nebraska, in 1885, by percentage of the total adult male
population.

TABLE 13

Potential Voting Population among German-American Adult Males of Jefferson
County, Nebraska, According to the Census of 1885

Precinct	Total Population	Total Adult Males	Potential German Voters	Per Cent of Total Adult Males	Rank
Plymouth	659	183	118	64.5	2
Gibson	523	137	80	58.4	4
Washington	532	143	41	28.7	7
Eureka	506	127	23	18.1	9
Meridian	698	175	54	30.7	6
Richland	688	208	16	7.7	13
Cub Creek	865	221	168[a]	76.0	1
Jefferson	386	108	38	35.2	5
Pleasant	732	206	38	18.5	8
Rock Creek	586	137	24	17.5	10
Fairbury	1886	555	67	12.1	12
Lincoln	468	110	67	60.9	3
Buckley	1021	258	33	12.8	11
Antelope	531	136	3	2.2	16
Endicott	759	200	14	7.0	14
Newton	1053	277	19	6.9	15
County	11,893	3532	803	17.6	

[a] Russian-born Germans were 44.3 per cent of the total number of adult males; 31.7 per cent were "regular" German stock.

Plymouth and Gibson townships, this community included a large number of Hesse-Darmstadters who had lived in Canada for many years before migrating to Nebraska. By 1885 two-thirds of the potential voters in Plymouth township were German. A third rural colony was located west of Fairbury in Lincoln township from whence it extended north into Meridian township. For the most part, the latter two settlements were strongly Lutheran and Evangelical in church affiliation. Catholics and Mennonites were not among them.[15]

Few other ethnic groups were represented in Jefferson County. A small number of Bohemians settled in Buckley precinct, and a few Irish families were scattered throughout the county. In general, the character of the county was strongly Yankee or native American and very Republican.

Figure 4, which charts the coefficients for Jefferson County over the two decades, reveals that in 1880 the Germans were much less inclined toward the Democratic party than the county as a whole. However, the woman suffrage and antimonopolist fights of 1882 modified this attachment significantly. When the German voters are associated with the votes won by the Republican party in 1882, a coefficient of −.43 is obtained, a complete

15 U.S. Bureau of the Census, *Religious Bodies: 1906* (2 vols.; Washington: Government Printing Office, 1910), I, 335 ff.

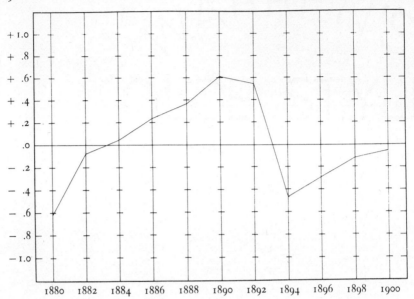

FIGURE 4. Coefficients of correlation between percentages of potential German voters according to the census of 1885 and the percentages of votes cast for Democratic candidates for President and governor in Jefferson County, Nebraska, 1880–1900.

reversal from the previous election, for which the coefficient is +.41. At the same time, the Anti-Monopoly party, which consisted largely of disaffected Republicans and ex-Greenbackers, did very well in Jefferson County. A correlation of the Germans with its vote produces a figure of +.32, indicating that, of the three competing parties, the Anti-Monopolists fared best among the Germans.[16]

With each succeeding election during the decade, the attraction of the Democratic party increased until the contest of 1890. The coefficient for that election is +.62. When the German voters are associated with the votes cast for the Republicans a figure of −.60 is obtained. The German rejection of Populism in 1890 was equally emphatic, as a coefficient of −.55 reveals.

In 1892 the Democratic percentage of the total votes cast in Jefferson County dropped to a mere 12.5 per cent. Yet the Germans were much more inclined to remain loyal to the Democrats than the total population, as a coefficient of +.54 indicates. As in other counties, the big change came in

16 The coefficient produced by correlation of German voters with votes cast against the woman suffrage amendment is a very high +.70. The data thus indicate that while the Jefferson County Germans were definitely opposed to woman suffrage they did not associate it with the Anti-Monopolist party, as one should expect because of its strong reformist character.

1894. Bryan's fusionist strategy was successful among the total population of the county, but the Germans would have none of it, as a coefficient of −.47 indicates. They were dedicated to sound money principles; they showed it by their support of the Gold Democrats, a splinter group of Democratic regulars of the Cleveland stripe, for whom Bryan's fusionist policy was anathema. Though the Gold Democrats garnered a mere 5.8 per cent of the total votes in the county, most of them seem to have been cast by German voters. The coefficient of correlation in this instance is +.76, a figure of extraordinary magnitude considering the size of the vote.

For the remaining elections in the 1890's the Germans were badly split, as they had been in Otoe and Seward counties. The election of 1898 illustrates the division. In that year the county as a whole was slightly Republican, 51.8 per cent to 47.8 per cent. But the Mennonite precincts (Cub Creek and Jefferson) gave 62.4 per cent and 73.0 per cent of their votes to the Republicans. Meanwhile, just a few miles north, the equally German but predominantly Lutheran Plymouth precinct cast 65.5 per cent of its votes for the Democratic candidate. Figure 4 suggests that in the county as a whole there may have been an improvement in the appeal of the Democratic party for German voters.

Thayer County

Adjacent to Jefferson County on the west is Thayer County (Map 8). A near duplicate of its neighbor in terms of geography and population, Thayer County was distinguished by having a precinct that was almost totally German Lutheran. While German stock constituted 19 per cent of the total number of adult males in the county in 1885 (Table 14), the figure for Friedensau township registered 93.4 per cent. The census lists seventy-one German adult males at a time when the records of Trinity Lutheran congregation of Friedensau reveal fifty-two voting members, all adult males. Besides these, others were members of Peace Lutheran congregation, a splinter group that had affiliated with the Ohio Synod. The colony extended westward into Kiowa and Spring Creek townships, where at least four additional Lutheran parishes were established by 1885. Except for a tiny German Congregational church, no other denomination seems to have been established among the Germans of this county.[17]

There were a few Swiss, Alsatians, and Russians among the Germans of Thayer County, but except for several Norwegian families, almost no other

[17] U.S. Bureau of the Census, *Religious Bodies: 1906*, I, 336 f.; [Lutheran Church—Missouri Synod], *Statistisches Jahrbuch, 1885*, pp. 45 f.; *Story of Peace Lutheran Church* (50th anniversary pamphlet), p. 7; *Minutes of the Twenty-Ninth Annual Meeting of the General Association of Congregational Churches of Nebraska* (Lincoln: State Journal Co., 1885), p. 20.

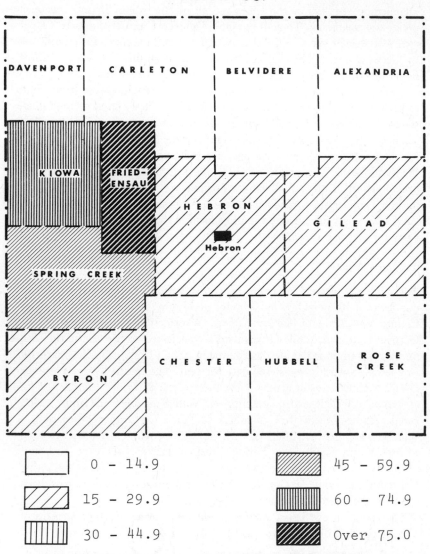

Map 8. Distribution of German-American adult males by townships in Thayer County, Nebraska, in 1885, by percentage of the total adult male population.

TABLE 14

Potential Voting Population among German-American Adult Males of Thayer
County, Nebraska, According to the Census of 1885

Precinct	Total Population	Total Adult Males	Potential German Voters	Per Cent of Total Adult Males	Rank
Alexandria	1083	297	33	11.1	9
Belvidere	1191	355	45	12.7	8
Carleton	1074	286	41	14.3	7
Davenport	750	219	16	7.3	11
Kiowa	357	98	69	70.4	2
Spring Creek	530	151	83	55.0	3
Friedensau	312	76	71	93.4	1
Hebron	1770	489	78	16.0	6
Gilead	774	203	53	26.1	4
Rose Creek	442	111	2	1.8	13
Hubbell	857	249	10	4.0	12
Chester	830	247	20	8.1	10
Harbine/Byron	360	108	27	25.0	5
County	10,330	2889	548	19.0	

non-English speaking immigrants were resident in the county. Native
Americans were most numerous of all groups, especially in the southeastern townships.

Unfortunately for purposes of statistical correlation, Thayer County made
minor changes in the boundaries of its precincts several times during the
period being studied. It is possible therefore to calculate correlations only
for the elections from 1882 to 1890, the years during which the census
districts were congruent with the voting precincts.

The coefficients of correlation charted in Fig. 5 indicate the overwhelming
preference which the Germans of Thayer County had for the Democratic
party during the 1880's. This was a time when the county as a whole
normally gave between 55 and 60 per cent of its votes to the Republicans.
The failure of the Germans to conform to the standards of the larger community of Thayer County may be explained by the fact that about half of all
the Germans in the county were concentrated in one area with Friedensau
as its center. Here, indeed, was a rural ghetto which reduced to a minimum
interpersonal contacts with people outside the ethnic group. Friedensau
regularly gave only 10 to 20 per cent of its ballots to the Republicans. In
1890, only one solitary vote in the precinct was cast for the Republican
candidate for governor.

At first the Germans of Thayer County rejected the siren song of Populism.
A correlation with Populist votes in 1890 produces a coefficient of − .54. In

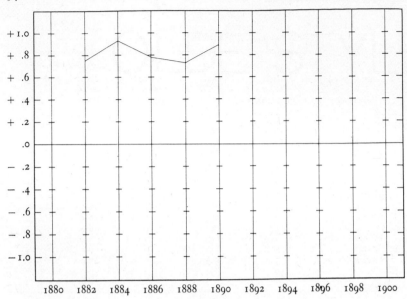

FIGURE 5. Coefficients of correlation between percentages of potential German voters according to the census of 1885 and the percentages of votes cast for Democratic candidates for President and governor in Thayer County, Nebraska, 1882–1890.

the next election, however, the Populist party achieved remarkable popularity in the German townships. Kiowa was its leading precinct with 72.9 per cent. All but one of the five most German townships exceeded the county-wide Populist vote of 36.2 per cent by more than 10 per cent. This popularity was sustained in 1894. However, a notable minority of Germans apparently objected to free silver and voted for the Gold Democratic candidate in that year. While the county gave only 5.2 per cent to those stalwarts, the German precincts gave them from 15 to 17 per cent.

By 1896 the heretofore solid ranks of the Germans of Thayer County began to break. Friedensau remained true to its strong Democratic tradition, free silver or no. Spring Creek and Kiowa, the other leading German townships, defected to the opposition, as they both exceeded the 52.2 per cent won by the Republicans that year. This conflict of political norms among German Lutherans continued to the end of the decade, with Kiowa among the leading Republican precincts and Friedensau at the head of the Democratic column.

Hall County

Hall County (Map 9), located astride the Platte River, is much like those counties from the southern part of the state already analyzed. Like Otoe

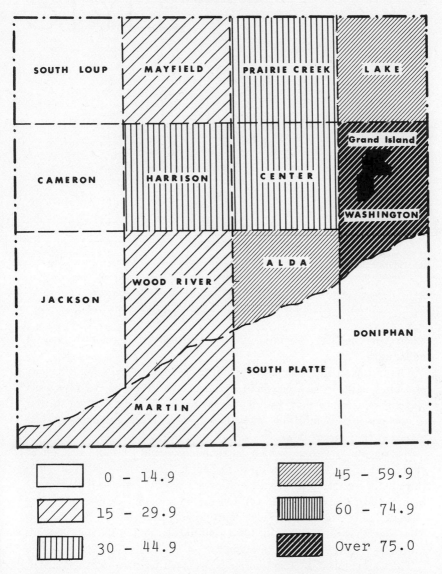

Map 9. Distribution of German-American adult males by townships in Hall County, Nebraska, in 1885, by percentage of the total adult male population.

TABLE 15

Potential Voting Population among German–American Adult Males of Hall County,
Nebraska, According to the Census of 1885

Precinct	Total Population	Total Adult Males	Potential German Voters	Per Cent of Total Adult Males	Rank
Grand Island	5040	1536	406	26.4	—
1st Ward	—	331	27	8.2	16
2nd Ward	—	523	217	41.5	4
3rd Ward	—	411	88	21.4	10
4th Ward	—	271	74	27.3	8
Lake	394	100	48	48.0	3
Prairie Creek	343	96	31	32.3	6
Mayfield	375	98	24	24.5	9
South Loup	259	82	10	12.2	13
Cameron	600	149	5	3.4	18
Harrison	494	130	40	30.8	7
Center	577	142	51	35.9	5
Washington	765	166	146	88.0	1
Alda	492	135	72	53.3	2
Wood River	1039	301	48	15.9	11
Jackson	864	233	10	4.3	17
Martin	322	85	13	15.3	12
South Platte	496	144	17	11.8	14
Doniphan	1050	269	27	10.0	15
County	13,130	3666	947	25.8	

County, its chief city, Grand Island, was a transportation center because of its location.

The German population of Hall County centered in and around the city of Grand Island, which had been founded by a group of Germans from Davenport, Iowa, in 1857. By 1885 Germans constituted about one quarter of the potential number of voters in the city. Their concentration was especially heavy in what was the second ward at that time.

Washington township, which surrounded Grand Island, was almost entirely German. Lake township to the north, Center and Harrison townships to the west, and Alda to the southwest were all from one-third to more than one-half German (Table 15). On the other hand, few Germans were to be found in the part of Hall County located south of the Platte River. Moreover, they carefully avoided the sand hills located in the northwestern townships of South Loup and Mayfield.

The total number of foreign-born who were not German was small. A few Scandinavians, principally Danes, had settled here and there. Irish were somewhat more numerous and, because they were concentrated in one district in Jackson and Wood River townships, they were more conspicuous.

Most other townships with small German populations were strongly Anglo-American in ethnic compositions.[18]

Holsteiners predominated among the Germans of Hall County. The leading church affiliation among them was consequently Lutheran. Within Grand Island there were three congregations; together they reflect the gradations of assimilation achieved by German Lutherans upon their arrival in the city. For the rapid assimilators there was St. Paul's English Lutheran congregation; for those who retained a higher regard for the mother tongue there was St. Paul's German Lutheran church, affiliated with the German Nebraska Synod; for the slow assimilators—appealing especially to the farmers outside the city—there was Trinity congregation, a member of the Missouri Synod, complete with a parochial school. In addition, several rural Lutheran parishes had been established in the county. A flourishing German Catholic congregation had been founded in Grand Island by 1876. The Evangelical Association, a Methodistic body which enrolled many German members, was also represented. Generally, however, the levels of church membership were low in Hall County compared to the state as a whole and to the other counties considered in this study.[19]

During the 1880's the Republican party had little appeal for the Germans of Hall County, despite the fact that several of their leaders, notably Fred Hedde and William Stolley, were among its staunch advocates. For each election from 1882 to 1892, as Fig. 6 shows, coefficients of correlation between German voters and the percentages of votes won by Democratic candidates average between +.50 and +.70. Throughout this period the Germans maintained an alliance with the Irish voters. Jackson precinct, where the latter were very strong, was regularly among the leading Democratic precincts. This fact has a substantial effect upon the magnitude of the coefficients, since Jackson was also one of the least German precincts. In 1888, for example, Jackson ranked second in Democratic strength, but it was seventeenth in terms of the size of its German population. Nevertheless, the coefficient for that election is +.69, a figure of considerable magnitude. But when Jackson precinct is omitted from the calculation, the coefficient soars to the extraordinary figure of +.93.

In 1890 a notable shift in traditional alliances occurred. The Irish of Jackson township abandoned the Democratic party and joined with the Yankees of Cameron and Martin townships to lead the Populist ranks.

18 Cf. A. F. Buechler, R. J. Barr, and Dale P. Stough, *History of Hall County Nebraska* (Lincoln: Western Publishing and Engraving Co., 1920), pp. 150–161.

19 U.S. Census Office, *Report on Statistics of Churches in the United States at the Eleventh Census* (Washington: Government Printing Office, 1894), p. 403; U.S. Bureau of the Census, *Religious Bodies: 1906*, I, 335; A. T. Andreas, *History of the State of Nebraska* (Chicago: Western Historical Co., 1882), p. 936; Buechler *et al.*, *History of Hall County*, pp. 328–347.

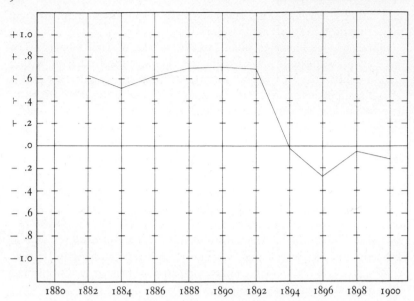

Figure 6. Coefficients of correlation between percentages of potential German voters according to the census of 1885 and the percentages of votes cast for Democratic candidates for President and governor in Hall County, Nebraska, 1882–1900. The precinct boundaries of 1880 do not correspond to the census districts of 1885, hence no coefficient of correlation can be calculated for that election.

Meanwhile the city of Grand Island voted with the Germans to give an unprecedented 57.6 per cent to the Democratic party (compared to 40.0 per cent for the county as a whole). The agrarian radicalism of the Populists seem to have caused the realignment. Grand Island's 13.0 per cent for the Populists was the lowest in the county. At the same time the German rejection of Populism in 1890 is indicated by a coefficient of − .63.

By 1892 disaster had caught up with the Democratic party. Unable to meet the challenge of Populism, its share of the vote in Hall County dropped to a trifling 11.9 per cent. The Germans nevertheless continued to vote much more heavily Democratic than the rest of the voters, as a coefficient of + .69 for that contest testifies. Heavily German Washington precinct, which surrounds Grand Island, behaved like a typical rural area dominated by a city as it gave 47.1 per cent of its votes to the Populists (compared to 41.0 per cent for the county).

Utter confusion reigned in 1894. County totals show an almost perfect division between the two parties at 48.2 per cent for the Republicans and 47.8 per cent for the "Demopop" fusion ticket. But these figures are deceptive because the range within the county on the precinct level was great.

Washington, the leading German township, was at the head of the Republican column with 65.1 per cent while Alda, which ranked second according to German population, gave the GOP a mere 26.5 per cent, the second lowest in the county. Here was another example of conflict in the transmission of group norms among the German ethnic group. Ethnicity seems to have been a factor in their voting behavior, for, if it was not, the percentages which the Germans gave the two parties are more likely to have approximated those of the county as a whole.

In 1896 the Republican party seems to have made some progress among the German voters. Both Washington and Alda exceeded the countywide 49.7 per cent for the Republicans. But confusion reigned again in 1898 and 1900, when the Germans were divided by the issue of imperialism, much as they were in other counties.

Platte County

Fifty miles down the Platte River from Grand Island is Platte County, (Map 10), one of the most interesting counties of Nebraska in terms of ethnic composition. Its chief city, Columbus, like Nebraska City and Grand Island, had a large minority of German-born citizens. Like many transportation centers it had a cosmopolitan population.

In 1885 more than a third of the potential voting population of Platte County was of German stock. Included within the German community were the largest Swiss German and Austrian German groups in the state. Alsatians were also common. Together these three subgroups constituted about one quarter of the German element (Table 16). Four geographically distinct communities of Germans were identifiable within the county. The first was in Columbus, which had been founded by a group of Germans and Swiss in 1856. A heterogeneous group, the Germans were especially numerous in the first ward. No one denomination held sway over the Germans of Columbus. A German Methodist and at least two Lutheran congregations had been formed. A German Reformed congregation reflected the Swiss origin of many of the people. Germans were the majority ethnic group in the large St. Bonaventure Catholic parish, which had maintained a sizable parochial school since 1878.[20]

Several miles northeast of Columbus was another German Lutheran community which surpassed Friedensau (Thayer County) in size and

[20] Margaret Curry, *The History of Platte County, Nebraska* (Culver City, Calif.: Murray and Gee, 1950), pp. 258, 265, 281; Eugene Hagedorn, *The Franciscans in Nebraska* (Humphrey and Norfolk, Nebr.: Humphrey Democrat and Norfolk Daily News, 1931), p. 254; Andreas, *History of Nebraska*, p. 1273; G. W. Phillips (ed.), *Past and Present of Platte County, Nebraska* (2 vols.; Chicago: S. J. Clarke Publishing Co., 1915), II, 122; *Columbus Journal*, November 13, 1878.

PLATTE CO.

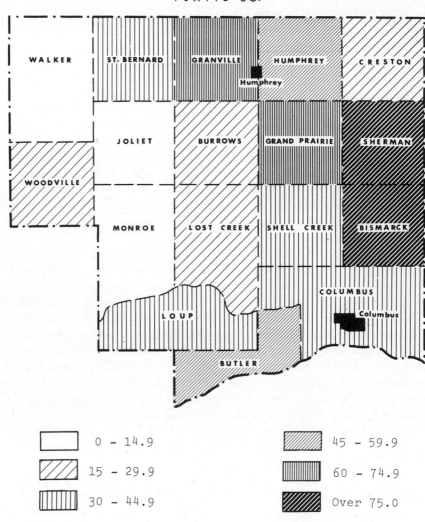

Map 10. Distribution of German-American adult males by townships in Platte County, Nebraska, in 1885, by percentage of the total adult male population.

TABLE 16

Potential Voting Population among German-American Adult Males of Platte County,
Nebraska, According to the Census of 1885

Precinct	Total Population	Total Adult Males	Potential German Voters	Per Cent of Total Adult Males	Rank
Creston	439	97	16	16.5	17
Humphrey	678	173	90	52.0	5
Granville	668	165	104	63.0	4
St. Bernard	514	149	54	36.2	9
Walker	668	196	4	2.0	20
Woodville	542	145	28	19.3	14
Joliet	486	129	16	12.4	18
Burrows	633	163	44	27.0	13
Grand Prairie	615	151	110	72.9	3
Sherman	575	147	140	95.2	1
Bismarck	567	138	115	83.3	2
Shell Creek	534	131	47	35.9	10
Lost Creek	877	238	41	17.2	16
Monroe	599	153	9	5.9	19
Loup	385	124	54	43.6	8
Butler	528	83	39	47.0	7
Columbus	709	207	63	30.4	12
City of Columbus	2573	766	262	34.2	—
1st Ward	—	252	131	52.0	6
2nd Ward	—	273	86	31.5	11
3rd Ward	—	241	45	18.7	15
County	12,590	3355	1236	36.8	

exclusiveness. This colony was located along Shell Creek and its tributary,
Loseke Creek, in Bismarck and Sherman townships. It consisted largely of
Oldenburgers, although Swiss Germans were also to be found there. The
community was served by no less than five Lutheran parishes, at least four
of which were large and flourishing. Two were affiliates of the Missouri
Synod and maintained parish schools from the time of their organization.
The others were affiliated with the German Nebraska Synod. The only other
church to be found in the area was a German Baptist congregation on the
western fringe of the settlement.[21]

The territory between the Loup and Platte rivers in Butler and Loup
townships was the site of a third German settlement. The great majority of
the adult males in this district were foreign-born. About half of them were

[21] Curry, *Platte County*, pp. 255–285; U.S. Census Office, *Report on Statistics of Churches*
(1890), pp. 443, 464; Lentz *et al.*, *Story of the Midwest Synod*, pp. 314, 316, 362; [Lutheran
Church–Missouri Synod. Nebraska District], *Dritter Synodal-Bericht des Nebraska
Distrikts der deutschen evang.-luth. Synode von Missouri, Ohio und anderen Staaten, A.D.
1885* (St. Louis: Luth. Concordia-Verlag, 1885), p. 4.

Germans, of whom the Swiss formed the largest subgroup. Poles from Austria and Prussia, as well as other Austrian Slavic peoples had settled there. The German churches located in the community were Catholic, German Reformed, and German Methodist.[22]

A fourth German colony in Platte County was located in St. Bernard, Granville, Humphrey, and part of Grand Prairie townships. In this area first- and second-generation Germans constituted from one-half to three-fourths of the population in 1885. Bavarians and Austrians predominated among the foreign-born Germans. Centered around the town of Humphrey, the community was overwhelmingly Catholic, though two small Lutheran congregations and a German Baptist church were established there during the period. Three large German Catholic churches served the area, each of which maintained a parochial school.[23]

Besides the Germans, three other ethnic groups occupied clearly defined geographical areas. A strong Irish settlement was located in Shell Creek township east of Platte Center. Burrows township contained the largest Polish community in the state. In the northwestern corner of the county, in Walker and spilling over into Woodville township, was a very strong community of Swedes and Danes. Anglo-American stock was strongest in Creston, Monroe, and Lost Creek townships, though each of them had sufficiently large numbers of Germans to support small Lutheran churches.[24]

The fact that there were significant numbers of other ethnic groups in the county whose voting patterns were likely to resemble those of the Germans had the effect of reducing the magnitude of the coefficients of correlation. As Fig. 7 demonstrates, the Germans of Platte County voted more strongly Democratic than did the total population. But the same was also true of Irish Shell Creek and Polish Burrows precincts. Thus, in 1880, even though every German precinct with one exception voted more heavily Democratic than the county as a whole, a correlation produces a coefficient of only +.50. Such was the pattern in every election before 1890. Meanwhile the Republican majorities always appeared in the Anglo-American and Scandinavian precincts. The Lutheran Germans were divided. Democratic candidates always fared well in Bismarck precinct where the Missouri Synod prevailed. Its twin to the north, Sherman precinct (in which most voters attended a German Nebraska Synod congregation) was regularly Republican.

22 Hagedorn, *Franciscans*, p. 413; Curry, *Platte County*, p. 281; [Methodist Episcopal Church. West German Conference], *Deutscher Kalender für das Jahr 1901* (Cincinnati: Jennings and Pye, n.d.), p. 78.

23 Hagedorn, *Franciscans*, pp. 298–522; Phillips (ed.), *Platte County*, I, 330–345; Curry, *Platte County*, pp. 235–261.

24 U.S. Census Office, *Compendium of the Eleventh Census: 1890. Part I. Population*, pp. 650 f.; Hagedorn, *Franciscans*, p. 392.

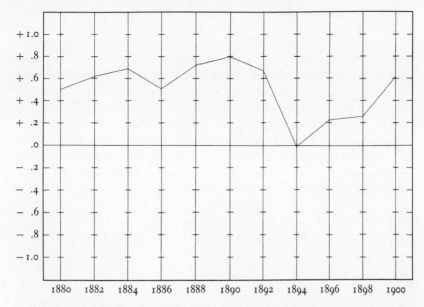

FIGURE 7. Coefficients of correlation between percentages of potential German voters according to the census of 1885 and the percentages of votes cast for Democratic candidates for President and governor in Platte County, Nebraska, 1880–1900.

In 1890 the prohibition issue moved Sherman township into Democratic ranks. The result was that the Platte County Germans, like those in every other county examined so far, registered their greatest tendencies toward the Democratic party in that year, the coefficient for which is +.80. The Democratic share in the county was 47.2 per cent but Sherman gave it 88.9 per cent. Meanwhile in Bismarck township Republican strength was reduced to a single vote. Ethnic block voting in 1890 is further displayed by the massive movement of Anglo-American and Scandinavian voters into the Populist column. Monroe precinct gave the new party 86.9 per cent, and Walker gave it an extraordinary 98.0 per cent. German refusal to vote Populist is shown by a coefficient of −.69.

In 1892 the Germans of Platte County tended to remain true to the cherished party of what they called "personal liberty" even though other traditional Democrats among the Irish and Poles defected to the Populist cause. But when Bryan used free silver to achieve "Demopop" fusion in 1894, the Germans, especially Lutheran Germans, abandoned the Democratic standard. Many voted Republican but others for whom the memory of 1890 was still too strong turned to the futile alternative of the Gold Democratic slate. The pattern was exactly like that of Jefferson and Thayer counties. (A correlation of German voters with Gold Democratic percentages produces a coefficient of $+.85$.) For these voters only the conservative Cleveland type of Democrat was untainted by prohibition and "funny money." The Scandinavians, however, flocked back to the Republicans after fusion in 1894. They were prepared to vote Populist but never Democratic.

With the passing of the economic crisis of the nineties, the Germans of Platte County returned to their traditional Democratic loyalties. Three of the four German colonies voted enthusiastically for Bryan in 1900. But the Lutherans of the Oldenburg colony held back. Both Bismarck and Sherman gave a greater percentage to McKinley than did the county as a whole. Republican imperialism seems not to have been a problem for them, as it was for many other German-American voters.

Madison County

Located directly north of Platte County, Madison County (Map 11) also had a tradition of Democratic strength. Situated on the high rolling prairie of the northeastern section of Nebraska, Madison County is crossed by the Elkhorn River in its northern tier of townships. Its county seat was Madison, though its largest city was Norfolk, a community of less than two thousand inhabitants in 1885. Norfolk had been founded by a group of Germans from Wisconsin in 1866.[25]

Germans were present in relatively strong numbers throughout the county except in the southwestern township of Shell Creek (Table 17).

TABLE 17

Potential Voting Population among German-American Adult Males of Madison County, Nebraska, According to the Census of 1885

Precinct	Total Population	Total Adult Males	Potential German Voters	Per Cent of Total Adult Males	Rank
City of Norfolk	1949	625	192	30.7	4
Norfolk	860	224	121	54.0	3
Battle Creek	908	244	69	28.3	6
Deer Creek	331	87	12	13.8	11
Jefferson/Burnett	713	171	10	5.9	13
Grove	476	119	12	10.1	12
Highland	364	88	17	19.3	9
Union Creek	1515	443	121	27.3	7
Fairview	472	118	34	28.8	5
Schoolcraft	438	106	22	20.8	8
Emerick	397	102	18	17.7	10
Shell Creek	444	123	4	3.3	14
Kalamazoo	492	111	68	61.3	2
Green Garden	512	131	106	80.9	1
County	9871	2692	806	29.9	

25 Andreas, *Nebraska*, pp. 1102 f.

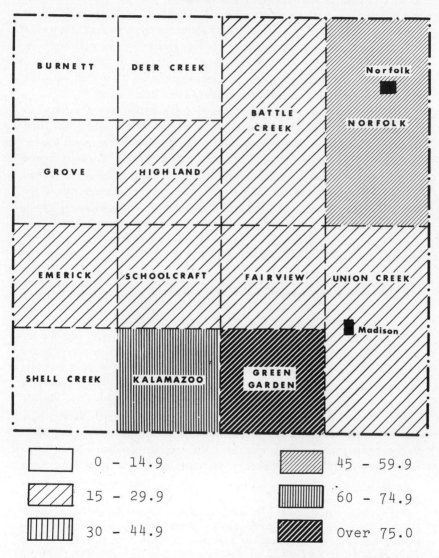

MADISON CO.

BURNETT	DEER CREEK	BATTLE CREEK
GROVE	HIGHLAND	
EMERICK	SCHOOLCRAFT	FAIRVIEW
SHELL CREEK	KALAMAZOO	GREEN GARDEN

Norfolk

NORFOLK

UNION CREEK

Madison

☐ 0 – 14.9	▨ 45 – 59.9
▨ 15 – 29.9	▥ 60 – 74.9
▥ 30 – 44.9	▨ Over 75.0

Map 11. Distribution of German-American adult males by townships in Madison County, Nebraska, in 1885, by percentage of the total adult male population.

There, directly north of the Swedes and Danes in Platte County, was a Norwegian settlement which constituted almost the entire population of the precinct. Germans were also sparse in the northwestern township of Jefferson, later called Burnett. Throughout the county, except where Germans and Norwegians were in the majority, Anglo-Americans predominated. A few Irish and Bohemians were scattered about the county. Together with a few Germans, they formed the basis for four small Catholic parishes. The Catholic influence was probably greatest in Schoolcraft and Kalamazoo precincts, the latter having many Germans who were associated with the Catholic colonization project at St. Bernard's in Platte County.[26]

Three distinct and widely separated German settlements developed in Madison County. The first of these was located at Norfolk and in the rural region north and east of the city. Within this group was organized a large Lutheran congregation of the Wisconsin Synod. A large Missouri Synod congregation was also founded in Norfolk in 1871. Both parishes maintained schools. The second German colony was located in the southern part of the county in Green Garden and Kalamazoo townships. Three Missouri Synod congregations served this area, one of which was located across the line in Platte County. No other denominations were represented by significant numbers among the Germans of the area. A third German settlement was located around the nucleus of a large Missouri Synod congregation located in Battle Creek. Its population was distributed over three and later four precincts and therefore cannot be analyzed statistically.[27]

The pattern created by coefficients of correlation plotted over two decades in Madison County varies somewhat from those that have been graphed for the other counties. Instead of German preference for Democratic candidates building up to a climax in 1890, it was already nearly as high as it could go in 1882. The coefficient calculated for the election of that year registers a very high +.87. This strong tendency continued throughout the decade to 1892. While Fig. 8 shows that the coefficients declined slightly during those years, an examination of the precinct returns shows that they were offset by the very high Democratic vote cast in Schoolcraft precinct, a township in which lived many Irish, Bohemians, Germans, as well as native Americans

[26] Hagedorn, *Franciscans*, pp. 379–387, 503; U.S. Census Office, *Report on Statistics of Churches* (1890), p. 242.

[27] U.S. Census Office, *Report on Statistics of Churches* (1890), pp. 464 f. and *passim;* *Directory of our Lutheran Churches of America, Missouri and Wisconsin Synod, Madison County, 1918* (n.p.: n.d.), Werkmeister Collection, Nebraska State Historical Society; *Eine kurze Geschichte der Ev.-Luth. St. Pauls-Gemeinde zu Norfolk.* According to Kriege et al., *Souvenir*, pp. 150, 158 f., there were two small German Methodist congregations near the Green Garden colony in Fairview and Kalamazoo townships. They are not, however, listed in the census of 1890.

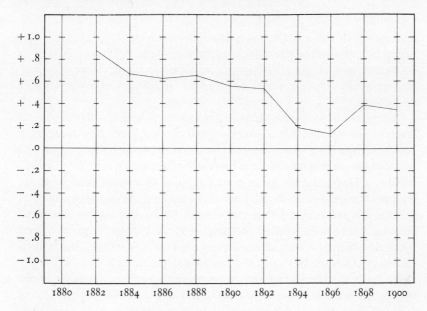

FIGURE 8. Coefficients of correlation between percentages of potential German voters according to the census of 1885 and the percentages of votes cast for Democratic candidates for President and governor in Madison County, Nebraska, 1882–1900. Census data and electoral data cannot be coordinated for the election of 1880.

from southern states. A rural Catholic parish was also located in the precinct.

In 1894 the German tendency to vote Democratic took its usual dip. Since Madison County tended to be Democratic, the rejection of the "Demopop" slate was not as thoroughgoing as it had been in the more Republican counties south of the Platte River. As usual, the Gold Democratic ticket was very attractive to the Germans. Green Garden gave it 30.2 per cent of its total vote compared to 5.3 per cent, which it won in the county as a whole. Association with the Gold Democratic percentages produces a coefficient of +.62. The tendency of Catholics to endorse Populism and fusion more readily than Lutheran Germans is also observable in Madison County, as it was in Platte and Hall counties.

The behavior of the Germans in the last two elections of the period conforms to the usual pattern in that their tendency to vote Democratic increased over what it had been in 1894 and 1896. The Democratic appeal to German fears of imperialism and conscription bore little fruit in Madison County. The percentages of the most heavily German precincts varied little from the pattern for the county as a whole in 1900.

Cuming County

Cuming (Map 12) was the most German county in Nebraska. In 1885 nearly half of all the potential voters were of German stock. There is no doubt that by 1900 the proportion had risen much higher. West Point, the largest town in Cuming County, was the most German city of any importance in the state.

The entire southwestern third of the county—those portions west and south of the Elkhorn River—were approximately 75 per cent German in 1885. The inhabitants who were not German were almost all Bohemian. The religious character of the district is revealed by the existence of three Catholic parishes, chiefly in St. Charles township, and of a half-dozen Lutheran congregations, mostly of the Missouri Synod, located in Bismarck, Elkhorn, and Lincoln townships. Except for a small Mennonite society, almost all of these churches maintained parochial schools. Within the city of West Point the Germans were served by two Lutheran churches and a large Catholic, a German Methodist, and an Evangelical church.[28]

As Table 18 reveals, Germans were numerous in every precinct of the county. There was, however, another area of concentration between the towns of West Point and Bancroft in Logan and Bancroft townships. Most of the Germans of this region were Lutherans, although a Catholic parish had been founded in Bancroft.

TABLE 18

Potential Voting Population among German-American Adult Males of Cuming County, Nebraska, According to the Census of 1885

Precinct	Total Population	Total Adult Males	Potential German Voters	Per Cent of Total Adult Males	Rank
Bancroft	1021	305	127	41.6	7
Logan	577	130	71	54.6	5
Cleveland	481	160	33	20.6	11
Wisner	1819	523	136	26.0	9
Bismarck	589	149	142	95.3	1
Elkhorn	669	169	154	91.1	2
Lincoln	365	91	59	64.8	4
St. Charles	983	223	154	69.1	3
West Point	2304	633	318	50.2	6
Garfield	758	193	59	30.6	8
Cuming	604	172	44	25.6	10
County	10,170	2748	1297	47.2	

[28] [Maurice] Bartlett and [P. F.] O'Sullivan, *History of Cuming County, Nebraska, with Complete Directory* (Fremont, Nebr.: Fremont Tribune, 1884), p. 175; C. H. Scoville (compiler), *History of the Elkhorn Valley, Nebraska* (Chicago: National Publishing Co.,

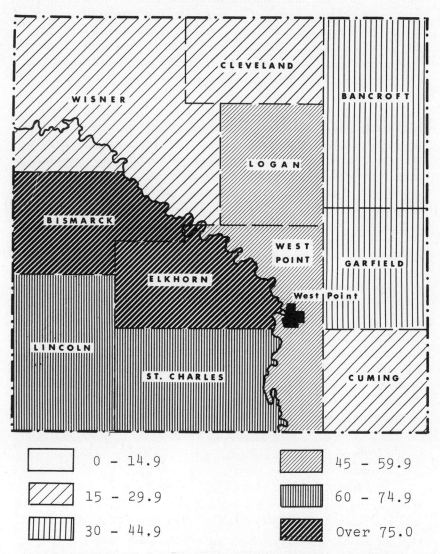

CUMING CO.

Map 12. Distribution of German-American adult males by townships in Cuming County, Nebraska, in 1885, by percentage of the total adult male population.

Other ethnic groups in Cuming County, besides the Bohemians of the southwestern part, were mostly Scandinavian. Swedes and Danes were common in Garfield and Cuming townships and a small group of Norwegians resided in the Wisner area. Impressionistic evidence drawn from newspaper sources suggests the existence of an important Irish element. Since census data do not reveal a significant number of Irish-born inhabitants, it is likely that many of them were third- and fourth-generation Americans. Whatever their number was, they together with the large proportion of Lutheran and Catholic Germans and Bohemians guaranteed a strong Democratic party within the county.

Because Cuming County changed its precinct boundaries in 1881 and 1887, coefficients of correlation can be calculated only for the three elections from 1882 to 1886.[29] The figures obtained for those years indicate an overwhelming preference of the Cuming County Germans for the Democratic party. For the election of 1882 the coefficient is +.89, for 1884 it is +.81, and for 1886 it is +.75. During those years the German precincts of the southwestern part of the county regularly gave from 75 to 95 per cent of their votes to the Democratic party. A climax was reached in 1890 when the prohibition amendment, which the Democratic party opposed with all its strength, garnered a total of four votes in the five southwestern precincts of the county.

In 1892 the Germans displayed ethnic bloc voting behavior in a most refined form. Responding to the editorial exhortations of the *Nebraska Volksblatt*, the Germans voted heavily for James B. Weaver, the Populist candidate for president, for J. Sterling Morton, the Democratic candidate for governor, and for Robert Kloke, the Republican candidate for representative in the state legislature.[30] In each case the winner exceeded the total won by his closest rival by about four hundred votes. The unusual control over German voting behavior is illustrated by Bismarck precinct, as shown by the following table.

	Republican	*Democratic*	*Populist*
For President	10.8%	8.6%	80.6%
Governor	11.8%	81.7%	6.5%
State representative	26.1%	59.8%	14.1%

While Weaver and Morton each won about 80 per cent, Kloke's margin was somewhat less at about 60 per cent. The failure of the Bismarck voters to

---

1892), pp. 193–218; E. Eckhardt, *Geschichte des Nebraskadistriktes* (Battle Creek, Nebr.: E. Eckhardt, n.d.), pp. 58–71; *Nebraska Volksblatt* (West Point), September 25, 1896, October 26, 1900.

29 Scoville, *History of Elkhorn Valley*, p. 159.

30 *Nebraska Volksblatt*, October 28, 1892.

support the Republican candidate for state representative with enthusiasm may be explained by the fact that Kloke was a prominent Catholic leader of West Point. The Catholic precincts made up the difference. St. Charles, for example, gave Kloke 70.4 per cent, and in the city of West Point his percentage was even higher. In other races, such as for state senator and lieutenant governor, Cuming County remained solidly Democratic.

Cuming County, unlike others analyzed in this study, sustained a large Democratic vote in 1894, the year in which fusion with the Populists was initiated. Except for the city of West Point, all of the most German precincts gave a higher proportion of their votes to the fusion slate than did the county as a whole. They did this despite the opposition which fusion evoked among the county Democratic leaders. As usual, the Gold Democratic ticket attracted support among the German voters. In Logan, Elkhorn, and Lincoln precincts the party won as much as 12 and 13 per cent of the total number of votes cast.

In each of the subsequent elections to 1900, Cuming County regularly voted about 55 per cent Democratic. The most-German precincts regularly exceeded this proportion. Meanwhile the most significant Republican majorities were won in West Point and in Garfield precinct, where there were many voters of Swedish origins.

Hitchcock County

Situated in the southwestern part of Nebraska, Hitchcock County (Map 13) is bisected by the Republican River. In 1885 nearly 40 per cent of the total population consisted of adult males, indicating that it was still in a frontier stage. Culbertson, the only village in the county at that time, was the center of an extensive cattle raising industry.[31] Yet the census schedules

TABLE 19

Potential Voting Population among German-American Adult Males of Hitchcock County, Nebraska, According to the Census of 1885

Precinct	Total Population	Total Adult Males	Potential German Voters	Per Cent of Total Adult Males	Rank
Culbertson	1009	370	80	21.6	1
Palisade	359	115	12	10.4	2
Driftwood	600	230	9	3.9	3
Frontier	420	202	6	3.0	4
County	2388	917	110	12.0	

[31] *Nebraska State Gazetteer and Business Directory for 1882–3* (Omaha: Herald Book Printing House, 1882), p. 102.

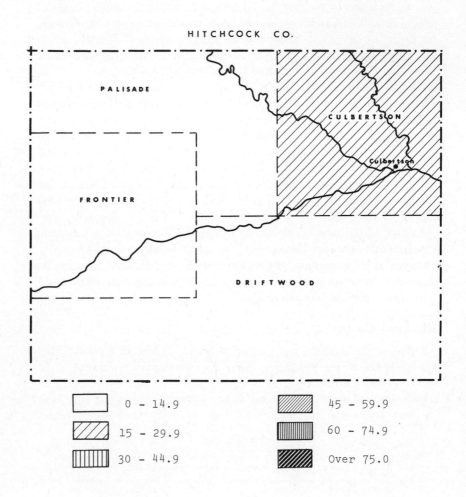

Map 13. Distribution of German-American males by townships in Hitchcock County, Nebraska, in 1885, by percentage of the total adult male population.

of 1885 (Table 19) demonstrate that many persons were attempting to cultivate the soil, despite the semiarid climate of western Nebraska. In many cases farmers had broken no more than five to twenty acres of sod on their holdings.

Many of these farmers were German immigrants. About three-fourths of them had settled along Blackwood and Frenchman Creeks north and northwest of the village of Culbertson in Culbertson township. Of the eighty adult males of German stock in that precinct in 1885, forty-three were *Volgadeutsch*, mostly from the Russian village of Frank. It often happened that in America the Volga Germans adopted a religious affiliation according to village origin. While one group affiliated with a Lutheran denomination, another might become associated, for example, with the German Reformed church. No Catholics and only a few Lutherans were among the *Volgadeutsch* of Hitchcock county. They seem to have found the German Congregational church the most congenial.[32] Smaller groups joined the Methodist, Baptist, and Evangelical churches.

The voting behavior of the Hitchcock County Germans is suggested by Fig. 9.[33] It is strikingly different from that of all other counties included in this study in that it consistently displayed a stronger tendency toward Republican party voting than did the total population. This pattern was also sustained in the 1890 election when the prohibition amendment appeared as a threat to the German element of the state. The vote for the amendment in Culbertson precinct was 59.9 per cent compared to 55.1 per cent registered for the entire county. At the same time, rural precincts containing most of the German voters gave up to 90 per cent of their votes to Populist candidates. Clearly prohibition was not the issue it was for most German citizens. The divergent behavior of these Germans may be explained by their adherence to non-Lutheran protestant churches which preached a morality that corresponded to the Puritan heritage of the native Anglo-Saxon establishment. In Nebraska this meant, in turn, a tendency to vote Republican.

After their brief flirtation with the agrarian radicals in 1890, the German voters of Hitchcock County, together with the voters in the villages of

[32] Richard Sallet, "Russlanddeutsche Siedlungen in der Vereinigten Staaten von Amerika," *Jahrbuch der Deutsch-Amerikanischen Historischen Gesellschaft von Illinois*, XXXI (1931), p. 86; George J. Eisenach, *A History of the German Congregational Churches in the United States* (Yankton, S.D.: Pioneer Press, 1938), pp. 66, 96 f.; U.S. Census Office, *Report on Statistics of Churches* (1890), pp. 403, 539.

[33] Prior to 1888 Hitchcock County kept no record of its votes on a precinct basis. Only county totals were registered. Hence analysis can begin only with that date. The small number of precincts precludes the use of the correlational formula. In 1888 Hitchcock County adopted the congressional township system. Voting data have therefore been grouped to conform to the census districts of 1885.

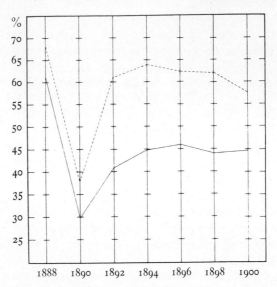

FIGURE 9. Percentages of votes cast for Republican candidates for President and governor in Hitchcock County, Nebraska, 1888–1900 (*solid line*) and in Culbertson precinct (*dashed line*).

Culbertson, Stratton, and Trenton, returned to the Republican party. The predominantly Anglo-Saxon rural precincts meanwhile stayed with the Populists as the Democrats were reduced to a mere 6.3 per cent in 1892. The pattern of German voting was not in the least disturbed by the fusion of the Democrats and Populists. German loyalty to the Republican party in this county remained strong to the end of the decade.

In any summary view of the mass of statistics that have been organized and interpreted in this chapter, it is essential to recall that the purpose has been to assess tendencies on the part of German voters toward one party or another by comparison to all voters in the same communities. Little emphasis has been placed on the party that happened to win a majority of German votes in a given election. By graphing coefficients of correlation over time, trends have been revealed that otherwise would never appear. In this respect Jefferson County (Fig. 4) offers a classic example. Though the coefficients for the elections from 1882 to 1886 are so close to zero that they reveal no partisan relationships when taken separately, they demonstrate an unmistakable trend away from the Republican and toward the Democratic party when placed in time sequence.

The general pattern over the twenty-year span is clear. At the beginning of the period, German bloc-voting was not pronounced except in those counties and precincts in which the German population was highly concentrated and somewhat uniform in its characteristics. In some districts the Democratic tendency was strong; in others the Republican party was more attractive. Usually causal relationships may be discovered in traditional partisan attachments, in the accidents of local leadership, and especially in the predominant church affiliation of the local German communities.

As the 1880's passed, the identification of the German voters with the Democratic party was strengthened under the pressure of continued agitation for woman suffrage, prohibition, and Sabbatarianism. By 1890 this tendency had been produced uniformly in every county save one. A remarkable consensus had been achieved among a diverse people as they embraced the Democratic party as the champion of personal liberty. But the eclipse of Republicanism in 1890 was brought about in part by the newly organized Populist party. This movement, which fed on agrarian discontent, was emphatically rejected by the Germans in 1890. Two years later, however, the Populists fared much better among the Germans, although their general adherence to the Democratic party remained strong.

In 1894 the most abrupt change in German political behavior occurred. Presumably in response to Democratic and Populist fusion and to William Jennings Bryan's emphasis on free silver policies, the Germans flocked to the Republican party. Others, whose memory of 1890 remained vivid, chose the futile alternative of the Gold Democratic ticket as an honorable solution to their dilemma. In counties like Otoe, Washington, and Jefferson (counties with strong Republican traditions), Germans tended to vote more strongly for Republican candidates than did their non-German fellow citizens.

The attraction of the Republican party for the Germans was sustained in 1896, but in the last two elections of the decade, the Democrats seemed to regain some of the ground they had lost. Presumably this was because of negative reactions to Republican policies of imperialism and expansion. Close inspection of precinct returns, however, shows that the Germans were badly split in 1900. One German precinct would vote strongly for one party, while another would vote just as strongly for its rival.

Within the larger pattern many variations may be observed. Catholic Germans regularly displayed the strongest Democratic tendencies. Lutheran Germans were only slightly less Democratic though there were some significant exceptions. Their behavior is in striking contrast to that of Scandinavian Lutherans. Having strong pietistic traditions, the latter supported the prohibition movement. Politically this meant that Scandinavian Lutherans were overwhelmingly Republican and later favorably disposed toward the Populist party. But differences may be discerned even among German

Lutherans according to synodical connections. Democratic tendencies paralleled Missouri Synod strength while Republican voting was more common in precincts where the German Nebraska Synod prevailed. Politically as well as theologically the latter synod seems to have been closer to the mainstream of American Protestantism, which was generally a bulwark of Republicanism in Nebraska. Republican tendencies were also apparent in regions where German-speaking congregations of non-Lutheran Protestant denominations were large or numerous. Thus it appears that church affiliation is the best guide to variation in political behavior among the Germans of Nebraska.

Differences in voting patterns also seem to have been connected with the density level of the German population. The higher the density of ethnic-group population, the greater was the tendency toward lopsided majorities in favor of one party. North of the Platte River the Germans usually constituted the largest single immigrant group, sometimes even surpassing the numbers of Anglo-Americans. There the Democratic tendency was strongest. This region was also the least affected by fusion in 1894. Apparently its traditional identification was so strong that the Germans were able to weather all storms. The character of interpersonal relationships within the immigrant group tended to produce uniformity in political behavior. Social pressure was strong; group political norms prevailed.

CHAPTER VI

An Economic Dimension :
The Case in Seward County

THAT A POSITIVE RELATIONSHIP existed between German ethnicity and electoral decisions is abundantly clear. The data examined thus far do not, however, exclude the possibility that there were other correlates of importance. Theoretically it is possible that the high level of association between German ethnic stock and Democratic party preference is in reality a dimension of the economic factor. To illustrate, if German immigrants were consistently among the lower economic groups, and if it can be established that lower economic groups regularly displayed preferences for Democratic candidates, then it may be argued that the economic factor was actually the foundation of ethnic political behavior. On the other hand, if German immigrants were distributed across the economic spectrum in approximately the same proportions as the total population, and if the German population, when ranked by precincts according to wealth rather than to numerical strength, displayed no special partisan preference, then one may conclude that economic factors were of less significance than ethnicity in determining the electoral decisions of German immigrants. The data presented in this chapter indicate that the latter was the case.

Possible relationships between the German population and economic variables that could be expected to impinge upon electoral decisions were explored in a series of correlations in which data from Seward County were used.[1] Average values of farmland and buildings according to the agricultural schedules of the state census of 1885 were employed as one yardstick. This source revealed an average value of $3,951 for 2,119 farms in the county. The range extended from an average of $2,329 in H township to $5,233 in C

---

[1] Seward County was selected because its German population paralleled that of the state in terms of proportion, religious affiliation, and distribution, because it was, like Nebraska, predominantly agricultural, and because wide variations in the value of farm land and income could be expected as a result of distinct variations in the topography and quality of the soil. Also its sixteen townships are equal in area (thirty-six square miles). See Map 6, Chapter V.

township. The average value of farms owned by German-stock residents of the county was nearly the same: 555 farms averaged $3,806 in value, ranging from $2,216 in A township to $5,713 in G township. Thus it appears that the agricultural wealth of the German population did not vary significantly from that of the total population of the county. This conclusion is supported by the use of the Spearman formula (see Appendix II). When the townships are ranked according to average values of farm lands and buildings according to the 1885 census and correlated with the percentages of German-stock adult males in the same townships, a coefficient of −.14 is produced.

In order to check the reliability of the agricultural data of the 1885 census, valuations of farm property were acquired from the tax lists maintained by the county treasurer for the same year.[2] These values were ranked by townships and correlated with the German population. In this instance a coefficient of −.08 was produced, indicating further that the German farmers of Seward County experienced a range of wealth that approximated that of the total population.

The evidence further indicates that there was no significant relationship between the economic status of the Germans and their partisan preferences. In I precinct, where the Germans tended to vote strongly Republican, the average value of all 129 farms was $3,653, while the average value of 56 German farms was $4,165, or more than $500 above the average for the precinct. But German farmers also were wealthier in Democratic C precinct, where 38 German properties averaged $5,565 in value compared to an average of $5,233 for all 137 farms in the precinct. At the same time, the data for D township, which shared the same geographical conditions and Democratic preferences as C township, demonstrate that 54 German farms were valued at about $400 *below* the average. Thus no consistent pattern of wealth in association with German immigrant population is revealed.

The sixteen townships of the county were then ranked according to the average value of farms operated by Germans as indicated by the census data and correlated with the percentages of votes cast for the Democratic candidate for governor in the election of 1886. A coefficient of −.02 was produced, indicating no relationship between the two variables. When the German economic data were associated with votes cast for the Republican candidate in 1886, a similar figure of +.02 was obtained.

These results carry striking implications for an understanding of immigrant voting behavior. As was shown in the preceding chapter, when percentages of German adult males were associated with Democratic voting in Seward County in 1886, a coefficient of +.50 was obtained, a figure which signifies a high-level relationship. But when the same persons are ranked according

2 The tax lists are in the office of the county treasurer, Seward, Nebraska.

to average values of farm lands and buildings the coefficient is so low (− .02) as to indicate no relationship at all. The data therefore suggests that ethnicity was much more important than agricultural wealth in determining the electoral decisions of German voters in Seward County.

If the distribution of wealth among the Germans did not differ significantly from that of the total population, and if the value of farmlands and buildings was not a significant correlate of German voting behavior, one must ask if this economic factor was also unimportant for the total population. In order to test this relationship, the total assessed values of farm lands as revealed by the tax lists for each election, ranked by townships, were correlated with the percentages of votes cast for the major party candidates for President and governor in each election from 1886 to 1898. This period of years spans the Populist era, a time when agricultural discontent presumably manifested itself in electoral decisions. The analysis is based on the assumption that the voters in the poorest precincts were the most likely to express their discontent by their preference for one of the parties. Hence townships were ranked from the least to the most wealthy and the electoral data were ranked from the greatest to the least percentages of votes cast for a given candidate. The results are recorded in Table 20.

TABLE 20

Coefficients of Correlation between Total Assessed Valuations of Farmland and the Percentages of Votes Cast for Major Party Candidates for President and Governor in Seward County, Nebraska, 1886–1898

	Republican	Democrat	Populist
1886	+.11	−.03	
1888	+.41	−.36	
1890	+.06	−.30	+.19
1892	+.08	−.16	+.24
1894	+.10	−.21[a]	
1896	+.17	−.07[a]	
1898	+.14	−.12[a]	

[a] In these elections the Democratic and Populist parties nominated the same candidates.

Several significant generalizations may be drawn from the data. In the first place, the coefficients produced by association of voting statistics with economic data are low compared to those obtained by correlation with ethnic data.[3] Secondly, when the several coefficients are taken individually they have significance only in a negative sense, that is, they indicate an absence

[3] See Figs. 1–8, Chapter V. Coefficients above +.50 were not uncommon for the elections from 1886 to 1892.

rather than a presence of a relationship between the economic and the electoral data. Thirdly, when the coefficients are considered collectively, they appear to be remarkably consistent in several respects. In every election the precincts with the lowest valuations of farm property displayed a slight tendency to prefer the candidates of the Republican party. Conversely, the Democratic candidates appear to have been slightly more attractive to the wealthier precincts. Moreover, when the Populist party entered the political arena in 1890 and 1892, the poorer precincts clearly found it to be the most attractive party of the three. At the same time, the Republican party maintained a middle position in both elections between the new agrarian radicals on one hand and the old, conservative Democratic party on the other. Furthermore, the data suggest that fusion of the Democratic and Populist tickets in 1894 and in subsequent elections did not succeed in attracting as many votes proportionally in the poorer districts as in the county as a whole.[4]

An attempt was made to verify these results through the use of economic data expressed in a different form. The Seward County tax lists for the years 1892 to 1896 permit agricultural property to be valued in terms of averages per acre per precinct. The data were also correlated with election statistics. The coefficients obtained in this manner are as follows:

	Republican	Democratic	Populist
1892	−.02	−.17	+.26
1894	+.23	−.36	
1896	+.13	.00	

They show the same relationships between partisan preferences and agricultural wealth that is revealed by Table 20.

The data of this chapter do not, of course, eliminate economic factors as causative agents in the political behavior of Seward County voters. It is possible that a high level of association may be discovered through the correlation of election statistics with economic data of a different kind. Moreover, the data employed in this study may not in fact be adequate

[4] Cf. Stanley B. Parsons, "Who Were the Nebraska Populists?" *Nebraska History*, XL (June, 1963), 95–99. In this study Parsons employed similar techniques to discover variables associated with Populist party voting. His data are organized on a county rather than a precinct basis. Since census data are published on a county basis, he uses a rich variety of economic data. He found that percentage of farmland in wheat and percentage of Protestant church affiliation were the most significant factors associated with the Populist vote. Parsons' study is limited to a correlational analysis of data for the year 1890; it does not offer coefficients obtained through the association of his social and economic data with the Republican and Democratic vote.

measures of the economic status of the persons being studied. The conclusion is clearly warranted, however, that wealth expressed as value of farm property was decidedly less significant than ethnicity in determining the electoral decisions of the German voters of Seward County.[5] While the coefficients obtained through the use of economic data are comparatively low, they are consistent enough to suggest a probable pattern that may be true for the state as a whole.

[5] It should be noted that the findings of this chapter are congruent with those of Chapter IV, which demonstrated that urban/rural residence and/or occupation was generally the least reliable index of party preference among the 653 German-Americans included in that part of this study.

CHAPTER VII

The Germans and Nebraska Politics, 1880–1890

EVER SINCE NEBRASKA ACHIEVED statehood in 1867 the Republican party had dominated its politics. Like most Republican state organizations in the North, the Nebraska GOP fed upon emotions stirred by the Civil War; it regularly stigmatized the Democratic party as the party of rebellion. The Republican party also laid substantial claim to being the instrument of prosperity and development in Nebraska. The Homestead Act and the railroad acts of the 1860's had been enacted under national Republican auspices over Democratic opposition, and most Nebraskans agreed that these measures had been essential to their state's growth.

The Democrats, meanwhile, seemed doomed to second place as they were outvoted on a statewide basis, sometimes by a two to one margin. They were led by dedicated and intensely partisan politicians like Dr. George Miller of Omaha and J. Sterling Morton of Nebraska City. Partisan rhetoric to the contrary, these Bourbon leaders held views not unlike those of the Stalwart Republicans.[1]

The Germans and Politics in 1880

Neither party was unified in 1880. In the Republican party, sharp conflict frequently broke out between the reform-minded progressive element and the regulars, who were dominated by the railroad companies.[2] Among the Democrats the struggle was between fiscal conservatives who regularly invoked Jeffersonian principles and a more radical band who were eager to

[1] Much useful information regarding the political parties and their leaders during the 1880's is contained in Stanley B. Parsons, Jr., "The Populist Context: Nebraska Farmers and Their Antagonists, 1882–1895" (unpublished Ph.D. dissertation, State University of Iowa, 1964), Chapter III, "The Politics of Economic Adjustment," pp. 75–121.

[2] J. Sterling Morton, Albert Watkins, and George L. Miller, *Illustrated History of Nebraska* (Lincoln: Western Publishing and Engraving Co., 1913), III, 195.

ally themselves with those who, as the conservatives saw it, whored after false money gods.

The platforms of the Nebraska political parties tended to reflect national concerns and issues in 1880. The Democratic document, adopted under the leadership of Morton and the conservative wing, contained a sharply worded plank calling for government regulation of the railroads and giant corporations. It also hit at Republican extravagance in the state and hinted at graft. Meanwhile, free trade and a revenue tariff were given perfunctory nods. The Republican state platform ignored state and local problems to concentrate on "waving the bloody shirt" and on problems of reconstruction in the South. The Greenbackers, who constituted the largest of the minor parties in Nebraska in 1880, emphasized the need for government control of the transportation and communication industries and endorsed woman suffrage.[3]

The Republicans were so firmly in control of the state government that a major problem for the Democrats was to find competent candidates who were willing to sacrifice themselves for the sake of the party. The gubernatorial candidate offered by the Democrats in 1880 was Thomas Tipton, an ex-Republican senator with a reputation as a prohibitionist.[4] Many Democrats feared that his candidacy would alienate foreign-born voters. Yet whatever negative influence Tipton may have had on the immigrant voters seems to have been balanced by the positive qualities which they normally associated with the Democratic party. Fiscal conservatism and a long established affinity with the foreign-born made the party attractive to many Germans.

The election of 1880 was a mild affair. The issues of the day aroused little interest and the candidates for the presidency, Garfield and Hancock, were neither distinguished nor well known. Though Germans constituted from 15 to 20 per cent of the voting population of the state, they were not ordinarily perceived as a potential voting bloc. Few newspapers of either political persuasion ever made references to the German vote in 1880. Publications such as the Omaha *Herald*, the Columbus *Journal*, the Fairbury *Gazette*, or Seward's *Blue Valley Blade*, all located in areas of heavy German population, never mentioned German voters, their attitudes, desires, strengths, or needs. Instead, local Democratic sheets like the Norfolk *Times* excoriated the Republicans for "fraud, intimidation, bribery, and every species of political villainy."[5] Political issues were not being articulated in terms that appealed

[3] [U.S. Work Projects Administration, Nebraska], *Nebraska Party Platforms* (Sponsored by the University of Nebraska, 1940), pp. 79–84. Hereafter cited as *Nebraska Party Platforms*.

[4] James C. Olson, *J. Sterling Morton* (Lincoln: University of Nebraska Press, 1942), pp. 252–259.

[5] Norfolk *Times*, September 16, 1880.

to the Germans as an ethnic group. Republican newspapers sometimes discussed politics in ways that could evoke negative reactions among German immigrants. A typical example was the Hebron *Journal* edited by Erasmus M. Correll. Fully committed to the Republican party as the only adequate vehicle for progress, reform, and human liberty, Correll was convinced that big business was a threat to civic stability, purity, and justice and that government regulation was a vital necessity. A second issue, as he saw it, was the temperance question. While the total suppression of the liquor traffic was his ultimate hope, Correll advocated a local option law as the most practical step that circumstances would permit at that time.[6]

Many German voters, particularly among the more rapid assimilators, would have applauded Correll's demands for reform. Such persons agreed that their prosperity as American citizens was due in part to Republican legislation. Moreover, they revered the memory of Abraham Lincoln. But while the Great Emancipator appeared to the Germans as the very embodiment of compassion and concern for the individual, the typical Republican did not. As one German-born journalist wrote in a column celebrating the founding in 1880 of *Der Herold* in Grand Island, it was the Democratic party that had proved itself to be the party of concern for the welfare of the people. The Democrats, he emphasized, treasured the German's "theuerestes Gut, die persönliche Freiheit."[7] Personal liberty could mean many things, but to the German immigrant it often meant the liberty to have his beer when and where he wanted it. Nevertheless, prohibition was in reality not a simple political issue. It was the political symbol of a general conflict of cultures that confronted the immigrant as he adjusted to the norms and standards of American society.[8]

One of the few newspapers that made much of the German vote in 1880 was the Nebraska City *News*, a Democratic publication. Its editor, Thomas Morton, delighted in pointing out that, though the Republicans expected to

[6] Hebron *Journal*, October 21, 1880. Correll's identification with small-town, Protestant values is further indicated by his wife's activity in the woman suffrage movement. See Ann Wiegman Wilhite, "Sixty-Five Years Till Victory: A History of Woman Suffrage in Nebraska," *Nebraska History*, IL (Summer, 1968), 149–164. Correll himself worked for both woman suffrage and prohibition in the Nebraska House of Representatives, of which he was a member. *House Journal of the Legislature of the State of Nebraska. Sixteenth Regular Session . . . 1881.*

[7] "Most cherished possession, personal liberty." *Der Herold* (Grand Island), October 20, 1887.

[8] This concept is fully developed by Joseph R. Gusfield in his *Symbolic Crusade: Status Politics and the American Temperance Movement* (Urbana: University of Illinois Press, 1963), especially in Chapter IV, "Coercive Reform and Cultural Conflict," pp. 87–110. See also Samuel P. Hays, "History as Human Behavior," *Iowa Journal of History*, LVIII (July, 1960), 196.

reap a rich harvest of German votes, they had no use for Germans as office-holders. The Democrats, by contrast, ran as many as five German candidates on their ticket for offices ranging from state treasurer to county commissioner.[9]

Many of the local editors paid precious little attention to national issues, such as they were in 1880, being more interested in chronicling the bitter clashes between local political factions for control of the party machinery.[10] The bloody shirt was waved and sometimes lampooned, but real fervor inspired the exhortations to party regularity and the maledictions on voters who were prepared to "scratch" their ballots in accordance with pre-arranged deals.[11] Germans sometimes played a role in such deals, as in Seward County, where collusion between German Democratic leaders and "Half-Breed" Republicans, led by the German-born editor of the *Nebraska Reporter*, allegedly resulted in the election of one of the three Democratic candidates elected to the state senate in 1880.[12]

The relative importance of Germans to the various parties may be estimated by a study of the membership lists of county central committees and of delegates to county conventions. Persons with German names were not often found in the councils of the Republican party, though there are some notable exceptions.[13] Paul Schminke, for example, enjoyed the postmastership of Nebraska City as a reward for his services to the Republican party. A native of Hesse-Kassel, Schminke was regularly characterized in the Democratic press as the "Republican Bismarck" of Otoe County. On the other hand, German names were comparatively common on Democratic party lists. In Platte County, for example, Germans dominated the county organization. They accounted for all the officers and half the membership of the central committee in 1880.[14]

Despite the fact that some editors believed that the Germans had voted Republican in 1880,[15] aggregated voting statistics reveal a trend in the opposite direction. As Table 21 indicates, the Democratic party exceeded its statewide average of 32.6 per cent of the total number of votes cast in those counties

[9] Nebraska City *News*, October 30, 1880.

[10] Cf. the sociohistorical conceptualization of this phenomenon developed by Samuel P. Hays, "Political Parties and the Community-Society Continuum," in William N. Chambers and Walter D. Burnham (eds.), *The American Party System: Stages of Political Development* (New York: Oxford University Press, 1967), pp. 152–187.

[11] E.g., see Fairbury *Gazette*, October 3, 1880.

[12] *Blue Valley Blade*, May 12, October 20, November 10, 1880.

[13] For example, German names are all but absent from such lists for Jefferson or Seward counties. See Fairbury *Gazette*, October 3, 1880; *Blue Valley Blade*, September 8, 1880.

[14] Columbus *Era*, October 14, 1880.

[15] See, for example, Nebraska City *News*, November 13, 1880.

with 8 per cent or more German-born in their populations. Conversely, the Democratic party won less than its state average in those counties with less than 8 per cent German-born inhabitants. Moreover, the rank orders of both categories are matched perfectly with one minor exception. The reverse tendency may be noted, though less clearly, in connection with Republican totals. The data furthermore indicate no relationship between the German population and the votes cast for the Greenback party candidate. It should be noted that all the counties in the state were included in the tabulation.

TABLE 21

Mean Percentages of Votes Cast for All Parties in the Election of 1880, by Counties, According to Percentages of German-Born Population[a]

Per Cent of German-Born[a]	Number of Counties	Per Cent Republican	Per Cent Democratic	Per Cent Greenback
20.0 and above	3	49.1	46.7	4.1
10.0–19.9	8	60.0	38.7	1.3
8.0–9.9	5	57.4	38.9	3.6
6.0–7.9	8	64.7	30.9	4.4
4.0–5.9	15	64.3	30.0	5.7
2.0–3.9	19	66.0	28.9	5.1
0.0–1.9	5	68.4	27.8	3.8
State[b]		62.9	32.6	4.5

[a] Percentages do not add to 100.0 per cent in every case, due to rounding.
[b] The German-born were 6.9 per cent of the population of the state as a whole.
SOURCE: *Nebraska Blue Book for 1901 and 1902*, pp. 173–175; U.S. Census Office, *Statistics of Population*, (*1880*), p. 519.

In Table 22 election results from 126 precincts are grouped according to percentage of German-born. The ethnic data are derived from the manuscripts of the population schedules of the Nebraska state census of 1885. The percentages of votes are taken from the election records of the ten counties analyzed in Chapter V, supplemented by data from Stanton County plus two precincts in York County and three in Clay County.[16] The percentage of potential German voters for the median precinct was 17.5. Because precincts are more homogeneous than counties, the range of the percentages in the categories is somewhat greater for the former, as may be observed by comparing Table 22 with Table 21. It should be noted, however, that the same relationship of German voters to party preference is

16 Stanton County, a sparsely populated area with only five precincts in the 1880's, was included because its German population was especially heavy. The precincts in Clay and York counties were studied because they contained concentrations of Germans from the Volga districts in Russia.

revealed in both tables. It appears therefore that even though the election of
1880 was largely a routine exercise with minimal salience for most voters,
German ethnicity was already a factor of importance in Nebraska politics
even at this early date.

TABLE 22

Mean Percentages of Votes Cast for all Parties in the Election of 1880, According
to Percentages of Potential German Voters in 1885 (126 Precincts)[a]

Per Cent of German-Born	Number of Precincts	Per Cent Republican	Per Cent Democratic	Per Cent Greenback
75.0 and above	4	42.2	51.9	5.7
60.0–74.9	10	52.7	44.9	2.1
45.0–59.9	11	61.8	36.7	1.5
30.0–44.9	18	56.2	39.1	4.6
15.0–29.9	26	60.6	33.9	5.5
0.0–14.9	27	67.0	26.8	6.2
State:		62.5	32.6	4.5

[a] Dates of election data and census data do not coincide. Since no census figures on the
precinct level have ever been published, the information was obtained by direct count
from census manuscripts. The census of 1885 was used for all tabulations. Percentages do
not add to 100.0 per cent in every case due to rounding.

The Election of 1882: The Woman Suffrage Amendment

In the Nebraska election of 1882 issues related to voter ethnicity increased
greatly in importance. Though prohibition was technically not an issue, the
political battle of that year was waged largely on its terms. Together
with the money question, which was emphasized by the Greenbackers, and
railroad regulation, which was the major concern of reform-minded Anti-
Monopolists, prohibition served to make 1882 a prelude to the more decisive
battle that was to be fought in 1890.

By the early 1880's the temperance movement had begun to gain ground
in the West. Under Republican leadership, a prohibition amendment had
been adopted in Kansas with a majority of 20,000 votes. A similar proposal
was before the Iowa legislature. In Nebraska a prohibition amendment had
been submitted to the legislature but in the early months of 1881 it fell two
votes short of the three-fifths majority necessary for adoption.[17]

The injection of the temperance issue into the bloodstream of politics was
not the action of the professional politicians. Responsibility belonged rather

[17] Nebraska City *News*, November 13, 1880; Omaha *Herald* (weekly edition), August 11,
1882. Addison E. Sheldon, *Nebraska: The Land and the People* (3 vols.; Chicago: Lewis
Publishing Co., 1931) I, 592 f. The *Nebraska House Journal, 1881*, reveals no action on the
bills beyond a third reading. See pp. 704–708.

with the puritanical social reformers who were eager to improve upon American society and to preserve its moral standards from dilution by alien attitudes imported by hordes of continental immigrants. The reformers, largely of Anglo-American ethnic origin, constituted a major part of the Protestant establishment in hundreds of the small towns that dotted the Midwestern landscape. More frequently found among the rank-and-file members of the Republican party than among Democrats, they attempted to force their party to endorse the antiliquor movement. Fired by a sense of righteousness, they blindly ignored the political implications of their actions.[18]

Having failed to achieve their primary aim in Nebraska, the prohibitionists succeeded in erecting a halfway house in the Slocumb Act of 1881. This legislation aimed to restrict the flow of liquor through a policy of high-cost licenses for its sale. By granting local authorities the power to set the amount of the license fee, a local option in effect had been passed. Minimum annual fees were set at $500 for villages and small towns and at $1,000 for cities with more than 10,000 inhabitants. Some legislators, conscious of the sensibilities of German voters among their constituencies, sought to lower the fee to $300 for beer halls, but the effort failed.[19]

As a concurrent step in the temperance campaign, the prohibitionists lent their considerable aid to the woman suffrage movement in Nebraska. They won legislative approval for the placement of a woman suffrage amendment on the 1882 ballot. The temperance and the woman suffrage movements were not, of course, identical in their goals, methods, or sources of support, and there were many suffragists who opposed linking their cause with prohibition.[20]

It is not likely that most voters made a significant distinction between the two movements. Certainly most immigrant voters did not. Germans, as well as other ethnic groups, tended to see woman suffrage as a mere device to create enough nativist votes to secure the passage of a prohibition amendment. They noticed that well-known prohibitionists like John B. Finch and Ada M. Bittenbender were conspicuously present at woman suffrage

[18] The various stages in the development of political action in the temperance movement is discussed by Joseph Gusfield in *Symbolic Crusade*. See also Horace S. Merrill, *Bourbon Democracy of the Middle West, 1865–1896* (Baton Rouge: Louisiana State University Press, 1953), p. 59.

[19] *Laws of Nebraska, 1881*, pp. 270–280; Sheldon, *Nebraska*, I, 593 f.

[20] *Laws of Nebraska, 1881*, pp. 398 f. Cf. Aileen S. Kraditor, *The Ideas of the Woman Suffrage Movement, 1890–1920* (New York: Columbia University Press, 1965), pp. 57–62. The suffragists were also eager to display the support of such German immigrants as could be enlisted. See the example of Mrs. Clara Newman in Wilhite, "Sixty-five Years Till Victory," p. 155.

meetings and rallies.[21] Rarely did anyone make the connection more explicit than Peter Jansen, the prohibitionist leader of the Russian-German Mennonite colony in Jefferson County. In a letter to the editor of the Fairbury *Gazette* he wrote:

Shall we allow women to help us suppress vice and immorality of every kind, or shall we let them look on how their sons . . . are sent to perdition and ruin of body and soul. . . . I appeal to every true temperance man in this county to do his duty at the polls. . . . Our opposition fully appreciates the situation. I have heard men say, "Why if we give women the ballot we will have prohibition upon us in no time." Well, this is just what we want and the readiness with which they oppose it ought to show us the importance of the issue.[22]

German liberals generally opposed woman suffrage because they believed it would strengthen "the fanatical regime of preachers and priests."[23] On the other hand, the conservative German preachers and priests opposed it because they thought its effect would be to take the *Hausfrau* away from her *Kinder*, *Küche*, and *Kirche*. The argument that women on the average stand higher morally than men and that therefore they should be given the right to vote was dismissed, for example, by the *Nebraska Staats Anzeiger* of Lincoln as another absurd notion of the Yankees, who considered their women to be angels despite experience to the contrary. Women, this newspaper observed, are noted for their hatred, spirit of vengeance, and intrigue; their vaunted morality is mere superficiality. The *Anzeiger* was sure that woman suffrage would have a demoralizing effect on society.[24]

German fears over woman suffrage were not without substance. There is no doubt that many nativists, especially in the West, did indeed conceive of woman suffrage as a means of defending traditional Protestant values from erosion by immigrant people. A doubling of the electorate, they believed, would greatly enhance their ability to impose native American cultural patterns upon the newcomers.[25] At the same time, other nativists opposed

[21] See the account of the woman suffrage convention held in Omaha in September, 1882, Omaha *Herald*, September 15, 1882.

[22] Fairbury *Gazette*, October 28, 1882.

[23] Carl Wittke, *The German-Language Press in America* (Lexington: University of Kentucky Press, 1957), p. 162.

[24] *Nebraska Staats Anzeiger* (Lincoln), March 22, 1894. Cf. Andrew Sinclair, *The Better Half: The Emancipation of the American Woman* (New York: Harper and Row, 1965), pp. 241–253.

[25] This theme is explored by Alan P. Grimes, *The Puritan Ethnic and Woman Suffrage* (New York: Oxford University Press, 1967). Robert H. Wiebe sees this conflict as one of many manifestations of crisis that attended the disintegration of the "island communities" that constituted American society in the nineteenth century. See his *The Search for Order, 1877–1920* (New York: Hill and Wang, 1967), pp. 55 f.

woman suffrage because of the alleged dangers that accompanied a doubling of the electorate to include, among other undesirables, ignorant foreign women.[26] Thus both the advocates and the enemies of the movement exploited nativist fears of immigrant hordes. Yet the immigrant saw woman suffrage as a threat to *his* traditional values. He was convinced that it would have a pernicious effect upon his family. It was nonsense, he believed, to consider suffragism as part of the woman's rights movement for that reduced it to a mere political struggle. It was rather a clash of cultures. Each group, whether native American or immigrant, was, as Joseph R. Gusfield expressed it, seeking "to preserve, defend or enhance the dominance and prestige of its own style of living within the total society."[27]

But temperance and woman suffrage were variations of one kind of reform. The Greenback party had been crying for monetary and political reforms since 1875. Many reform-minded Republicans had meanwhile become convinced that big business had corrupted the GOP to a point where it was beyond redemption. Some of them, whose sense of alienation was strong, organized the Anti-Monopoly party which had begun to denounce regularly and vehemently corporate privilege and domination of government. It was natural that these two minor parties should come together, as they did in September, 1882. Although the Greenbackers had condemned the state legislature for defeating the bill which would have submitted prohibition to a popular vote, the various pronouncements of the Anti-Monopolists skirted the issue. When the two parties met with the Farmers' Alliance in Hastings on September 22, 1882, they ignored the prohibition question as they adopted a joint platform. Meanwhile a variety of proposals—abolition of free railroad passes, controls on corporations, equal taxation, all currency as legal tender, postal savings banks—helped to assuage German fears of moralistic legislation that might be expected to emanate from these sources.[28] Consequently in the November election some heavily German precincts gave as much as 40 and 50 per cent of their votes to the Anti-Monopoly ticket.[29]

The Republican party presented something of a dilemma for Germans who normally voted Republican. Many of them tended to be reform-minded and hence gravitated toward the insurgent, progressive, antimonopolist wing of the party led by Senator Charles H. Van Wyck and by Edward

26 Kraditor, *Ideas of the Woman Suffrage Movement*, pp. 29–33. Miss Kraditor analyzes the rationale of antisuffragism in her second chapter.

27 Gusfield, *Symbolic Crusade*, p. 3.

28 *Nebraska Party Platforms*, pp. 89–98.

29 Examples: Sherman (Platte County), 42.4 per cent; Cub Creek (Jefferson County), 59.6 per cent; Henderson (York County), 43.8 per cent; Alda (Hall County), 42.5 per cent. In each instance German-stock voters accounted for more than 50 per cent of the adult male population in 1885.

Rosewater, the foreign-born publisher of the Omaha *Bee*. But the Germans discovered to their embarrassment that espousal of economic and political reform measures usually meant fellowship with moralistic nativists. It seemed impossible to favor reform and to oppose sumptuary legislation at the same time. Paul Schminke, the so-called "dictator" of the Republican party in Otoe County and a leading Van Wyck lieutenant, tried to disengage himself from prohibitionist hangers-on by the conspicuous public consumption of beer.[30] Stalwart Republicans, on the other hand, were not troubled with this conflict. They could denounce woman suffrage and railroad regulation with equal gusto.[31]

The lack of unity in the Republican party was revealed in its platform of 1882. A brief collection of generalities, this document was taken seriously by no one. It evaded the woman suffrage/prohibition issue but included an anticorporation plank that the Anti-Monopolists dismissed as "political clap-trap."[32] James W. Dawes, a bright young lawyer from Crete, was nominated for the governorship. The Hastings *Democrat* proclaimed that Dawes was a "red hot prohibitionist and a woman suffragist" and predicted that if this fact became widely known, the 22,000 Germans in Nebraska would vote against him.[33] Dawes himself said nothing on the issue, while Paul Schminke, according to the antagonistic Nebraska City *News*, insisted that Dawes was not a temperance man "because on a certain occasion he drank more beer than Paul did."[34] Other prominent Republicans like Charles Manderson, who was later elected to the United States Senate, publicly condemned prohibition because it eventually would contribute to a contempt for law.[35]

The relationship of the Democratic party to the Germans in 1882 was relatively uncomplicated. J. Sterling Morton, who accepted the gubernatorial nomination, continued to provide conservative leadership. As the Democrats chose their candidates, they were shrewd enough to place two Germans, Henry Grebe and Charles Speice, on the state ticket.[36] In an attempt to attract reformist votes, the Democrats denounced in their platform the alleged efforts of corporate capital to influence government. Prohibition was roundly condemned as "contrary to the fundamental rights of the individual,

[30] The source for this observation is the very Democratic Nebraska City *News*, October 21, 1882. This paper took special delight in baiting Schminke.

[31] E.g., *Blue Valley Blade*, February 22, April 5, 1882.

[32] *Nebraska Party Platforms*, pp. 91, 96 f.

[33] Quoted in Omaha *Herald* (weekly edition), October 27, 1882.

[34] Nebraska City *News*, October 28, 1882.

[35] Sheldon, *Nebraska*, I, 602.

[36] Morton *et al.*, *Illustrated History of Nebraska*, III, 206.

and to the fundamental principle of social and moral conduct."[37] As members of the only party to make a statement on this issue, the Democrats much preferred to alienate the few temperance people among them, like the well-known John B. Finch of the Red Ribbon Movement, in order to attract the "wet vote," as it would be called in a later day. Morton published a letter to Finch in which he asserted that "Nebraska democrats are against prohibition in all its Puritanical and persecuting phases" and that he, as the Democratic gubernatorial candidate, would denounce "all sumptuary laws which invade domestic life, destroy man's independence as a free-will agent and obliterate, by more votes, the sacred right of property."[38]

Republican fears of losing German votes were given substance when the *Nebraska Staats Zeitung* of Nebraska City, normally a Republican newspaper, decided to back Morton and the Democrats because of their antiprohibition views. In an obvious pitch for German votes, the Nebraska City *News* coupled James Dawes with Archibald Weaver, the Republican candidate for Congress. Both candidates, this paper declared, were prohibitionists, woman suffragists, and machine politicians. "Can liberal-minded citizens of this state, can Germans of this state," it asked, "vote for either Dawes or Weaver?"[39]

Apparently many voters could not. The results of the election of 1882 showed that, though the Republicans won a plurality of the votes, they lost their majority party status. Their share of the total vote cast for governor was reduced to 48.8 per cent; the Democrats attracted 32.1 per cent and the Anti-Monopolists 19.1 per cent. Had the last two parties been able to agree on common candidates, it is possible that they could have swept the field, as they did in the state treasurer race. Yet Democratic fusion with monetary radicals and progressives was not likely so long as conservatives like Morton were in control of the party. Rather than gamble on the support of unstable radicals, the Democratic leadership employed the traditional strategy of seeking the support of immigrant groups. The alliance was natural and comfortable because most Germans, Irish, and Bohemians also were conservatives; they were new Americans interested in conserving an old way of life.

Aggregated voting statistics reveal the success which the Democrats experienced in their attempt to win German votes in 1882. Table 23 shows a pattern similar to that of the election of 1880 except that the Democratic tendency was greatly strengthened. As the percentage of German voters

37 *Nebraska Party Platforms*, pp. 88 f.
38 Nebraska City *News*, October 28, 1882.
39 Syracuse *Journal*, November 3, 1882. Copies of the *Staats Zeitung* for the period are no longer extant. Nebraska City *News*, October 28, 1882.

TABLE 23

Mean Percentages of Votes Cast for All Parties in the Election of 1882, According to Percentages of Potential German Voters in 1885 (116 Precincts)

Per Cent of German Voters	Number of Precincts	Per Cent Republican	Per Cent Democratic	Per Cent Anti-Monopoly
75.0 and above	6	18.6	64.4	17.0
60.0–74.9	10	26.0	61.1	13.0
45.0–59.9	13	31.4	53.8	15.4
30.0–44.9	20	38.6	49.9	11.5
15.0–29.9	34	41.8	40.5	17.6
0.0–14.9	33	55.0	29.3	15.6
State:		48.8	32.1	19.1

increased in the 116 precincts tested, the percentage of votes cast for the Democratic candidate for governor expanded correspondingly. The Republican pattern was precisely the opposite. No discernible relationship existed between German votes and the Anti-Monopoly party percentages. Successful as the Democratic party was in capturing large numbers of German votes, the ultimate goal of winning the election remained as elusive as ever.

The observation that the movement of German voters into Democratic ranks in 1882 was the consequence of the woman suffrage movement is supported by aggregated voting statistics. While the state as a whole turned down the suffrage amendment by a two to one margin, the ratio was ten to one in sample precincts in which Germans constituted more than half the potential voting population.[40] The Germans were joined on this issue by the other non-English-speaking immigrant groups, especially the Scandinavians and Bohemians.[41]

The Election of 1884: The Resurgence of Nativism

The lessons of 1882 were not lost on the Republicans. For the first time in the history of the state there had been a specific issue that could be used to measure the electoral power of immigrant groups. Ethnic bloc-voting was becoming a recognized fact of political life in Nebraska.

[40] In St. Charles and Bismarck precincts (Cuming County) and in Grand Prairie precinct (Platte County) every vote was cast against the amendment. In these instances the German element accounted for more than 70 per cent of the potential electorate.

[41] Examples: Walker precinct (Platte County), Scandinavian: 97.1 per cent against; Burrows (Platte), Polish: 96.6 per cent against; Jackson (Hall), Irish: 86.3 per cent.

Noting the overwhelming defeat of the woman suffrage amendment, many Republicans, especially those in the Stalwart camp, made conscious efforts to shake off the onus of prohibition. In January of 1883 another attempt was made in the legislature to submit a prohibition amendment to the electorate. Its defeat by a vote of sixty-eight to twenty-eight reveals the changed political climate.[42]

The Republican nominee for the presidency in 1884 was James G. Blaine. While his nomination was hardly the consequence of antinativist sentiment, the players of ethnic politics in the Republican party were delighted to advertise Blaine's Irish Catholic connections. At the same time, Republican newspapers in Nebraska announced that Blaine had a high regard for German culture and education, so high, indeed, that he had his son educated at Heidelberg.[43]

Further efforts were made to refurbish the Republican image as pro-immigrant. The *Blue Valley Blade* of Seward reminded its readers that the Republican party had "always been the friend of the oppressed of every land," that thousands of Germans had secured homes under the Homestead Act and had grown rich under Republican rule. Other efforts included publicizing xenophobic statements allegedly made by Democrats, the organization of German Republican clubs, and smearing Democratic candidates as crypto-Know-Nothings.[44] At the same time other Republican editors continued to assume that waving the bloody shirt was an effective tactic.[45]

The new pro-immigrant orientation of the Nebraska GOP included entering German-born candidates in various electoral contests. In Seward County the Republican managers selected John F. Goehner, a German-born hardware merchant, as their candidate for state senator. Goehner had a record of support for the Stalwart faction and, by allegedly agreeing to support submitting a prohibition amendment to popular vote, had even won the support of a temperance paper like the Milford *Ozone*. Yet Goehner was strictly a tool; his nomination by acclamation was arranged by a county central committee that included no Germans. When Republican editors promoted Goehner's candidacy, they often mentioned his ethnic origins.

[42] Milford *Ozone*, October 18, 1884. *House Journal of the Legislature of the State of Nebraska. Eighteenth Regular Session . . . 1883*, p. 577; Sheldon, *Nebraska*, I, 616.

[43] Eugene H. Roseboom, *A History of Presidential Elections* (New York: Macmillan Co., 1957), p. 271; *Blue Valley Blade*, June 25, 1884; Fremont *Tribune* quoted in the Nebraska City *News*, June 21, 1884; Columbus *Journal*, October 15, 1884.

[44] *Blue Valley Blade*, June 25, October 1, 1884; Columbus *Journal*, October 15, 1884; Syracuse *Journal*, October 31, 1884; Milford *Ozone*, October 3, 1884; Nebraska City *News*, August 23, 30, 1884.

[45] For examples see Syracuse *Journal*, October 24, 1884; *Blue Valley Blade*, June 25, 1884.

On the other hand, when they attacked Oscar E. Bernecker, an important Democratic leader in the county, they always ignored the latter's German birth.[46]

Of course, not all Republicans resorted to these tactics. The reform-minded *Nebraska Reporter* flatly stated that prohibitionists had better vote Republican because it was "the only party that has espoused their principles and assisted to enforce the same."[47] Editors of this stripe, however, insisted that the Republican party was not committed to prohibition in the political sense (they merely wanted to let the people decide), but that if the people chose prohibition they stood for its enforcement.

In their state platform of 1884, the Republicans also chose to soft-pedal the prohibition issue. Not a word was said about it or any other issue that arose out of the clash of cultures. Meanwhile the Prohibition party decided that the situation called for a separate slate of candidates. In their platform, the prohibitionists demanded "submission" and explicitly linked woman suffrage with their moralistic crusade.[48]

Democratic strategy was considerably more pragmatic in 1884 than it had been two years earlier. There was strong sentiment within the party for fusion with the Anti-Monopolists and Greenbackers. J. Sterling Morton, who was again the Democratic gubernatorial candidate, received the endorsement of these parties. Nevertheless, Morton insisted on campaigning on his conservative monetary and tariff principles.[49] While the Democratic party adopted its usual plank denouncing prohibition as unconstitutional, it did not hesitate to endorse the Anti-Monopolist candidate for lieutenant governor, L. C. Pace, who was well known as a "rampant, red-hot, uncompromising Prohibitionist."[50] But a plank in the Democratic platform had a special appeal for immigrant voters: It insisted that the rights of naturalized American citizens be respected by foreign powers. This was in response to several incidents in which German-born American citizens had been impressed into the German army when they returned to their *Vaterland* for a visit.[51]

The new solicitude of Blaine and the Republicans for the foreign-born was summarily dismissed as vote-catching soft soap by the Nebraska City

[46] *Blue Valley Blade*, August 20, October 8, 1884; Milford *Ozone*, September 26, 1884. The Seward *Democrat* insisted that Goehner did not dare proclaim publicly whether he was for or against submission. See Milford *Ozone*, October 18, 1884.

[47] *Nebraska Reporter* (Seward), October 9, 1884. See also the Milford *Ozone*, October 18, 1884.

[48] *Nebraska Party Platforms*, pp. 111 f.; Nebraska City *News*, August 23, 1884.

[49] Olson, *J. Sterling Morton*, pp. 302–307.

[50] *Blue Valley Blade*, September 17, 1884.

[51] *Nebraska Party Platforms*, p. 109; Nebraska City *News*, August 16, 1884.

News, as this paper embarked upon a campaign to smear Blaine with charges of Know-Nothingism. He was accused of having been a member of the Know-Nothing party in 1854 and 1855 and of having "done what he could to increase the prejudice which then prevailed to such an extent against the Germans and Irish."[52] Other Democratic newspapers chimed in with an exposé of Blaine's "Madigan circular." This was a pamphlet allegedly written and distributed by Blaine in 1875 in which he urged the defeat of Madigan, a candidate for Congress, solely on the grounds of his membership in the Catholic church.[53] Dr. George Miller's Omaha *Herald* labeled Blaine a confirmed demagogue, a hypocrite, and "a more dangerous foe to liberty than even the most unreasonable prohibitionist."[54]

While Republicans failed to nominate a German for any office on the state ticket, the Democrats had the good judgment to run Judge Gustav Beneke, an Omaha jurist, for state auditor. Beneke's contribution to the campaign was a tour of the German communities, during which he addressed large groups in the German language. Although he made all the charges against Blaine that regularly appeared in the English-language press, Beneke emphasized his belief that the Republican candidate was actually a prohibitionist.[55]

Democrats were also particularly active in getting German immigrants to take out papers declaring their intentions of becoming American citizens. The law required that such declarations had to be certified at least thirty days before the election in order for an alien to qualify for the franchise. The *Blue Valley Blade* of Seward reminded Republicans to watch the polls carefully on election day because many Germans had voted illegally in the past. Several German residents of the community, this newspaper noted, had declared their intentions too late to entitle them to vote.[56]

It is not possible to know exactly how the several German newspapers of the state stood politically in 1884. Few copies of these publications for the 1880's are extant. However, the Nebraska City *News*, a not unbiased source, asserted that of nine German papers being published in the state in 1884, five (Omaha *Post und Telegram*, Grand Island *Herold*, Fremont *Platte River Zeitung*, Norfolk *Demokrat*, and West Point *Nebraska Volksblatt*) were "straight-out" for Cleveland; two (*Omaha Tribüne* and Sutton *Freie Presse*)

52 Nebraska City *News*, August 2, 23, 30, 1884.

53 *The Democrat* (Columbus), July 17, 1884. This newspaper, published in a county with a heavy Catholic population, was unrelenting in its smear of Blaine as a nativist bigot.

54 Reprinted in *The Progress* (West Point), September 18, 1884.

55 Omaha *Herald* (weekly edition), October 17, 1884; *The Progress*, October 16, 1884.

56 *Blue Valley Blade*, October 15, 1884.

were independent, and two (Nebraska City *Nebraska Staats Zeitung* and the *Nebraska Staats Anzeiger* of Lincoln) were Republican.[57]

As the survey of German papers suggests, not all German voters were convinced that "personal liberty" was the only vital issue dividing the two major parties. Differing views among Germans were contrasted in the pages of two Columbus newspapers in the last three weeks of the 1884 campaign. By means of letters to the editor of the Columbus *Journal*, Melchior Brugger, a young Columbus banker, born and educated in Switzerland, strongly defended Blaine from charges of Know-Nothingism and prohibitionism that had appeared in the Columbus *Wochenblatt*. Brugger typified the rapid assimilator, anxious to conform to the norms and standards of the dominant cultural group. He was a well-educated, business-oriented urbanite, a member of the Congregational church, a Mason, a Republican, and a staunch temperance worker. The opposing view was taken by Fred Luchsinger, also Swiss-born, but a Lutheran, a Democrat, apparently a farmer, and clearly a champion of the values of German immigrant culture. None of the arguments employed by these two antagonists were new, and they need not be repeated here, but they were aptly summarized and well expressed. Brugger seems to have won the letter-column debate. Rational discussion ended when the *Wochenblatt* smeared Brugger as a pharisee who consumed cheap whiskey as he practiced the vice of drunkenness in secret.[58]

As election day neared, the charges and countercharges of prohibitionism, bigotry, xenophobia, and corruption were hurled furiously back and forth. With remarkable prescience, the editor of the Fairbury *Gazette* observed that

prohibition seems to develop as slavery did, in opposition to both parties. It is now as slavery was, the Banquo's ghost of American politics; it will not down; and when prohibition does prevail, as it will in the distant future, both parties can say with Macbeth: "Thou canst not say I did it; never shake thy gory locks at me."[59]

Nativism in its several aspects was not the only issue of the campaign. The gubernatorial contest between Dawes and Morton in particular sank to new depths of cynicism and vituperation, yet aggregated voting statistics on the precinct level reveal a continuation of the movement of German

---

[57] Nebraska City *News*, August 8, 1884. The list of German-language newspapers is not complete. The *Wochenblatt* of Columbus, for example, is not mentioned.

[58] Columbus *Journal*, October 15, 22, 29, 1884; Columbus *Democrat*, October 17, 1884.

[59] Fairbury *Gazette*, September 13, 1884.

voters into the Democratic party (Table 24).[60] Even though the Republicans
fared better than they had in 1882, it was apparent that their efforts to woo
the German immigrant vote had been unsuccessful. This fact, of course,
improved the prospects of the temperance-reform wing to capture the
Republican party in future elections.

TABLE 24

Mean Percentages of Votes Cast for Republican and Democratic
Candidates in the Election of 1884, According to Percentages of
Potential German Voters in 1885 (126 Precincts)

Per Cent of German Voters	Number of Precincts	Per Cent Republican	Per Cent Democratic
75.0 and above	8	27.4	72.8
60.0–74.9	10	38.6	61.1
45.0–59.9	15	48.2	51.0
30.0–44.9	22	50.6	48.8
15.0–29.9	38	56.2	42.2
0.0–14.9	33	64.6	33.9
State:		57.3	40.5

The Election of 1886: The Tempo of Temperance

By the election of 1886, temperance sentiment had grown so strong in
Nebraska that the Republican party was unable to ignore it officially any
longer.[61] The final plank of the 1886 Republican platform endorsed the
submission of a prohibition amendment to the electorate. Adopted by a vote
of 341 to 189 in its state convention, the resolution evoked anguished cries
from German Republicans. The *Nebraska Staats Anzeiger* of Lincoln
fumed: "The devil gets the 341! Down with submission, prohibition, and
all the other works of the devil! Germans, make every candidate for the
legislature and the senate clarify his position on submission no matter what
party he belongs to."[62]

The effect of continued agitation for prohibition, as well as woman
suffrage and Sabbath laws, was to intensify the self-consciousness of the
German minority group. With each succeeding election the tendency
increased for Germans to vote as Germans rather than as Republicans or
Democrats. Partisan loyalties became increasingly unstable, even though the
Democrats continued to attract the majority of German votes in the state.

60 Because the census data and the election data are separated in time by only seven
months, the reliability of this table may be assumed to be the highest for any election of the
period.

61 Omaha *Weekly Herald*, October 7, 1886; Grand Island *Herald*, October 1, 1886.

62 Reprinted in *Der Herold* (Grand Island), October 6, 1886.

The *Nebraska Volksblatt* of West Point abandoned party identification as early as 1885. Independence permitted the consistent endorsement of any candidate who gave promise of advancing the good of *das Deutschtum* as the *Volksblatt* conceived of it. Opponents of prohibition were consistently endorsed, regardless of party. "Better a liberal, anti-prohibitionist Republican," this newspaper announced, "than a Democratic temperance bigot."[63]

The Democratic party, under the chairmanship of W. O. Hambel, a German of Jefferson County, denounced prohibition as usual. The National Union party, which had been assembled from scattered fragments of the old Greenback and Anti-Monopoly parties, with support from the Farmers' Alliance, Knights of Labor, and disaffected Van Wyckers, endorsed "absolute prohibition" and woman suffrage. The Prohibition party also seemed to be gaining strength as it attempted to marshal the forces of righteousness. In some communities the Prohibition and National Union parties fused to nominate the same candidates for local office.[64]

For the general public as well as for the German element, prohibition increasingly tended to crowd out other issues, notably the tariff and railroad regulation. In the Omaha *Weekly Herald* it was virtually the only issue discussed.[65] The *State Democrat* of Lincoln, which believed that liquor was the major cause of Democratic defeats, argued that "with most men prohibition is a close, tangible and present thing, of more importance than the distant and difficult tariff. The majority of men can wait to adjust the tariff and regulate the railroads, but they want the whisky question settled now."[66] The results of the election of 1886 were similar to those of 1884. The Republicans easily overcame all opposition with 55 per cent of the total number of votes cast. Aggregated voting statistics also reveal that the German leanings toward the Democratic party were almost unchanged. In precincts in which Germans constituted three-fourths or more of the electorate, the Democratic percentage was 70.1 per cent; in the least German precincts it dropped to 30.8 per cent. The only surprise of the election was the easy victory of Democrat John McShane of Omaha, Catholic Irish and very "wet," over Church Howe in the race for congressman in the First District.

Having gained the victory, the Republicans honored their platform pledge to try to secure submission of a prohibition amendment in the legislative session of 1887. In the struggle that followed, the resolution failed by eleven

63 *Nebraska Volksblatt*, October 16, 1885; October 29, 1886.

64 *Nebraska Party Platforms*, pp. 121, 123; Fairbury *Gazette*, October 23, 1886.

65 The point is illustrated by a headline of October 21, 1886: "Prohibition the Issue: The Sentiment Generally Prevalent that Prohibition is the Issue of the Day: The Democratic Opposition to it is Open and Pronounced—The Republicans for it."

66 Reprinted in the *Blue Valley Blade*, November 23, 1887.

votes to reach the requisite three-fifths majority, largely due to anti-prohibition Republicans who dared not risk the wrath of their constituents.[67] The result was that prohibition was destined to plague Nebraska politics for nearly another four years.

The Election of 1888: Repeat Performance

The distinctiveness of the German vote continued unchanged in 1888 in regard to prohibition, woman suffrage, and Sabbatarian legislation. These were virtually the only issues which distinguished German voters from the rest of the electorate. The tariff, railroad legislation, soldiers' pensions, immigration restriction, alien land ownership, and other issues did not evoke distinctive political attitudes among German voters.

The professionals in both parties made an effort to play down the prohibition issue in 1888. The Democrats abandoned their traditional denunciation of prohibition for a mere expression of support for the Slocumb high-cost liquor license law as "the best and most practicable solution of the liquor traffic question."[68] The Republican platform committee had hoped to get by with a harmless expression of sympathy for "all wise and well-directed efforts for the protection of temperance and morality." However, a resolution calling for submission of the issue to the voters was introduced from the floor of the convention and, after prolonged and excited debate, was adopted as part of the Republican platform.[69]

In the campaign of 1888 the tariff issue seemed to dominate the scene. William Jennings Bryan, newly arrived in Nebraska from Illinois, developed a statewide reputation by speaking tirelessly on behalf of tariff reform.[70] Yet prohibition continued to alienate German Republicans. In the wake of the national convention, the normally Republican *Nebraska Staats Zeitung*

[67] *House Journal of the Legislature of the State of Nebraska. Twentieth Regular Session . . . 1887*, p. 1138. Sheldon, *Nebraska*, I, 648 f.

[68] *Nebraska Party Platforms*, p. 135. Morton *et al.* interpret this action as constituting the adoption of a strong anti-prohibition plank. *Illustrated History of Nebraska*, III, 219. Sheldon agrees, *Nebraska*, I, 653. It is true, of course, that the Democrats had fought the Slocumb Act in 1881. Their support of that law seven years later is a measure, not of altered attitudes within the Democratic party but of the changed political climate in Nebraska. While the consensus had shifted, the basic attitudes of the two major parties toward prohibition remained unchanged in 1888.

[69] *Nebraska Party Platforms*, pp. 138 f. The eloquent John M. Thurston spoke at length to convince "his rural brethren" that submission would ruin the Republican ticket in Omaha. As the Nebraska City *News* expressed it, "the fanatics admired his oratory, [but] they refused to swallow its sentiments," August 30, 1888.

[70] Paolo E. Coletta, "William Jennings Bryan's First Nebraska Years," *Nebraska History*, XXXIII (June, 1952), 79.

described Republican enthusiasm as the kind born of the monopolist, the gold king, the officeseeker, the nativist, and the hater of foreigners.[71] Later the same paper refused to support any candidate that espoused submission. The issue so embarrassed Republican Paul Schminke that he temporarily retired from Otoe County politics. Meanwhile, organizations like the German Anti-Prohibition Club of Omaha denounced the Republican willingness to placate its prohibitionist faction at the same time as it endorsed the Democratic party's support of the high-cost liquor license law.[72] The Omaha *Weekly Herald* asserted that the effect of prohibition would be the stagnation of trade and a loss of $250,000 annually in revenue.[73]

Nothing was changed at the end of election day in 1888. The Republicans won as usual although the Democrats gained about two percentage points over the previous contest; Republican percentages among German precincts remained about the same. In the legislative session which followed, a resolution to submit a prohibition amendment to the voters of Nebraska finally succeeded by a margin of one vote.[74] To most Germans this action was a call to arms. Its effect was to invest prohibition with a new measure of salience. Except for the minority whose religious convictions opposed the use of alcoholic beverages, most Germans of the state, regardless of occupation or class, were united in their support of the Democratic party as the only party committed to their interests in the matter. They were joined, of course, by many others whose opposition was economic or political, if not cultural.

The Election of 1890: Prohibition Vanquished

By a curious twist of history two unrelated issues, prohibition and agrarian discontent, came to a head in Nebraska politics at the same time. By 1890 the Farmers' Alliances throughout the West and South had entered the political struggle on a partisan basis. In some states, notably Kansas, they experienced spectacular successes. The grievances of the farmers had become so acute and their protests so insistent that the entire party system was shaken to its foundations. Yet in Nebraska the agrarian revolt was clouded by the prohibition issue, which, in turn, was compounded by attempts to enact compulsory school legislation. In some country newspapers the liquor question was the only issue. This was true not only of German-language

[71] Reprinted in translation in the Nebraska City *News*, July 6, 1888.

[72] Nebraska City *News*, August 24, 30, September 21, 1888; Columbus *Democrat*, September 21, 1888.

[73] Omaha *Weekly Herald*, September 3, 1888. In this paper prohibition easily displaced tariff reform as the chief issue.

[74] The Nebraska constitution required a three-fifths majority for passage. Sheldon, *Nebraska*, I, 658; *Laws of Nebraska, 1889*, pp. 629–631. See also *Nebraska House Journal, 1889*, pp. 557 f.; *Nebraska Senate Journal, 1889*, pp. 280, 371.

papers but of some others as well.[75] Prominent Nebraska politicians like Lorenzo Crounse and John Watson believed that prohibition figured so largely in the campaign that the traditional issues dividing the parties were swallowed up.[76]

After nearly a decade of debate there was very little left to be said. The old arguments were endlessly repeated and new ones were sought out. The campaign of 1890 saw new emphasis on the economic aspects of prohibition, particularly by the business community.[77] In Omaha a nonpartisan Businessman and Bankers Association was established which engaged Edward Rosewater of the Omaha *Bee* to lead the antiprohibition forces. Intense efforts were made and large sums of money were expended to defeat the amendment. The railroads also were delighted to assist any group which promised to divert popular attention away from themselves and onto other issues. At the same time, the prohibitionists tended increasingly to identify the liquor interests as the dominant cause of intemperance. According to Joseph R. Gusfield, this view coincided with the Populist "assumption of business malevolence," thereby strengthening the nexus between the two movements. Inevitably conflicts between native and immigrant value systems received new emphasis as the cultural groups were increasingly differentiated by their political orientations.[78]

The year 1890 also saw an increase in arguments reflecting cultural conflict. The *Nebraska Volksblatt*, for example, contrasted the drinking habits of Germans with those of Anglo-Americans to the detriment of the latter, who were characterized either as militant abstainers or as intemperate consumers of hard liquor. This same paper matched the fanaticism of the puritanizers by reporting that a conspiracy was afoot to forbid by law the use of wine in the celebration of Holy Communion.[79]

[75] For examples, see *Hitchcock County Republican, Cuming County Advertiser*, or the Blair *Courier*. Articles on the venture of the Alliancemen into politics are all but absent from the pages of these papers. The *Blue Valley Blade* stated that "the saloon question has taken prominence above everything else," March 25, 1891. See also Parsons, "The Populist Context," p. 220. This is not to say, of course, that Alliance agitation did not pervade the newspapers of other communities. *Ibid.*, pp. 176 ff.

[76] Grand Island *Daily Independent*, September 6, 1892; Paolo E. Coletta, "The Morning Star of the Reformation: William Jennings Bryan's First Congressional Campaign," *Nebraska History*, XXXVII (June, 1956), 114.

[77] For an example, see Blair *Courier*, September 13, 1890.

[78] Victor Rosewater, "The Life and Times of Edward Rosewater" (typewritten MS, Nebraska State Historical Society), p. 165; Grand Island *Daily Independent*, September 24, 1890; Helen Storms, "A Study of the Nebraska State Election of 1890" (unpublished Master's thesis, University of Nebraska, 1924), p. 86; Gusfield, *Symbolic Crusade*, pp. 94–98.

[79] *Nebraska Volksblatt*, April 11, 1890.

Most commonly the appeal to the German vote in 1890 was on the basis of "personal liberty." This term included more than the right to enjoy a friendly stein of beer at the local saloon. To many Germans beer drinking was a matter of indifference, but "personal liberty" meant the freedom to educate their children as they saw fit.[80] The slow assimilators in particular felt threatened by the wave of compulsory school laws that were being enacted across the country. Laws that had originated with a nativistic, anti-Catholic "Committee of One Hundred" in Boston were being passed in several states, notably Wisconsin and Illinois. These laws placed parochial schools under state supervision and, more significantly, specified that reading, writing, arithmetic, and United States history be taught in the English language.[81]

An attempt was made to enact such legislation in Nebraska in 1889. A bill to amend Nebraska's compulsory school attendance law in conformance with nativist sentiments was introduced in the state legislature at the suggestion of the state superintendent of schools. In the end, opponents of the bill assured its defeat by having it postponed indefinitely.[82] According to the *Lincoln Freie Presse*, this *deutschfeindliche* bill, which the Germans called the *Schulzwanggesetz*, was prevented from coming to a vote in the legislature by the intervention and influence of Robert E. Moore, a Republican, who was later (in 1894) elected lieutenant governor of Nebraska.[83] It is possible that this legislative battle, which attracted minimal attention in the native-American press, stimulated the Germans to united action as much as did prohibition.

By the time the Republican state convention was held in July, 1890, it was apparent that the People's Independent party was going to be a genuine

[80] *Grand Island Anzeiger*, October 7, 1892.

[81] *Laws of Wisconsin, 1889*, chap. 519, quoted in Walter H. Beck, *Lutheran Elementary Schools in the United States* (St. Louis: Concordia Publishing House, 1939), p. 229. The Massachusetts matrix of compulsory school legislation is examined briefly by Barbara M. Solomon, *Ancestors and Immigrants: A Changing New England Tradition* (New York: John Wiley and Sons, 1956), pp. 49–53. See also Daniel F. Reilly, *The School Controversy (1891–1893)* (Washington: Catholic University of America Press, 1943), pp. 43–45, 56 f.

[82] *House Journal of the Legislature of the State of Nebraska. Twenty-First Regular Session . . . 1889*, pp. 162, 389, 1989.

[83] *Lincoln Freie Presse*, August 30, October 25, 1894. Compulsory school legislation provides an outstanding example of an ethnocultural issue oriented to community concerns. As such, it had greater relevance for voter experience than issues deriving from national and cosmopolitan perspectives. See Samuel P. Hays, "Political Parties and the Community-Society Continuum," in William N. Chambers and Walter D. Burnham, eds., *The American Party System: Stages of Political Development* (New York: Oxford University Press, 1967), p. 158.

threat to Republican dominance. It was also clear that the prohibition amendment was not likely to receive popular approval. According to Addison Sheldon, the Republican leadership was "scared stiff"—and the party platform showed it. Several popular demands for reform were adopted, such as the remonetization of silver, adoption of the Australian (secret) ballot, reduction of railroad rates, the abolition of free railroad passes, and the end of discrimination by owners of elevators and railroad companies in the handling of grain. An attempt to endorse the prohibition amendment was sidetracked by the platform committee.[84] Bourbon control was very much in evidence. It was apparent that great numbers of agrarian reformers and puritanizers had taken their leave.

Many of them had gone into the new People's Independent party. Meeting in Lincoln just a week after the Republican convention, the Populists, as the members of this party were later known, adopted a platform that espoused all their hoped-for reforms. On the subject of prohibition, however, the Populists, like the Republicans, chose to remain silent.[85] Though many Populist leaders were known to be committed privately to temperance reform, they had no desire to further antagonize immigrant voters.

The Democratic party alone was in a position to take a stand on the prohibition issue. Managed by the Omaha "ring" under the leadership of the conservative James E. Boyd, the Democratic party first declared for free coinage of silver, tariff reform, equitable freight rates, and a stringent usury law. But the Germans were especially interested in the final plank of the platform which declared "that the social habits of the people are [not] proper subjects for constitutional provisions." Following a reaffirmation of support for the high-cost liquor license law, it taunted the Republicans for having been responsible for the submission of the prohibition amendment to the popular vote, "thereby creating uncertainty, injuring business, unsettling values, and depressing trade," and then, as the day of decision approached, for having purposely dodged the issue in its convention.[86]

Of the several gubernatorial candidates in 1890, only the Democrat James Boyd stood openly and solidly against the prohibition amendment, which, he said, "was paramount to all other issues."[87] The Populist nominee, John Powers, was an avowed prohibitionist and had announced his intention to vote for the amendment. The Republican standard-bearer was Lucius D.

[84] *Nebraska Party Platforms*, pp. 155 f.; Morton *et al.*, *Illustrated History of Nebraska*, III, 228; Sheldon, *Nebraska*, I, 684 f.

[85] *Nebraska Party Platforms*, pp. 149 f.

[86] *Ibid.*, pp. 148 f.; Morton *et al.*, *Illustrated History of Nebraska*, III, 229.

[87] Nebraska City *News*, October 24, 1890; Grand Island *Daily Independent*, October 13, 1890.

Richards, a Fremont banker. While Richards had private prohibitionist sentiments, he steadfastly refused to commit himself on the issue. If elected governor, he stated over and over again, he would enforce whatever law the people of Nebraska decided upon. His refusal to take a stand cost him the support of the Omaha *Bee* and its influential publisher, Edward Rosewater.[88]

The attitude of the *Nebraska Volksblatt* was typical of many German newspapers. Powers was ignored while Richards was dismissed as never having done anything in the interest of the immigrant people of Nebraska. On the prohibition issue Richards was evasive; on the school question he naïvely announced that it made no difference to him which language was taught in private schools, so long as English was given the greatest importance. Boyd, on the other hand, had declared himself against *Schulzwang* (compulsory education legislation) and prohibition. Therefore every German, urged the *Volksblatt*, should vote for Boyd. Meanwhile, Republican newspapers like the *Nebraska Staats Zeitung*, partly owned by Paul Schminke, and Fred Hedde's Grand Island *Daily Independent* endorsed the Democratic slate.[89] The case was summed up neatly for the Germans by the Nebraska City *News:* "Richards and Powers are covertly hand in glove with the prohibitionists. Boyd is openly opposed to them. Take your pick."[90]

Newspapers were not the only means for the transmission of group standards. The church also played a significant role. The Lutheran Synod of Nebraska endorsed Boyd for the governorship and C. D. Rakestraw, the Democratic nominee for superintendent of public instruction. Circular letters were distributed among its members throughout the state explaining the Synod's action and elaborating upon the candidates' views.[91] When pressed for his views, the Reverend F. H. W. Bruechert, pastor of the First German Evangelical church of Omaha, publicly branded prohibition as a farce. Meanwhile, nonimmigrant church organizations like the Nebraska Baptist convention and the Presbyterian Synod of Nebraska resolved to support the prohibition amendment.[92] Inevitably their action caused them to serve as negative reference groups for the Germans, whose political behavior became increasingly distinctive.

[88] Omaha *Daily Bee*, August 29, 1890; Fairbury *Gazette*, October 4, 1890; Parsons, "The Populist Context," p. 239; *Morning World Herald* (Omaha), September 20, 1890; Columbus *Telegram*, October 16, 1890; Morton *et al.*, *Illustrated History of Nebraska*, III, 228 f.

[89] *Nebraska Volksblatt*, October 10, 17, 1890; Columbus *Telegram*, April 24, 1890; Nebraska City *News*, October 17, 1890; Grand Island *Daily Independent*, October 17, 1890.

[90] Nebraska City *News*, October 31, 1890.

[91] *Ibid.*

[92] Omaha *Daily Bee*, October 29, 5, 18; November 1, 1890.

The Lutheran Germans were particularly anxious about compulsory school legislation. The Nebraska district of the Lutheran Church—Missouri Synod, in convention in Arlington, was told by the main speaker to address the group that the attempts in Wisconsin and Illinois to control parochial schools were works of the devil. One political party, he asserted, was all stirred up with hatred for foreigners, their languages, and religions. The district convention resolved to use its power at the polls to urge Lutherans to vote only for those candidates who publicly promised to oppose compulsory school legislation. A political action committee was also elected to coordinate the effort and to confront the various candidates with the school question.[93]

German Lutheran clergymen were also active in the work of the Personal Rights League, an organization with headquarters in Chicago, which worked primarily through *Turnvereine* and other culturally based institutions. The League was very active in Nebraska. With the help of a full-time organizer, it attempted to establish member leagues in as many communities as possible. Primarily organized in Nebraska to defeat prohibition and to defend German schools against impending regulatory legislation, it encouraged immigrants to take out their first naturalization papers and sought to convince them to vote Democratic on election day.[94]

In June the Personal Rights League scheduled a convention to meet simultaneously with a statewide *Turnfest* in Lincoln. In this way the hundreds of German citizens who converged upon the city were exposed to the goals and objectives of the League.[95] In October another large meeting was held in Lincoln, at which the replies of the candidates for state office to the issues as posed by the Personal Rights League were discussed. Richards, as usual, endeavored to straddle the issues, and Powers made no reply at all. But Boyd responded to the League's questions with satisfactory answers on both prohibition and the school question. Hence, his candidacy was endorsed. All candidates for lieutenant governor, secretary of state, treasurer, and auditor declared themselves in accord with the League's platform, and were commended to German voters without reference to party. In the race for superintendent of public instruction, the Democratic candidate, Rakestraw, was endorsed. Finally, the League decided to issue a circular publicizing its

93 [Lutheran Church—Missouri Synod. Nebraska District], *Sechster Synodal-Bericht des Nebraska-Districts der deutschen evang.-luth. Synode von Missouri, Ohio, und anderen Staaten. 1889* (St. Louis: Luth. Concordia-Verlag, 1890), pp. 57–60. See also *Nebraska Volksblatt*, June 20, 1890, for activity of the Iowa Synod.

94 *Nebraska Volksblatt*, June 13, August 22, 29, September 5, 1890; *Daily Nebraska State Journal* (Lincoln), October 15, 1890; *Personal Rights Advocate* (Chicago), June 7, November 22, 1890.

95 *Nebraska Volksblatt*, June 13, 27, 1890.

endorsements and the stands taken by the several candidates on questions of "personal liberty."[96]

Another organization which gave itself fully to the political problems of prohibition and compulsory school legislation was the Association of German Agricultural Societies of Nebraska. Ethnic politics crowded almost every other issue off the agenda at its annual meeting in 1890. In order to assist German farmers in their comprehension of these difficult issues, this organization decided to circulate pamphlets in support of personal rights.[97]

It is apparent that a remarkable degree of unity was achieved among the German voters of Nebraska in 1890. News media, churches, cultural societies, commercial groups, and farmer organizations had all sounded the alarm. The result was the heaviest turnout and the first Democratic gubernatorial victory in the history of the state. The race was remarkably close, with each of the candidates winning about one-third of the total. Despite some evidence of irregularities at the polls in Omaha, where Boyd piled up an overwhelming lead, subsequent investigation revealed that it had been an orderly election by comparative standards.[98] There was an unusual amount of vote-trading and vote-scratching in the election. Many Republican ballots were voted straight except for the governorship, in which case Richard's name was scratched and Boyd's was written in.[99] Hence, with the exception of the commissioner of public buildings and lands, Boyd was the only Democrat on the state ticket to be elected. All other state executive offices were swept by the Republicans, while the Peoples Independent party won control of both houses of the state legislature.

The distinctiveness of German voting behavior in the Nebraska election of 1890 is indicated in Table 25, which groups the votes cast for governor in

[96] Nebraska City *News*, October 17, 1890; *Daily Nebraska State Journal*, October 15, 1890; Lincoln *Weekly Herald*, October 18, 1890; Lincoln *Evening News*, October 15, 1890.

[97] *Nebraska Volksblatt*, September 19, 1890.

[98] Rosewater, "Edward Rosewater," p. 170. For charges of ballot box stuffing, see Morton *et al.*, *Illustrated History of Nebraska*, III, 230; Jesse E. Boell, "William Jennings Bryan Before 1896" (unpublished Master's thesis, University of Nebraska, 1929), pp. 63 f.; and Storms, "Study of the Nebraska State Election of 1890," p. 90. Boell's comments are the most detailed. Comparative statistical analysis is offered but it is not satisfactory. It ignores, for example, the fact that nearly five thousand foreign-born residents of Omaha took out their first papers in time to vote in the election. See the Lincoln *Daily Call*, October 15, 1890. Though the flood of applications for naturalization was hardly the consequence of newfound patriotism, it was an exercise of legitimate politics. It was partisan but not fraudulent.

[99] Lincoln *Weekly Herald*, November 1, 1890; Storms, "Study of the Nebraska State Election of 1890," p. 88; Coletta, "Morning Star of the Reformation," p. 115.

136 precincts. It clearly documents the German rejection of both Republican and Populist candidates. At the same time, Boyd's narrow victory seems to have been made possible by German bloc-voting. The same pattern is revealed by Table 26, which groups voting data on the prohibition amendment in 145 precincts. The table offers remarkable proof of the overwhelming rejection by German voters of the prohibition amendment.

TABLE 25

Mean Percentages of Votes Cast for Major Candidates for Governor in the
Election of 1890, According to Percentages of Potential German Voters in
1885 (136 Precincts)

Per Cent of German Voters	Number of Precincts	Per Cent Republican	Per Cent Democratic	Per Cent Populist
75.0 and above	8	10.3	81.1	7.7
60.0–74.9	9	17.5	61.8	17.1
45.0–59.9	17	21.3	55.7	21.7
30.0–44.9	24	21.4	47.9	29.1
15.0–29.9	39	27.7	33.4	37.0
0.0–14.9	43	31.6	21.8	45.0
State:		32.2	33.3	32.8

TABLE 26

Mean Percentages of Votes Cast for and Against the Prohibition
Amendment in the Election of 1890, According to Percentages of
Potential German Voters in 1885 (145 Precincts)

Per Cent of German Voters	Number of Precincts	For Prohibition	Against Prohibition
75.0 and above	8	7.7	92.3
60.0–74.9	9	14.9	85.1
45.0–59.9	19	20.7	79.3
30.0–44.9	26	28.2	71.8
15.0–29.9	41	41.4	58.6
0.0–14.9	42	54.6	45.4
State:		42.1	57.9

The Religious Factor

While the data offer conclusive evidence that German ethnicity was a correlate of Democratic party voting throughout the decade of the 1880's, climaxing in 1890, it would be a mistake to assume that ethnicity was the only factor of importance related to immigrant political behavior. Careful examination of the election records reveals that church affiliation was also fundamental. Unfortunately, however, the statistics of church membership are inconsistent and unreliable; hence they are not subject to accurate or comprehensive grouping techniques.[100] Instead, the assessment of the religious factor must be based upon impressions gathered from strongly German precincts that are generally identifiable as predominantly Lutheran, Catholic, Mennonite, or some other denomination, by the presence of parishes of these denominations within their borders.

This approach indicates that certain general patterns were present. The voting behavior of Lutheran Germans, the most numerous religious group, corresponded closely to that of the German immigrant community as a whole. Though the percentages derived from distinctively Lutheran precincts vary widely, the data reveal that Democratic party voting increased dramatically in 1882, presumably as a negative response to agitation in favor of woman suffrage. In the following year Democratic proportions among German Lutherans were reduced, but the trend toward Democratic voting resumed in subsequent elections, reaching a high point in 1890. Table 27 shows that Democratic percentages in German Lutheran precincts ran as high as 85 and 95 per cent in that year, apparently the consequence of the prohibition and compulsory school legislation movements. Throughout the period of the 1880's, Democratic tendencies seem to have been

TABLE 27

Percentages of Votes Cast for Democratic Candidates in Representative Precincts of High German Population in Nebraska, According to Dominant Church Affiliation, 1880–1890

Precinct	County	1880	1882	1884	1886	1888	1890
				Lutheran			
Rock Creek	Otoe	45.6	92.6	71.9	61.3	60.0	88.9
Bismarck	Platte	63.0	87.6	69.7	89.5	80.0	86.0
Sherman	Platte	37.8	54.3	55.2	53.7	52.8	88.9
H	Seward	38.0	53.4	42.6	42.1	47.4	63.2
Friedensau	Thayer	—[a]	—[a]	81.1	83.0	86.3	95.9
				Catholic			
St. Charles	Cuming	71.2	93.7	89.5	84.4	75.8	—[a]
St. Bernard	Platte	88.0	87.9	83.5	91.5	93.0	75.9
Granville	Platte	65.4	68.0	71.4	69.5	75.1	71.9
				Non-Lutheran Protestant			
Cub Creek	Jefferson	15.2	23.4	63.8	65.1	50.0	66.2
Lincoln	Jefferson	13.9	27.0	27.9	27.0	18.1	24.3
Berlin	Otoe	30.6	64.2	33.1	34.4	45.6	65.1
Henderson	York	32.8	34.3	41.6	27.4	35.0	16.0

[a] Precinct boundaries changed.

[100] For a valuable discussion of the uses of religious statistics, see Seymour Martin Lipset, *The First New Nation : The United States in Historical and Comparative Perspective* (New York : Basic Books, Inc., 1963), pp. 143–150.

strongest in precincts dominated by Lutheran churches affiliated with the conservative Missouri Synod. Harboring large numbers of slow assimilators, such precincts responded quickly to what they perceived as threats to their life style and value system.[101]

Throughout the decade of the 1880's precincts identifiable as German Catholic regularly gave from 65 to 90 per cent of their votes to Democratic candidates. Since their association with the Democratic party was high from the outset, the woman suffrage and prohibition issues affected their partisan preferences only slightly. They would have voted Democratic anyway. In 1890 Catholics generally were not as aroused as Lutherans. Indeed, the Populist movement appears to have been attractive enough in some rural Catholic precincts to have reduced Democratic majorities by several percentage points in 1890 from what they had been in the previous election of 1888.

The pattern in non-Lutheran protestant precincts is much less clear. Because their numbers were smaller, non-Lutheran Protestant groups rarely dominated the population of a given precinct. In a few cases Mennonite precincts can be identified. But since Mennonites often eschewed political activity it is doubtful that they voted in proportion to their numbers. Nevertheless, it is apparent that the Republican party regularly enjoyed substantial majorities in non-Lutheran Protestant precincts. In some places, such as Berlin precinct in Otoe County, where the mother congregation of German Methodism in the state was located, significant Democratic increases occurred in 1882 and 1890. It does not follow, however, that these shifts were brought about by Methodist voters, because Lutherans and Catholics were also resident in the township. On the other hand, Henderson precinct in York County was strongly Mennonite with almost no Lutherans or Catholics. Since Mennonites leaned toward prohibition, it is not surprising that this precinct gave its smallest percentage of the decade to the Democrats in 1890. In any case, the data suggest a close relationship between church affiliation and voting behavior. These findings correspond closely to those obtained by the multiple biography technique employed in Chapter IV.

101 It is important to recognize that the political behavior of Scandinavian Lutherans was markedly different from that of Lutherans of German origin. Much more pietistic than the Germans, a great many Norwegians and Danes welcomed prohibition and Sabbatarian legislation. Not having parochial schools, the Scandinavians sensed no threat in the proposed compulsory school legislation. This helps to explain why Scandinavians regularly preferred the Republican party and why many of them found the Populist party congenial. In 1890, Walker precinct in Platte County, heavily Swedish and Danish in population, gave 96 per cent of its ballots to the Populist candidate for governor. Swedish precincts in Phelps and Polk counties responded similarly.

Paul Schminke

Fred Hedde

Henry Sprick

Peter Jansen

Governor Charles H. Dietrich

Republican Gubernatorial Candidate Dietrich fishing for the German vote.

Courtesy of the Nebraska State Historical Society

Cartoon attacking Dietrich's "beer and sauerkraut" campaign for the governorship of Nebraska in 1900. From the Dietrich Scrapbook in the Nebraska State Historical Society. The newspaper in which it appeared has not been identified.

Theodore Roosevelt, the Republican vice-presidential candidate in 1900, campaigning in Nebraska with Charles H. Dietrich. Dietrich appears second to the left of Roosevelt, and slightly behind.

CHAPTER VIII

_____

The Germans and Nebraska Politics
in the Populist Era

IN 1890 THE GERMANS of Nebraska tended to categorize the Populists among their chief foes. Nativist sentiments were occasionally voiced in the Populist press, and leading Populist figures were known to be prohibitionists. Omar M. Kem, the successful Populist candidate for Congress in 1890, for example, was reputed to have said that no foreign-born person had any right to be in politics. Labor leaders, often found in Populist ranks, were among the most outspoken advocates of immigration restriction. Terence V. Powderly, the national leader of the Knights of Labor, earned a reputation among the Germans as a formidable *Deutschenfresser*. According to the distinguished immigration historian Marcus Lee Hansen, the immigrant clergy consistently spoke out against Populist political heresies, and theological conservatism, the hallmark of many immigrant churches, was against any movement which fostered unconventional political and social ideas.[1] As fanatic as their antagonists, many German leaders were blind to all issues in 1890 other than prohibition and *Schulfreiheit*. Their energies had been almost exclusively devoted to a defense of their cultural heritage against what they perceived as attacks of nativist bigotry from Republicans— and Populists as well. It was apparent that the leadership of the Populist party was overwhelmingly Anglo-American.[2] To the hypersensitive German

[1] *Hamilton County Register* (Aurora), April 4, 1889; *Cuming County Advertiser* (West Point), June 17, 1890; Grand Island *Independent*, October 21, 1890; *Nebraska Biene* (Columbus), September 21, 1900; Marcus Lee Hansen, *The Immigrant in American History* (New York: Harper Torchbooks, Harper and Row, 1964), p. 91.

[2] This generalization is verified by a study of the names of delegates and committee members in the Populist county organizations. A recent study of 311 delegates from Seward county to state, district, and county conventions of the three parties from 1890 to 1892 reveals that 80.7 per cent of the Populist party delegates were native-born compared to 77.7 per cent of the Republicans and 46.8 per cent of the Democrats. Sixty-two of the 311 delegates were Germans. Of these, 3.2 per cent were Populists, 22.6 per cent were Republicans, and 74.2 per cent were Democrats. David Stephens Trask, "Anti-Populism in

of 1890 there was little point in distinguishing the Populist from the Republican as far as the issues of that year were concerned.[3]

The Election of 1892: Populists and Nativists

By 1892 conditions had changed somewhat. Although traditional voting habits continued to cause many Germans to identify with the Democratic party and to expect the worst from the Republicans, some began to look at the Populists in a different light. Populist reforms sounded good, particularly to the rapid assimilators, those of the Per Hansa psychology. Out of consideration for Germans and other immigrant groups, the Populists had excluded any reference in their platform to prohibition, woman suffrage, and similar issues. Moreover, the Nebraska Populist statement on money was mild in that year; it was expressed in terms of legal tender, not free silver. The platform of the national convention held in Omaha included a strong silver statement, but it was only one of many reforms being recommended.[4] In 1892 the currency issue lacked the salience it was to acquire later at the hands of William Jennings Bryan.

In some parts of the state the Populists appealed directly to the Germans and tried to create an image of a *Volkspartei*.[5] None of the German newspapers, however, accepted this. Indeed, none supported the Populist movement in 1892; most tended to ignore it. Only the *Lincoln Freie Presse* condemned the Populists as a serious threat to "our rich and flourishing state."[6] Although Charles H. Van Wyck, the Populist candidate for governor,

Nebraska" (unpublished Master's thesis, University of Nebraska, 1968), pp. 104 f. See also the comment of *The American* (Omaha), August 31, 1894: "The Populists are in the main, Americans, native born, who have nothing in common with ecclesiastical politicians."

[3] This is not to say that the Populist party was nativist, anti-Catholic, or anti-Semitic, or that it officially advocated measures productive of xenophobia. Indeed, it is likely that nativists found the Republican party more congenial to their prejudices than the Populist party. Rather than Populists cultivating nativists, as has been suggested by some historians, the opposite seems to have been the case. Nonetheless, German immigrant perceptions of the agrarian radicals in 1890 did not recognize these distinctions, and the Populists were unhesitatingly coupled with the Republicans.

[4] [U.S. Work Projects Administration, Nebraska], *Nebraska Party Platforms* (sponsored by the University of Nebraska, 1940), pp. 175 f. Hereafter cited as *Nebraska Party Platforms*. John D. Hicks reports that the ovation given the anti-railroad plank at the Omaha convention exceeded the applause given free silver; see his *The Populist Revolt: A History of the Farmers' Alliance and the People's Party* (Lincoln: University of Nebraska Press, 1961), p. 231; Addison E. Sheldon, *Nebraska: The Land and the People* (3 vols.; Chicago: Lewis Publishing Co., 1931), I, 717.

[5] William F. Zimmerman, "Legislative History of Nebraska Populism, 1890–1895" (unpublished Master's thesis, University of Nebraska, 1926), p. 86.

[6] *Lincoln Freie Presse*, September 10, 1892.

was occasionally condemned as a free silverite and a prohibitionist, James B. Weaver, the presidential nominee, was rarely mentioned in the German-language press. In general, it seems that group political norms among the Germans with respect to the Populist party were less clear in 1892 than they had been in 1890.

It was apparent to most political observers that the Nebraska Democratic party was facing disaster in the election of 1892. Boyd's tenure as governor had not been happy. As a conservative politician saddled with a radical legislature, he had labored under impossible conditions. The party had slipped back into the control of J. Sterling Morton and other fiscal conservatives, who with great effort had staved off an attempt by William Jennings Bryan to insert a silver plank into the Democratic platform.[7] Though the Democrats generally had no hope of being elected in the state, they continued to attract German support in 1892. Grover Cleveland was often billed as a great friend of the Germans and an opponent of prohibition and of all forms of nativism.[8] Morton, once again the Democratic nominee for governor, was well known for his opposition to nativist legislation and to free silver. Besides, the Democrats had nominated several Germans for state office. Samuel N. Wolbach, a Grand Island merchant who allegedly "remained a German in speech and customs," was nominated for the lieutenant governorship; a Bavarian, Matthew Gering of Plattsmouth, was the candidate for attorney general; and for the office of superintendent of public instruction, a post about which Germans were always sensitive because of nativist threats to their schools, the Democrats chose J. A. Hornberger of Norfolk.[9] Moreover, the Democratic state platform was silent on the silver issue and included the traditional declaration that prohibition was "contrary to fundamental principles of social and moral conduct." It announced its opposition to all nativist movements by denouncing "any attempt to deprive our citizens of their political rights and privileges as such because of their race or religious faith."[10]

The Republican state platform of 1892 attracted little attention. It managed to avoid most significant issues, though a few gestures were made in the direction of reform. Lorenzo Crounse was nominated for governor as a

---

[7] Paolo E. Coletta, "The Nebraska Democratic State Convention of April 13–14, 1892," *Nebraska History*, XXXIX (December, 1958), 317–333; James C. Olson, *J. Sterling Morton* (Lincoln: University of Nebraska Press, 1955), pp. 338 f.; J. Sterling Morton, Albert Watkins, and George L. Miller, *Illustrated History of Nebraska*, III (Lincoln: Western Publishing and Engraving Co., 1913), 239–243.

[8] *Nebraska Volksblatt*, July 15, 1892; October 7, November 4, 1892; *Omaha Tribüne*, October 17, November 5, 1892; *Grand Island Anzeiger*, October 14, 1892.

[9] *Lincoln Freie Presse*, September 1, 1892; *Nebraska Volksblatt*, October 7, 1892.

[10] *Nebraska Party Platforms*, pp. 172 f.

compromise candidate capable of uniting the party; a wheelhorse of the old guard, Thomas Majors, was the nominee for lieutenant governor. Neither choice was popular with the Germans. Both, but especially the latter, were regularly attacked as prohibitionists or as members of the militantly anti-Catholic American Protective Association (APA).[11]

The chances of Republican success among the Germans were dimmed by *The American* of Omaha, the organ of the APA in Nebraska. Delighted with Major's nomination, which it had advocated, this paper announced that the Catholic church was centering its fight against his candidacy. It also leveled an attack on Edward Rosewater, the Bohemian-born publisher of the Omaha *Bee*, who had strenuously opposed Majors at the time his nomination was being considered. Rosewater had pointed out that the great majority of APA members were Republicans and therefore Majors could add nothing to the ticket. On the other hand, many foreign-born voters would be alienated.[12]

Of the German-language newspapers in the state, the *Lincoln Freie Presse* was the most outspoken in its condemnation of the APA, which it grouped with the Patriotic Order of the Sons of America and the Junior Order of United States Mechanics. These secret societies allegedly furthered patriotic ideas, the *Freie Presse* stated, but in the interpretation of their basic principles they made bitter enemies of all immigrants and their schools and churches. The APA wanted to prohibit the foreign-born from holding political office. According to the *Freie Presse*, it had

declared a war of annihilation against German schools . . . which remain the best agencies of German language and customs. A thorn in the flesh of the nativists, the German schools are immune to the influence of prohibition and other false teachings and are the strongest defenses of personal liberty. . . . The mere existence of these secret societies is an infamous insult to all immigrants and all Catholics of the land.[13]

But the American Protective Association insisted that it was neither partisan nor nativist.[14] As though to prove the point, it endorsed the candidacy

[11] Nebraska City *News*, August 26, September 30, 1892; *Sunday World Herald*, November 6, 1892; Blair *Courier*, October 22, 1892; *Grand Island Anzeiger*, October 14, 1892; *Nebraska Volksblatt*, October 28, 1892. For a thorough study of the American Protective Association on the national level, see Donald L. Kinzer, *Episode in Anti-Catholicism: The American Protective Association* (Seattle: University of Washington Press, 1964).

[12] *The American* (Omaha), September 2, 1892; Omaha *Daily Bee*, November 4, 1894.

[13] *Lincoln Freie Presse*, October 6, 1892.

[14] *The American*, August 19, September 2, 1892; September 28, 1894. Cf. John Higham, *Strangers in the Land: Patterns of American Nativism, 1860–1925* (New Brunswick, N.J.: Rutgers University Press, 1955), p. 83. Higham notes that in Minneapolis so many Scandinavians joined the movement that the APA organ there merged with a Scandinavian-language newspaper.

of Andrew Beckman, a Swede who was running for state treasurer on the Democratic ticket. Moreover, many non-Catholic Germans saw no cause for alarm in the APA.[15] German editors, few of whom were Catholic, were often strangely silent on the issue. Some became aroused only after they had got their fingers burned.[16] Actually the strongest journalistic opposition to the APA came from the foreign-born publishers of two English-language Republican newspapers, Edward Rosewater of the Omaha *Bee* and Fred Hedde of the Grand Island *Independent*.[17]

An extraordinary amount of ticket-splitting and vote-trading occurred in the November election, a phenomenon reflecting the first use of the Australian ballot in a presidential election in Nebraska. Although the Republicans won the major state contests, Bryan won reelection to Congress in the First District by a margin of 140 votes. The Democratic managers, recognizing that their party had no chance of election, had advised their adherents to vote for Weaver electors.[18] Hence Cleveland mustered a mere 12.8 per cent of the total number of votes cast for President, while Morton, who had campaigned almost exclusively against Van Wyck, outpolled Cleveland by 20,000 votes.

Though the Democratic party had been reduced to shambles in Nebraska in 1892, the Germans generally continued to display their preference for it, compared to the total voting population, as Table 28 demonstrates.[19] The rejection of the Republican party likewise continued as strong as ever. The most notable change occurred with respect to the Populist party: In 1890 the Germans classed the Populists as nativists, along with Republicans, but in 1892 the German vote for the Populist candidate does not appear to have been distinctive. In other words, whatever caused approximately 40 per cent

[15] Martin E. Carlson, "A History of the American Protective Association in Nebraska" (unpublished Master's thesis, Colorado State College of Education, 1947), pp. 52–55, 143–145. While the Nebraska APA endlessly attacked Catholic schools, no word was ever said about Lutheran schools, which were actually more numerous in Nebraska at the time.

[16] For example, the *Nebraska Staats Anzeiger* of Lincoln did not attack the APA until after the election of 1893, when it became apparent that its favorite candidate, Fred Schmidt, had been shamelessly used by the nativists. See the *Staats Anzeiger*, November 9, 16, 1893. In the same election, West Point's *Nebraska Volksblatt* was silent on the APA until its last issue before the election, when it became evident that Joseph Zajicek, Democratic candidate for Cuming County treasurer, had been victimized by the society. *Nebraska Volksblatt*, November 3, 1893.

[17] Ruth Knox Stough, "The American Protective Association" (unpublished Master's thesis, University of Nebraska, 1931), p. 16; Victor Rosewater, "The Life and Times of Edward Rosewater," unpublished MS, Nebraska State Historical Society, p. 16.

[18] Addison E. Sheldon, *Nebraska: The Land and the People* (3 vols.; Chicago: Lewis Publishing Co., 1931), p. 722.

[19] Cf. the graphed coefficients of correlation recorded for individual counties in Chapter V above.

of the Germans to vote for the Populist candidates does not seem to have been connected to their ethnic origins. Thus, Germans did not vote as a bloc for or against Populists in 1892, as they had voted in a bloc *for* the Democrats and *against* the Republicans in 1890.

TABLE 28

Mean Percentages of Votes Cast for Major Candidates for President in the Election of 1892, According to Percentages of Potential German Voters in 1885 (139 Precincts)

Per Cent of German Voters	Number of Precincts	Per Cent Republican	Per Cent Democratic	Per Cent Populist
75.0 and above	8	24.4	26.6	47.9
60.0–74.9	9	30.4	23.9	44.5
45.0–59.9	18	36.4	26.9	35.7
30.0–44.9	23	37.4	25.6	35.8
15.0–29.9	40	39.7	16.5	41.4
0.0–14.9	41	43.1	13.1	42.0
State:		44.9	12.8	42.3

The Election of 1894: Political Realignment

The most extraordinary realignment of partisan loyalties among the Germans occurred in 1894.[20] Largely the consequence of Bryan's political ambitions, of economic depression, and of unprecedented crop failures, the Democratic party endorsed Populist demands for free and unlimited coinage of silver at the ratio of sixteen ounces of silver to one ounce of gold. Other Populist demands were also grafted onto Democratic roots so that the party was transformed from an organization led by fiscal conservatives of Jeffersonian traditions to one which espoused an expanded role of government acting in behalf of the common people.[21] Moreover, Bryan led the Democratic party into an endorsement of most of the Populist candidates, headed by Silas A. Holcomb, the nominee for governor. Believing that a majority of the people wanted free silver, Bryan planned to use the silver issue to fuse

[20] Recent historians have recognized that the election of 1894 heralded the beginning of a new era in American politics that has traditionally been identified with the election of 1896. Cf. Carl N. Degler, "American Political Parties and the Rise of the City," *Journal of American History*, LI (June, 1964), 41–59. See also his *The Age of Economic Revolution, 1876–1900* (Glenview, Ill.: Scott, Foresman and Co., 1967), pp. 137 f., 149; Samuel P. Hays, "Political Parties and the Community-Society Continuum," in William N. Chambers and Walter D. Burnham, eds., *The American Party System: States of Political Development* (New York: Oxford University Press, 1967), p. 159.

[21] James C. Olson, *History of Nebraska* (Lincoln: University of Nebraska Press, 1955), pp. 189 f.

Democratic and Populist strength and to put the Republicans to rout. As a personal reward for his efforts, he expected that a Democratic-Populist majority in the state legislature would elect him to the United States Senate.[22]

In 1894 the Republican gubernatorial nominee was Lieutenant Governor Thomas Majors. Backed by the Burlington railroad, Majors was a stalwart who had the active support of the American Protective Association. His candidacy was bitterly opposed by Edward Rosewater, who resigned his position as a Republican national committeeman in order to fight Majors and to support Holcomb for the governorship.[23]

The German voter who viewed the political scene in 1894 was confronted by a series of contradictory choices. Traditionally he had thought of the Republican party as the political vehicle of nativism and moralistic fanaticism. Yet in 1894 the party seemed to be controlled by the regulars who had customarily fought off prohibition and woman suffrage. Moreover, the Republican candidate for lieutenant governor was Robert E. Moore, whom the Germans fondly remembered as a great help in their fight in 1890 against compulsory school legislation. Yet German endorsement of the Republican slate was inhibited by Thomas Majors' connections with the anti-Catholic APA and by the memory of his efforts on behalf of submission of the prohibition amendment in the legislature of 1889.[24] The Republicans were sound enough on the currency question, but it was clear that their election was tantamount to the end of reform and to continued domination of the railroads and the corporation in Nebraska politics.

Populist reforms no longer looked as attractive as formerly. To the dismay of most Germans, free silver was given a pre-eminence it had not had in 1892. At the same time agitation among Populists for prohibition and woman suffrage seemed to be resurgent, as several Populist county conventions had endorsed both measures. Silas Holcomb, the Populist gubernatorial nominee, was known as a prohibitionist and as favoring *Weiberstimmrechts-Humbug*,

[22] Morton *et al.*, *Illustrated History of Nebraska*, III, 254–260; Sheldon, *Nebraska*, I, 740–742, 748–750; Paolo E. Coletta, *William Jennings Bryan: Political Evangelist, 1860–1908* (Lincoln: University of Nebraska Press, 1964), pp. 99–102. For sample comment in the German-language press, see *Omaha Tribüne*, October 25, 1894, and *Nebraska Volksblatt*, October 19, 1894.

[23] Carlson, "A History of the American Protective Association in Nebraska," p. 152; *The American*, November 2, 1894. Rosewater, "Life of Rosewater," pp. 184–187. Almost every issue of the *Bee* from September to November, 1894, contains violent attacks on Majors as an incompetent corruptionist. Although Rosewater was equally opposed to the APA, he never mentioned the connection between Majors and that organization, perhaps out of fear of reaping a whirlwind.

[24] *Lincoln Freie Presse*, September 6, October 18, 1894; *Nebraska Vorwaerts* (Omaha), September 27, 1894; Omaha *Daily Bee*, October 31, 1894.

as the woman suffrage movement was sometimes referred to in the German-language press. Worse, the Populist candidate for lieutenant governor, James W. Gaffin, had been active in the Prohibition party several years earlier.[25] Yet these men were now the standard-bearers of the Democratic party, which had always been the Germans' bulwark against Puritanism and nativism.

While the Democratic platform made no mention of its traditional opposition to prohibition (to do so would have jeopardized Bryan's courtship of the "Pops"), it contained a strong statement directed against the religious bigotry of the American Protective Association, which was becoming a major power factor within the Republican organization.[26] Above all, the Germans could not swallow free silver. Ultraconservative in money matters, Germans typically regarded the proposal as a swindle or as an impractical chimera. Max O. Gentzke, the fiery editor of the *Nebraska Volksblatt*, blasted Bryan's free silver arguments as puerile, naïve, and transparent. Bryan himself, who unquestionably had enjoyed much German support in 1890 and 1892, became the *bête noire* of conservatives like Gentzke.[27]

As a futile but honorable alternative to the Republican party and to "Popocratic" fusion, many Germans turned to the Gold Democrats, who had walked out of the Democratic convention when the Bryan forces had won the day. A full slate of candidates was nominated, headed by Phelps Sturdevant. Untouched by nativism or Puritanism, the Gold Democrats stood firmly for sound money. Not opposed to other reforms, these stalwarts offered everything the typical German was looking for except the possibility of victory. Some observers suspected that the party was a conservative conspiracy designed to drain off German votes that would otherwise have gone to the fusion candidates.[28]

According to the *Lincoln Freie Presse*, eight of the thirteen German-language newspapers in the state, all of which had been Democratic or independent in the past, had decided to support Majors and the Republicans.[29]

[25] *Grand Island Anzeiger und Herold*, October 19, 26, November 2, 1894; *Nebraska Staats Anzeiger*, October 18, 1894; Omaha *Daily Bee*, November 4, 1894; *Nebraska Volksblatt*, November 2, 1894; *Omaha Tribüne*, October 25, 1894.

[26] *Lincoln Freie Presse*, October 4, 1894; Nebraska City *Daily News*, September 22, 1894; Carlson, "A History of the American Protective Association in Nebraska," p. 150. Carlson states that the APA "had become the dominating and controlling influence in the Republican camp" in 1894.

[27] Omaha *Daily Bee*, October 31, 1894; *Nebraska Vorwaerts*, September 27, 1894; *Nebraska Volksblatt*, October 12, 19, 1894; *Omaha Tribüne*, October 25, 1895.

[28] Omaha *Daily Bee*, October 9, 1894.

[29] *Lincoln Freie Presse*, November 8, 1894. Among these were the *Omaha Tribüne*, *Grand Island Anzeiger und Herold*, *Nebraska Staats Anzeiger* of Lincoln, the *Volksfreund* of Hastings, and *Nebraska Volksblatt* of West Point. Omaha's *Nebraska Vorwaerts* and the *Lincoln Freie Presse* generally supported Fusion candidates.

The *Freie Presse* itself remained a staunch supporter of Holcomb and Bryan. It styled Majors as a "*Liebkind* of the Know-Nothings," thoroughly corrupt, and a threat to the honor of the state. Yet it supported Republican Robert E. Moore for the lieutenant governorship and any candidate for the legislature who promised to vote for Bryan as United States senator. On the other hand, the *Nebraska Staats Anzeiger*, also of Lincoln, asserted that it could never support a party which "is rotten on the coinage question, which attempts to destroy the credit of the state, and which seeks to help the cause of woman suffrage and the prohibition swindle." [30]

The data tabulated in Table 29 reflects confusion with respect to the expected political behavior of the German community. What the German read in one newspaper he found contradicted in another. Since the transmission of group standards lacked clarity he tended to vote much more like the total voting population than he had in the past. The distinctiveness of the German vote as Democratic was entirely lost in 1894.[31] Fusion strength was as strong in the least-German precincts as it was in the communities with large numbers of German residents. The data clearly indicate the attraction of the Gold Democratic slate for the Germans while the traditional animosity for the Republican party is shown to have been sustained, though greatly weakened compared to what it had been in 1890 and 1892.

TABLE 29

Mean Percentages of Votes Cast for Major Candidates for Governor in the Election of 1894, According to Percentages of Potential German Voters in 1885 (138 Precincts)

Per Cent of German Voters	Number of Precincts	Per Cent Republican	Per Cent Fusion	Per Cent Gold Democratic
75.0 and above	8	34.5	49.3	15.3
60.0–74.9	9	41.9	44.6	11.9
45.0–59.9	20	40.5	50.6	7.3
30.0–44.9	25	39.5	52.8	6.0
15.0–29.9	39	42.5	50.9	4.6
0.0–14.9	41	46.0	49.2	3.0
State:		46.4	48.2	3.4

The Republicans scored remarkable victories across the nation in 1894. This was true of Nebraska as well, where they captured every state office save the governorship, which went to Silas Holcomb. Equally successful in

[30] *Lincoln Freie Presse*, September 6, October 11, 1894; *Nebraska Staats Anzeiger*, October 18, 1894.

[31] These data are remarkably congruent to those presented in Chapter V, which demonstrated that coefficients of correlation between percentages of German voters and Democratic party percentages dropped sharply in 1894 from what they had been in 1892.

the state legislature, the Republican party won majorities in both houses. Nebraska's United States Senate seat was thus denied William Jennings Bryan, whose fusionist plans fell far short of the victory that he expected them to produce. But fusion in Nebraska in 1894 set the pattern for the nation in 1896, when Bryan headed the Democratic-Populist ticket as candidate for the presidency of the United States.

The Election of 1896: A Trend Confirmed

The election of 1896 completed the bloodless political revolution in Nebraska that had begun in 1890. The distinctiveness of the German vote, which attained its highest level in 1890 as a response to pressures that had been mounting for a decade, was greatly reduced in 1894. The realignment brought about in that election persisted for the next several years. In this sense, the election of 1896 was a confirmation of a trend brought about two years earlier.

Free silver had become the overriding issue and William Jennings Bryan had done everything in his power to make it so. The Germans were vitally interested in it, but no more so than the rest of the voting public. While it is probably true that a majority of German citizens opposed free silver as a fraud or as a foolish attempt to get something for nothing, it is also true that some of them were strong supporters of Bryan and the Democratic-Populist ticket in Nebraska.[32] In 1894 the German-language press had been decidedly in favor of sound money; in 1896 the press was more evenly divided, probably in a proportion that differed little from the English-language press. The Nebraska City News reported that of seventeen German newspapers in the state, Bryan could claim the support of ten. Among those with circulations exceeding one thousand copies were the Nebraska Vorwaerts of Omaha, the Lincoln Freie Press, the Grand Island Anzeiger und Herold, and the Platte River Zeitung of Fremont. Ranged behind McKinley and the gold standard were the Omaha Tribüne, the Nebraska Staats Zeitung of Nebraska City, the Nebraska Staats Anzeiger of Lincoln, the Nebraska Volksblatt of West Point, and the Nebraska Biene of Columbus.[33]

[32] The standard comment is that Germans were almost unanimously opposed to free silver. Carl Wittke, The German-Language Press in America (Lexington: University of Kentucky Press, 1957), pp. 160 f.; Nebraska Staats Anzeiger, October 22, 1896; Seward County Democrat, June 18, 1896.

[33] Nebraska City News, August 25, 1896; N. W. Ayer and Son's American Newspaper Annual (Philadelphia: Ayer and Son, 1895), p. 1310. Earlier the News had printed a release which stated that of 581 German-language papers in the country, 499 favored the gold standard, 39 were for free coinage or bimetallism, and 43 were doubtful. Nebraska City News, July 17, 1896.

Like other such lists, however, this one was probably inaccurate. Some papers supported Bryan in spite of, rather than because of, his monetary policies.[34] The *Lincoln Freie Presse*, a large and influential paper, was at first emphatically in support of Bryan. Midway in the campaign it underwent a change in ownership with the result that a neutral stance was adopted thereafter. Arguments on both sides were printed without editorial comment.[35] Max O. Gentzke of the *Volksblatt*, strongly influenced by *Coin's Financial School*, practically withdrew from the political stage. As election day neared, however, his traditional prejudices won out as he decided that, as a sound-money Democrat, he had no choice but to support McKinley.[36]

For the most part, the arguments in the German-language press differed little from those found in English-language papers. Yet both political parties were conscious of the German vote and appealed directly to it. Both imported prominent German speakers to plead their cases.[37] German pressure groups and campaign bureaus were established and pamphlets were prepared and distributed.[38]

The most widely used propaganda device in the election was the technique of endorsement. Column after column appeared in the Democratic papers describing how ex-Chancellor Otto von Bismarck, in a letter to Governor Culberson of Texas, had endorsed free silver as an appropriate solution to America's particular problem. Republicans responded with Carl Schurz's strong statements on behalf of the gold standard. The Democratic *Nebraska Vorwaerts* observed that while Bismarck was himself a *Landswirth* who thoroughly understood agriculture, Carl Schurz knew as much about farm problems as a cow knows about Sunday.[39]

Some attempts were made to picture Bryan as a foe of prohibition and of the American Protective Association. The *Grand Island Anzeiger und Herold* went so far as to claim that it was due to Bryan's forensic skill that

[34] *Ibid.*, July 17, 1896.

[35] *Lincoln Freie Presse*, June 18, July 23, November 5, 1896.

[36] *Nebraska Volksblatt*, September 25, October 30, 1896.

[37] Robert Schilling, a Democrat running for Congress in Wisconsin, spoke frequently in favor of Bryan. West Point *Progress*, September 11, 1896. Among Republican speakers was Joseph Brucker, an editor of the *Illinois Staats Zeitung* of Chicago. Grand Island *Daily Independent*, September 29, 1896; *The Advertiser-News* (Sutton), October 2, 1896; *Nebraska Volksblatt*, October 9, 1896.

[38] *Nebraska Vorwaerts*, July 23, 30, 1896; *Die Beatrice Post*, August 27, October 15, 1896; *Nebraska Volksblatt*, October 23, 1896; Grand Island *Daily Independent*, September 24, 1896.

[39] Humphrey *Democrat*, October 2, 1896; *Grand Island Anzeiger und Herold*, October 2, 1896; Blair *Courier*, September 24, 1896; *Nebraska Vorwaerts*, October 8, 1896.

prohibition had been beaten in 1890.[40] Perhaps the most ridiculous charge made in the German-language press during the 1896 campaign was the allegation in the *Volksblatt* that the APA was linked with the Democratic party.[41] Actually, the APA was unalterably opposed to Bryan, whom it called the "special pet and champion of the Romanists" and the father of the anti-APA resolution that had been adopted by the Democratic convention.[42]

When all the ballots had been counted in 1896, it was found that Nebraska's Bryan had put the state in the Democratic column for the first time in a presidential election. Holcomb was re-elected governor and the "Demopops" took all the state elective offices. They also captured an overwhelming majority of the seats in the state legislature, as well as four of Nebraska's six seats in Congress.[43] But these victories were not due to any distinctive voting behavior by the German element. As Table 30 demonstrates, there is no relationship, positive or negative, between the German voters and the votes cast for either party.

TABLE 30

Mean Percentages of Votes Cast for Republican, Fusion, and Gold Democratic Candidates for President in the Election of 1896, According to Percentages of Potential German Voters in 1885 (142 Precincts)

Per Cent of German Voters	Number of Precincts	Per Cent Republican	Per Cent Fusion	Per Cent Gold Democratic
75.0 and above	8	45.1	52.7	2.0
60.0–74.9	9	47.0	49.9	2.4
45.0–59.9	20	46.3	51.8	1.6
30.0–44.9	25	45.0	52.6	2.1
15.0–29.9	41	43.1	52.2	1.6
0.0–14.9	39	46.3	51.9	1.2
State:		46.0	51.8	1.2

The Urban-Rural Dimension

The election of 1896 has frequently interested historians as one of the most critical contests in American politics. The urban-rural dimension in particular

[40] *Grand Island Anzeiger und Herold*, October 16, 1896. Bryan had indeed campaigned against the amendment in 1890, despite his well-known personal sentiments regarding alcoholic beverages.

[41] This charge was based upon a statement allegedly made by Constantine J. Smyth, Democratic candidate for attorney general. Probably no one in the state had suffered more abuse from the APA than Smyth. See *Nebraska Volksblatt*, October 30, 1896.

[42] *The American*, September 25, 1896.

[43] Sheldon, *Nebraska*, I, 765 f.

has been studied intensively.[44] It is not, however, within the scope of this study to treat the problem except for the ways in which place of residence was related to the voting behavior of the German ethnic group in Nebraska. In general, the data indicate that in 1890 the party preference of rural Germans did not differ significantly from that of their kinsmen in Nebraska's towns and villages. Thereafter, however, place of residence increased in importance as a correlate of German electoral decisions and achieved its greatest significance in the election of 1894. The evidence further suggests that in the later elections of the Populist era the German behavior was not unlike that of the voting population in general.

These findings are based upon average percentages of votes cast for Populist, Democratic, and Republican candidates for the President and governor from 1888 to 1896 in approximately thirty precincts in which Germans constituted more than 50 per cent of the potential voting population, as indicated by the Nebraska state census of 1885. These precincts were grouped into two categories. The first group consisted of precincts in which there were no villages plus precincts in which such hamlets as there were totaled less than 250 inhabitants. The typical rural precinct in Nebraska *circa* 1890 contained approximately 500 inhabitants. Thus, if a given precinct had within its borders a village of less than 250 persons, the farmers were likely to predominate numerically. The second category included farm area precincts in which the nonfarm population predominated plus those precincts with strictly town populations. Although a category for urban voters only would be desirable, the number of such precincts in which German ethnic voters were in the majority was too small for meaningful grouping.

Table 31 documents the town and country factor as related to partisan preferences in predominantly German precincts. In 1890 the country precincts cast an average of 16.6 per cent of its votes for the Populist candidate while the town precincts cast 14.8 per cent. The difference of less than two percentage points indicates that place of residence had minimal influence on the electoral decision of Germans in that election. In 1892 the Populist candidate attracted 45.0 per cent of the vote in the rural precincts and 38.1 per cent in the towns, a difference of nearly 7 per cent. By 1894, when the Democrats and Populists joined forces to nominate the same gubernatorial candidate, the spread increased to 11.5 percentage points, as the rural units cast 53.0 per cent for the fusion candidate and the towns 41.5 per cent.

[44] William Diamond, "Urban and Rural Voting in 1896," *American Historical Review*, XCVI (January, 1941), 281–305; Degler, "American Political Parties," pp. 47–49; Stanley B. Parsons, Jr., "Who Were the Nebraska Populists?" *Nebraska History*, XLIV (June, 1963), 83–99; David F. Trask, "A Note on the Politics of Populism," *Nebraska History*, XLVI (June, 1965), 157–161.

Thereafter the town and country factor declined in importance among the Nebraska Germans, although it never disappeared completely. No matter how small the margin of difference was, however, Populist and fusion voting among Germans tended throughout the period to be more common in the countryside than in the towns.

TABLE 31

Average Percentages of Votes Cast for Populist, Democratic, and Republican Candidates for President and Governor in Predominantly German Precincts in Nebraska, 1888–1896

	1888	1890	1892	1894	1896
		For Populist Candidates			
Country precincts	—	16.6	45.0	53.0[a]	51.4[a]
Town precincts	—	14.8	38.1	41.5[a]	48.5[a]
Differences	—	1.8	6.9	11.5	2.9
		For Democratic Candidates			
Country precincts	59.9	65.4	25.5	53.0[a]	51.4[a]
Town precincts	58.0	62.2	25.3	41.5[a]	48.5[a]
Differences	1.9	3.2	.2	11.5	2.9
		For Republican Candidates			
Country precincts	38.6	15.8	28.5	34.8	43.8
Town precincts	40.1	20.4	35.9	46.5	49.0
Differences	1.5	4.6	7.4	11.7	5.2

[a] Populists and Democrats nominated the same candidates.

The data presented in Table 31 also demonstrate that place of residence was not an important factor when associated with Democratic party voting in predominantly German precincts. Only in the election of 1894, following William Jennings Bryan's use of free silver proposals to achieve fusion with Populism, did the town-country dimension achieve significance, as the rural Germans displayed a notably stronger tendency to support the "Demopop" candidate. In the case of Republican party voting, the margin of difference between town and country precincts steadily increased with each election from 1888, when it registered a mere 1.5 per cent, to 1894, when it reached 11.7 per cent. In each election, preference for Republican candidates was stronger among German residents of the towns and villages than it was in the countryside.

To assert that place of residence of German voters increased in importance after 1890 is to imply that there was a concurrent decrease in importance of ethnocultural considerations. If valid, this interpretation should be supported by data which demonstrate (1) that in 1890 the partisan preference of German voters diverged noticeably from that of Nebraska voters generally and (2) that by 1894 the margin of difference between Germans and the mass of voters was reduced to a minimal level. This phenomenon may be illustrated by data from rural precincts in association with Populist party voting. In 1890 the rural German precincts voted 16.6 per cent Populist while one hundred rural precincts in fifteen counties recorded 47.6 per cent—a difference of 31.0 per cent between the groups.[45] In 1892 rural German precincts voted 45.0 per cent Populist, while the country precincts in general scored 47.3 per cent, a difference of only 2.3 per cent. A dramatic shift in German perceptions of the Populist party had indeed taken place. In 1894 the trend was sustained as the German farm precincts cast 53.0 per cent of their votes for the Democratic-Populist candidate compared to 56.9 per cent for the countryside in general, a difference of 3.9 per cent. In 1896 the rural German vote was 51.4 per cent compared to 55.9 per cent for the larger group of farm precincts, a difference of 4.5 per cent. Besides documenting the sharp reduction in the differences between the two groups, these data also demonstrate that throughout the period German voters were less inclined to support agrarian radicalism than the Nebraska farm population in general.

[45] These precincts were all the precincts in fifteen counties in which there were no villages of more than 250 inhabitants.

CHAPTER IX

The End of the Century :
A Return of Ethnic Politics

As THE NINETEENTH CENTURY drew to a close, there was a resurgence of ethnocultural politics in Nebraska. The distinctiveness of German political behavior had been minimal during much of the Populist era in contrast to the previous decade. Some differences were apparent, but on the whole the electoral decisions of German-American citizens in Nebraska had been conditioned largely by concerns of occupation and income, social relationships, and residence (rural or urban), as well as by habit and tradition. This pattern subsequently was modified by reactions to the foreign policies of the McKinley regime. Strident charges of imperialism, expansionism, militarism, and violations of the spirit of the Declaration of Independence evoked a variety of ethnopolitical appeals and responses. Imperialism became for many Germans what prohibition, woman suffrage, and compulsory school legislation had been a decade earlier. Yet this issue never achieved the salience that nativist reform had had for the German community.

The Nebraska election of 1898 was transitional. Some politicians continued to argue the old issues of the Populist era, while the new issues related to imperialism were introduced in the wake of the Spanish-American War. But the old rhetoric could no longer excite and the issues of the new debate were not yet sharply defined. The result was that the election of 1898 was generally a dull affair, especially for the Germans. No great issues were at stake. The German-language press generally agreed that the election was as uninteresting as it was unimportant. The *Nebraska Volksblatt* of West Point stated as late as mid-October that it had no intention of boring its readers with long political articles. The *Nebraska Staats Anzeiger* of Lincoln made no reference to the contest on its editorial page until two weeks before election day. The *Lincoln Freie Presse* addressed itself to the issues but never mentioned parties or candidates by name throughout the entire campaign.[1]

[1] *Nebraska Volksblatt*, October 21, 1898; *Nebraska Staats Anzeiger*, October 20, 1898; *Lincoln Freie Presse*, November 2, 1898.

This low-key quality was reflected in the smallest voter turnout since the election of 1886.

Many Germans continued to feel that they had no party which suited them. The nativism that they had always associated with the Republicans had been partially transferred in 1894 to the Populists, who dominated the Fusion ticket. In German eyes fusion was a fiction; the choice actually lay between the Republican and Populist parties. According to the *Nebraska Biene* of Columbus, the once strong and energetic Democracy was slowly but surely being swallowed by the boa constrictor of Populism. The only way the Democratic party could prevent its total destruction, the *Biene* advised, was to repudiate the "undemocratic and illogical doctrine of free silver."[2]

In general, free silver could no longer evoke much enthusiasm, pro or con. The *Volksblatt* and the *Grand Island Anzeiger* insisted that as a valid issue it was dead, having been killed by Bryan's defeat in 1896 and by economic prosperity. The *Freie Presse* pointed out that nothing could be done about it so long as the McKinley administration was in office; hence, it asserted, free silver was no longer a real issue in 1898.[3]

Expansionism and imperialism were the issues that most excited the *Lincoln Freie Presse*. While this paper agreed that colonies would open new frontiers for American capital, it pointed out that colonies also would open the floodgates of cheap labor into the homeland. Far worse, it argued, was the impact of imperialism on the free institutions of a democracy. Colonies meant a strong army and navy, a corresponding increase in the influence of the military, and the transformation of the nation's manhood into cannon fodder. Like imperialism itself, anti-imperialism drew strength from widespread racist attitudes. Imperialism implied the acquisition of lands peopled by Negroes, the *Freie Presse* asserted, and of these people America already had too many.[4]

Given the lack of vital issues, the political debate tended to degenerate into charges of prohibitionism and nativism. The *Nebraska Biene* repeatedly labeled William Poynter, the Fusion gubernatorial candidate, as a fanatic, a prohibitionist, and a friend of the American Protective Association.[5] When the state central committee of the Prohibition party endorsed Poynter's candidacy, the *Biene* gleefully announced that the Fusion nominee was one

[2] *Nebraska Biene* (Columbus), September 23, 1898. See also *Nebraska Volksblatt*, October 21, 1898, and *Cuming County Advertiser*, October 25, 1898.

[3] *Nebraska Volksblatt*, October 14, 1898; *Grand Island Anzeiger und Herold*, October 21, 1898; *Lincoln Freie Presse*, November 2, 1898.

[4] *Lincoln Freie Presse*, September 7, November 2, 1898.

[5] *Nebraska Biene*, August 12, 26, September 2, October 28, 1898.

for whom even the *kälteste Wassermann* could vote. The *Volksblatt's* last-minute decision to support the Republican ticket was based on its fear that Poynter's election would jeopardize "personal liberty."[6]

Other newspapers sprang to the defense of the Populists. The *Grand Island Anzeiger und Herold*, after dismissing the charges of prohibitionism as simple lies that had originated in the pages of *The Nebraska Liquor Dealer*, said that Poynter was "conscientious and liberal-thinking, and a friend of personal liberty." The *Nebraska Staats Anzeiger* stated that Germans had tended to look with contempt upon the Populist party without placing any value on the excellent administration it had given the state.[7]

The election of 1898 put William Poynter in the governor's chair with 50.2 per cent of the votes cast. Fusion candidates were elected to other state offices with slightly larger majorities. The state legislature, however, went Republican, and with it went Populist William V. Allen's United States Senate seat.[8] The political preferences of the Germans were no more distinctive than in 1896.

As the decade drew to a close, there was an increase in cultural nationalism among the Germans.[9] Their self-awareness as a minority ethnic group had been heightened through the years by moralistic legislation and by rampant nativism. As far as the Germans were concerned, the configuration of issues had been confused and distorted by the Populist movement and by the subsequent fusion of parties against the Republicans. Inevitably these two factors served to weaken party loyalties. The Germans were repeatedly urged to vote independently for the party which promised most to advance the interests of *das Deutschtum*. As the largest non-English speaking ethnic group in the state, they believed that their numbers were sufficiently large to force the several parties to do their bidding.

The trouble with this approach was that the Germans rarely were united. While they often were motivated in their voting behavior by ethnic considerations, they did not effectively vote as a bloc. A diverse people, they could not often agree on the issues, the parties, or the candidates. Most German leaders urged political involvement but on a nonpartisan basis. At the same time, they could not understand why they were rarely accorded a political importance commensurate with their numbers. The *Nebraska Biene*, for example, complained bitterly that even though there were 75,000

6 *Nebraska Biene*, October 7, 1898; *Nebraska Volksblatt*, November 4, 1898.

7 *Grand Island Anzeiger und Herold*, October 28, 1898; *Nebraska Staats Anzeiger*, October 27, 1898.

8 Addison E. Sheldon, *Nebraska: The Land and The People* (3 vols.; Chicago: Lewis Publishing Co., 1931), I, 770, 774.

9 For an enlightening discussion of this phenomenon, see G. A. Dobbert, "German-Americans Between New and Old Fatherland, 1870–1914" *American Quarterly*, XIX (Winter, 1967), 663–680.

German voters in Nebraska, there was not a single German on the Republican state ticket, whereas the Scandinavians, who numbered no more than 12,000, were regularly represented.[10] The *Biene* vented its frustration by a strong endorsement of Cenek Duras, a Bohemian who was the Republican nominee for secretary of state. Duras was "one of their own," according to the *Biene*, because he had been educated in Germany and had been associated with Carl Schurz in the newspaper business in St. Louis.[11]

Ethnic bloc-voting in 1900 played a larger role in the election than in any since the prohibition amendment had been defeated in 1890. On the level of national politics impassioned appeals were made by Democrats to German voters against the Republican policies of expansion and imperialism; in state politics the Republicans sought to balance this liability by the nomination of a German, Charles H. Dietrich, for governor. This was the first time that the Nebraska electorate was given an opportunity to vote for a gubernatorial candidate who was not of British-American antecedents.

A very great amount of propaganda was prepared and distributed to German readers. Both parties maintained German press bureaus and each denounced the other's materials as idiotic mispresentations and as insults to German intelligence.[12] During the campaign, many English-language newspapers of Democratic persuasions printed column after column of German articles against imperialism.[13] The endorsement technique was again fully exploited. Carl Schurz's repudiation of Republican imperialism was cited dozens of times in both the English- and German-language press.[14] Prominent German-American personages were imported to speak against the new threat. One of the most effective was John W. Habercorn, a former head of the German bureau of the Republican congressional campaign committee. "A government with imperial powers over our possessions cannot long remain a republic at home," Habercorn announced. "As the government could not have lived half slave and half free, so it cannot live half imperial and half republic."[15]

---

10 *Nebraska Biene*, August 12, 1898. This is a repeated theme in the 1890's in county politics. Democratic editors often exploited this sentiment to their advantage—e.g., see Seward *Independent-Democrat*, October 28, 1897.

11 *Nebraska Biene*, October 28, 1898.

12 *Grand Island Anzeiger und Herold*, October 5, 1900; *Lincoln Freie Presse*, October 17, 1900.

13 E.g., see the September and October issues of Blair *Courier*, Seward *Independent-Democrat*, and *Adams County Democrat.* When they ran out of material they reprinted articles that had been published earlier.

14 E.g., *Nebraska Biene*, August 10, 24, 1900; *Grand Island Anzeiger und Herold*, August 10, 1900; *Morning World Herald*, October 27, 1900.

15 Seward *Independent-Democrat*, July 26, August 9, 1900; *Grand Island Anzeiger und Herold*, August 31, 1900.

Most of the German-language newspapers were united in their attack upon imperialism. Any number of reasons were offered to convince Germans of the evils of Republican foreign policy. The most substantial basis for German opposition was stated simply by the *Nebraska City News*: The Germans believed that militarism was an inevitable concomitant of imperialism; they had been forced into military service in the *Vaterland* and they had been taxed heavily for the support of the military establishment; they did not wish to have those circumstances repeated in America.[16] Some Democrats deliberately played with German fears of conscription. The Omaha *Bee* charged that certain persons posing as Republicans toured the German districts of the state with the announced purpose of getting the names of all males between sixteen and thirty years of age. Allegedly in the employ of the Democratic state central committee, they hoped to frighten Germans into voting for Bryan.[17]

The *Grand Island Anzeiger und Herold* charged that imperialism not only impinged upon principles of enlightenment, independence, and public freedom of individuals, but also on the freedom of religion. As this newspaper capitalized on a denunciation of pacifism by the ebullient Theodore Roosevelt, it pointed out that about 4,000,000 Americans had as a chief tenet of their religious belief the refusal to bear arms. The Mennonites in particular were cited as having emigrated from Prussia and Russia to America out of respect for this doctrine.[18] *Die Beatrice Post*, which had been staunchly Republican in 1896, carried its anti-imperialism to the extreme of stating that the leaders of the Republican party intended to convert America from a republic to an empire with a monarchical form of government.[19]

Some Germans were also excited about the Boer War in South Africa and bitterly resented the Republican failure to support a resolution in Congress that expressed sympathy for the Boers. They linked this action with a pro-British foreign policy based on a hatred of Germany and on what they called the *anglosächsischen Verbrüderungshumbug* (nonsense about the brotherhood of Anglo-Saxon peoples).[20] Running through much of this propaganda was a subtheme that linked imperialism with chauvinistic nativism.[21]

16 Nebraska City *News*, August 29, 1900. See also Seward *Independent-Democrat*, November 2, 1899, for a similar statement.

17 Omaha *Daily Bee*, October 30, 1900. See also the Fairbury *Gazette*, October 6, 1900.

18 *Grand Island Anzeiger und Herold*, September 28, 1900.

19 Quoted in translation in the *Morning World Herald*, October 24, 1900.

20 *Grand Island Anzeiger und Herold*, August 3, 1900; *Morning World Herald*, October 9, 1900. See also the *Nebraska Biene* for frequent articles on the Boer War.

21 See Julius Goebel, "Warum protestieren wir Deutsch-Amerikaner gegen den Imperialismus?" in *Der Kampf um deutsche Kultur in America* (Leipzig: Verlag der Dürr'schen Buchhandlung, 1914), p. 45. In this speech delivered at Stanford University, Goebel,

The Republican party continued to be vulnerable to German charges of xenophobia. There were strenuous objections when President McKinley replaced a German as Immigration Commissioner with "the well-known nativist and German-hater, Terence Powderly." Theodore Roosevelt was often the object of ridicule. The *Anzeiger und Herold* asserted that Roosevelt's whole *Rohreiter Comödie* was in bad taste and his *theaterhaften Reiter-Schlapphut* was a disgusting anachronism. Some Germans resented the fact that Roosevelt, who had a reputation as a nativistic jingo among them, also campaigned crassly for immigrant votes.[22]

The unity of the German leadership in Nebraska in 1900 is also evident in that most of the German-language newspapers were either independent or Democratic. Only the *Omaha Tribüne* held firm to its traditional Republicanism. It dismissed German concerns about imperialism and militarism as baseless Bryanite propaganda devoid of any real prospect of scaring people into voting for the Democratic ticket. Germans, the *Tribüne* said, were attracted by the conservative policies of the McKinley administration and by the economic prosperity these policies were bringing to the country.[23] Edward Rosewater's Omaha *Bee* ridiculed the charges of militarism. It pointed out that the ratio of soldiers in the American army to the total population was less than 1 to 100,000. To hear German alarmists talk, the *Bee* observed, one would think that the United States army consisted only of German immigrants.[24]

In order to assess German sentiment, the independent *Lincoln Freie Presse*, which had a circulation of 100,000 throughout the Midwest,[25] conducted a poll that received a great amount of publicity. Returns from its readers were received in quantity from Nebraska, Iowa, Kansas, Illinois, and Wisconsin, as well as other states. The poll gave 3,106 votes to McKinley, 5,861 to Bryan, and a scattering to minor party candidates. Nebraska's total was 433 for McKinley and 769 for Bryan. The Omaha *Bee* dismissed the poll as meaningless and charged that many ballots had been forged at the Populist headquarters in Lincoln.[26] The significance of the survey lies less

---

an intellectual leader of the German-American community, objected to the religious content of imperialism with particular reference to the concept that the Anglo-Saxons, as God's chosen people, were to rule the world.

[22] *Grand Island Anzeiger und Herold*, August 3, 1900; *Nebraska Biene*, September 28, 1900; *Lincoln Freie Presse*, August 29, 1900.

[23] Reprinted in translation in the Grand Island *Independent*, September 11, 1900.

[24] Omaha *Daily Bee*, November 3, 4, 1900.

[25] [Rowell's] *American Newspaper Directory* [1901] (New York: Geo. P. Rowell and Co., 1901), p. 1330.

[26] *Lincoln Freie Presse*, October 31, 1900; Omaha *Daily Bee*, October 31, November 3, 1900.

with the alleged majority won by Bryan than with the conviction of the newspaper that a poll of its readers would be an effective tactic in the campaign.

McKinley beat Bryan in Nebraska, Bryan's home state, in 1900. He received 50.5 per cent of the votes cast while Bryan got 47.2 per cent. The voter turnout was the largest in the state's history. Table 32 indicates that

TABLE 32

Mean Percentages of Votes Cast for Major Candidates for President in the Election of 1900, According to Percentages of Potential German Voters in 1885 (142 Precincts)

Per Cent of German Voters	Number of Precincts	Per Cent Republican	Per Cent Fusion
75.0 and above	8	45.5	54.0
60.0–74.9	9	47.8	51.2
45.0–59.9	20	46.9	52.5
30.0–44.9	25	48.3	50.2
15.0–29.9	41	49.6	49.2
0.0–14.9	39	51.4	47.1
State:		50.5	47.2

the great propaganda effort of the Democrats was moderately successful among the German voters. For the first time since 1892 there was a positive relationship between precincts ranked according to strength of potential German voting population and the percentages of votes cast for the Democratic candidate; at the same time, a negative relationship may be observed with respect to the votes cast for McKinley. The range is low—only six to seven percentage points—but its consistency suggests that German ethnic origins were indeed a factor of some importance in influencing voter decisions in these precincts.

The Republicans of Nebraska had anticipated this loss of German votes. Some party leaders hoped to counteract this desertion by nominating German-Americans for high office. They assumed that the Germans would ignore the issues in order to vote for a *Landsmann*. Ultimately, both parties employed this strategy. The Democrats and Populists nominated George Berge, a young Lincoln lawyer, for a seat in Congress and Theodore Griess, a Russian-German of Clay County, for state auditor. The Republicans chose William Stuefer of West Point for state treasurer and Charles H. Dietrich of Hastings for governor. Never before had so many Germans been nominated for so many high offices.

Dietrich's nomination was not, however, a last-minute effort to fend off disaster. It was the consequence of an arduous campaign managed by

Dietrich's close friend, Adam Brede, the editor and publisher of the Hastings *Tribune*.[27] While Brede himself did not emphasize Dietrich's ethnic origins, others who supported Dietrich did. Frank McCartney, an influential Republican of Otoe County, advised Dietrich to

go into our German precincts for there, in my mind, lies our greatest danger in the coming campaign. Bryan and his followers have tried in every way to make our German farmers believe that if McKinley is elected it means a large standing army and that their boys will be compelled to serve as in the old Countries and that in many ways the rights of the people are to be disturbed.[28]

McCartney's counsel apparently gained favor among the Republican managers. Following his nomination, Dietrich's campaign was conducted on the basis of extensive personal contacts, a minimum discussion of issues, and an overt appeal to the voters of the German element.[29]

A glowing campaign biography of article length was prepared and distributed across the state. Dietrich was characterized as the son of a Forty-Eighter who had fled political oppression in Germany. At the same time, Dietrich's panegyrist emphasized that after his birth (in humble circumstances in Illinois) the Republican gubernatorial candidate was baptized and raised in the German Lutheran faith. Through industry and thrift, Dietrich's biographer averred, he worked his way up the ladder of success. As a courageous and law-abiding frontiersman he had participated in the gold rush to the Black Hills of South Dakota. His persistent exercise of virtue allegedly led to his development as a competent and generous businessman, founder and president of the German-American National Bank of Hastings. Thus Dietrich's candidacy was expected to attract the business community as well as the German element; the prohibitionists, on the other hand, were not expected to defect from the Grand Old Party of virtue and morality.[30]

Dietrich's candidacy caused more than one Teutonic pulse to quicken. The Norfolk *News* commented that Dietrich's personal appearance bore a marked resemblance to that of Emperor William II of Germany.[31] The *Nebraska Courier*, a Grand Island German-language newspaper, published twenty stanzas of doggerel entitled "Karl Heinrich Dietrich für Gouverneur!" A few sample stanzas follow:

[27] Hastings *Tribune*, March 16, April 27, May 4, 25, 1900.

[28] Frank McCartney to C. H. Dietrich, Nebraska City, May 19, 1900, Charles H. Dietrich MSS, Nebraska State Historical Society.

[29] *Nebraska Biene*, September 21, 1900; Norfolk *Times Tribune*, November 2, 1900, *Blue Valley Blade*, July 4, 1900.

[30] Omaha *Daily Bee*, May 3, 1900; Grand Island *Daily Independent*, September 12, 1900; *Blue Valley Blade*, May 16, 1900; *Nebraska Tribüne* (Omaha), September 20, 1900.

[31] Norfolk *News*, undated clipping, Dietrich Scrapbook.

Deutsche giebt's in grosser Zahl
In der Stadt und auf dem Land;
Und bei der nächsten Wahl
Reichen Sie Dietrich die Hand.

Als Gouverneur-Kandidat
Passt er Allen herzlich gut;
Denn er gilt im ganzen Staat
Als ein Mann von Recht und Muth.

Mit jedem Mann spricht er gern
Im Geschäft und auf der Strass,
Blässt sich nicht als grossern Herrn
Und trägt nicht hoch die Nas.

Parteilichkeit legt bei Seit!
Zweitracht lasst aus dem Spiel!
Deutsche wollen keinen Streit;
Das führt sie nicht zum Ziel.[32]

Dietrich's special appeal to the German element had been widely advertised throughout the campaign in the English-language press. The Nebraska City *News* warned that "when a man goes campaigning for German votes on a beer and sauerkraut platform he'll find that many a German who drinks beer and eats sauerkraut will vote for someone else who asks for support on more tangible grounds."[33]

Two basic tactics were used by Dietrich's enemies to ruin his chances of election. One was to reveal the counterfeit quality of his German-ness; the other was to mobilize the forces of righteousness against him. The amount of lying, misrepresentation, slander, defamation of character, and fraud that ensued has rarely been rivaled in Nebraska history. Dietrich was accused of having struck a bargain with the liquor dealers whereby he allegedly promised to work for the repeal of the Slocumb high-cost liquor license law in return

[32] *Nebraska Courier,* undated clipping, Dietrich Scrapbook. A rough translation: There are great numbers of Germans / in the city and the countryside; / and in the next election / they will lend Dietrich a hand. / As gubernatorial candidate / he suits everyone very well; / he is esteemed throughout the state / as a man of honesty and courage. / He gladly speaks with each man / in business places and on the street, / he does not pretend to be a great man / nor does he hold his nose high in the air. / Lay partisanship aside! / Dissension must be left out of the game! / Germans want no strife; / that does not lead them to the goal.

[33] Nebraska City *News,* July 31, 1900. For similar comments see the Fremont *Leader,* quoted in the Seward *Independent-Democrat,* August 30, 1900, and undated clippings from the Blair *Republican* and the Crawford *Bulletin* in the Dietrich Scrapbook.

for their support.[34] Several members of the Protestant ministerial association of Hastings printed and distributed a widely reprinted statement to the effect that they, as Republicans, could not support Dietrich, the saloon candidate, because he was a man of "pronounced immoral propensities" who had "no regard for law and order."[35] The phraseology of this letter was similar to a circular published over the names of the officers of the Anti-Saloon League. In it Dietrich was called the pet of the rum sellers and was characterized as intemperate and dissolute in his personal habits.[36] A prohibitionist publication stated that "if everyone votes for [Dietrich] who drank beer at his expense, his election is assured." As for itself, this paper stated that it would prefer to "vote for the devil himself."[37] Mrs. Helen M. Gougar, a Populist of well-known prohibitionist propensities, allegedly branded Dietrich as a drunkard and as "the author of the ruin of twenty-two girls now supported in state institutions."[38] By the end of October, the rumor had spread that Dietrich was the proprietor of a house of prostitution.[39]

The Republicans made a considerable effort to counteract the slander. Published statements by Catholic, Lutheran, and German Evangelical pastors, together with the signatures of dozens of Dietrich's neighbors and business acquaintances, defended his character. The Hastings city council (which included some Democrats) passed a resolution that attested to Dietrich's respectability and denounced the slanders as "cruel and inhuman political warfare."[40] Meanwhile the Omaha *Bee* sought to expose the fraudulent and libelous character of the letters circulated by the Anti-Saloon League.

[34] *Morning World Herald*, October 27, 1900; Omaha *Daily Bee*, undated clipping, Dietrich Scrapbook.

[35] Open letter signed by the Reverend H. G. Wilkinson, Pastor, Church of Christ, Hastings, Nebr., October 25, 1900. A printed copy is in the Dietrich MSS in the Nebraska State Historical Society. Other ministers who signed the document were of the Methodist, Presbyterian, Congregational, Episcopal, United Brethren, Evangelical, and Baptist denominations, all known for their temperance proclivities. Another letter printed in the *World Herald* included as a signatory the Reverend Kirchstein of the Christian Church. The *Bee* disclosed that Kirchstein was not even a resident of Hastings. *Sunday World Herald*, October 28, 1900; Omaha *Daily Bee*, October 31, 1900.

[36] A copy is in the Dietrich MSS, Nebraska State Historical Society. The *Bee* subsequently exposed the fraudulent character of this effort as well. Omaha *Daily Bee*, November 3, 1900.

[37] Reprinted in English and German, *Nebraska Tribüne*, September 20, 1900.

[38] Unidentified clipping, Dietrich Scrapbook.

[39] Hubbell *Standard*, undated clipping, Dietrich Scrapbook; Grand Island *Daily Independent*, October 30, 1900.

[40] Omaha *Daily Bee*, October 21, 31, 1900; Hastings *Tribune*, November 2, 1900; Columbus *Journal*, November 7, 1900.

It was impossible, however, to refute the charges that Dietrich's German-ness was not authentic. Unfortunately, these rumors were true. Dietrich's reluctance to speak the German language was given publicity, as was his refusal to support German cultural organizations. Although his campaign biography stated that he had worked hard to defeat the prohibition amend-ment in 1890, the *World Herald* challenged this by producing an affidavit sworn to by Philip Andres, the Nebraska state organizer of the Personal Liberty League in 1890, asserting that Dietrich refused to participate in the League's activities for business reasons. Although Dietrich had promised Andres a monetary contribution for the organization, not a cent was forth-coming. Morever, Dietrich's coarse exploitation of his German ethnic origins alienated his well-assimilated brethren. A German-born professional person of Lincoln complained that on a visit to his office, Dietrich had barely crossed the threshold before he began effusively to describe his fondness for beer and sauerkraut.[41]

These charges were, of course, politically inspired and for that reason may be discounted. Evidence suggests, however, that Dietrich was in fact well assimilated into American society. Prior to the campaign of 1900 it is unlikely that he thought of himself as a German-American, even though he was president of a German-American bank. His interpersonal contacts seem to have been primarily with non-Germans. English was his native tongue; he spoke and wrote it well. He had long since given up his association with the immigrant church into which he had been baptized. He sent his daughter to Bryn Mawr to be educated. He married a non-German. He was a wealthy businessman and a Republican, a part of the protestant establishment of Hastings. Moreover, it is not likely that the managers of the Republican party would have permitted the gubernatorial nomination to go to someone who was not of their own kind. Yet, as the candidate in 1900, he was expected to exploit his ethnic origins to get votes that might otherwise go to Bryan. Here, indeed, was a conflict. The poor man was forced by circumstances to display close relationships with his ancestral ethnic group, a people with whom he had in fact few casual relationships outside the business world. As a German he was a fraud; his appeal was crude, inept, and unnatural; and many Germans resented the masquerade.

Dietrich did not enjoy the support of the German-language newspapers in Nebraska. Since most were either Democratic or independent in their politics, they tended to ignore Dietrich as a candidate, not wanting to give his candidacy the advantage even of negative publicity. The *Nebraska Biene* was the most outspoken against him. The *Nebraska Staats Anzeiger* re-

[41] *Morning World Herald*, October 27, 1900; Nebraska City *News*, July 31, 1900; Seward *Independent-Democrat*, July 26, 1900.

mained silent until its last issue before the election. At that time it expressed its disgust with Dietrich for having turned his back on *das Deutschtum* until he needed German votes. Moreover, this paper stated that it could not in good conscience support a man who once had charged 30 per cent interest per month on a loan to one of his fellow citizens.[42]

Republican strategy, it will be recalled, was to use Dietrich's candidacy to compensate for German antipathies toward imperialism. Instead of Dietrich pulling McKinley through to victory in Nebraska, the opposite took place. In terms of raw votes, McKinley outpolled Dietrich in every county of the state. A total of 232,307 ballots were cast for governor; Dietrich won by a margin of only 861 votes.

The Nebraska election of 1900 was the only contest in the history of the state in which one of the major party candidates for President or governor was of German stock and made a direct appeal to the German element. As such, this contest affords an opportunity to measure statistically the relative drawing power of a German candidate as compared to a non-German candidate of the same party. It is possible to determine not only if the votes Dietrich received were proportional to the German-born population in each county but also whether he received more German votes than McKinley, his running mate. To illustrate, Dakota County gave Dietrich, the German Republican candidate, 47.6 per cent of its vote for governor, while McKinley, the non-German Republican candidate, received 46.3 per cent of its votes for president. Thus, McKinley ran 1.3 percentage points behind Dietrich in Dakota County. After determining the positive or negative percentage point differences for every county in the state, all the counties may be grouped according to the percentage of total population who were German-born; the mean percentage point differences between the two candidates' votes may then be calculated. If the Republican strategy was correct, Dietrich should have demonstrated a superior drawing power in the more-German counties as compared to the less-German counties.

Table 33 groups the data as described above. The statistics do not support Republican expectations. Dietrich recorded a negative percentage point difference in every category. Moreover, his lack of attraction was as low in the most-German counties as it was in the least-German. He fared best (or least poorly) in the middle range, where the percentage of German-born approximated the state average. It is possible that Dietrich served as a negative reference point at both ends of the continuum—in the most-German counties as a counterfeit German not worthy of support and in the least-German counties as an undesirable representative of foreign stock. What-

[42] *Nebraska Biene*, September 21, November 2, 1900; *Nebraska Staats Anzeiger*, November 1, 1900.

TABLE 33

Mean Percentage Point Differences between the Votes Cast for Dietrich,
Republican Candidate for Governor, and for McKinley, Republican
Candidate for President, According to the Percentage of German-Born
in the Election of 1900, by Counties

Per Cent German-Born[a]	Number of Counties	Mean Percentage Point Difference, Dietrich over McKinley
10.0 and over	10	−2.1
8.0–9.9	6	−1.6
6.0–7.9	10	−1.1
4.0–5.9	34	−1.4
2.0–3.9	22	−2.1
0.0–1.9	7	−2.2
State:	89	−1.5

[a] Percentage of German-born in the entire state in 1900 was 6.3.
SOURCES: *Nebraska Blue Book for 1901 and 1902*, pp. 176, 177, 260, 261;
U.S. Census Office, *Twelfth Census, 1900. Population*, I, 768 f.

ever the reason, the data demonstrate that the Republican managers seriously erred when they planned Dietrich's campaign. The Hastings banker won the election in spite of, not because of, his German-ness and his bid for the support of the German element.

Despite the failure of Dietrich as a German candidate, the election of 1900 was a high point in the practice of ethnic politics in Nebraska. This contest was essentially different from the climactic election of 1890 in that the clear-cut identification of the Republican party with nativism and moralistic legislation growing out the clash of cultures had been thoroughly obscured. Nor was it possible any longer to associate the Democratic party with "personal liberty." The unity which had characterized the voting behavior of the Germans in 1890 could not be regained.

CHAPTER X

A Summary View

THE DISTINCTIVE ROLE of the German element in Nebraska politics did not end with the election of 1900. Even though emigration from Germany had virtually ceased by that time, the Germans continued to have an importance which politicians could not afford to ignore. During World War I the German community suffered from a wave of chauvinistic intolerance.[1] This blind "Americanism" was not without a political effect, nor did it end with the return of peace. A conflict over the use of the German language in Lutheran schools continued into the 1920's when it was climaxed with the United States Supreme Court's ruling against the state in *Meyer* v. *Nebraska* in 1923.[2] During this period the cultural nationalists, who so earnestly desired to protect their ethnic way of life in America, continued to be politically active through such organizations as the *Deutsche Staatsverband* and the *Deutschamerikanischen Bürgerbundes von Nebraska*.[3]

Although most German ethnic organizations and German-language newspapers in Nebraska had atrophied by the end of the Great Depression in the 1930's, voting patterns based upon ethnic origins seem to have continued to the present time.[4] Many of the solidly German precincts which voted overwhelmingly Democratic in 1890 are strongly Republican today. Contemporary political analysts, notably Samuel Lubell, have attributed this

[1] Robert N. Manley, "Language, Loyalty, and Liberty; The Nebraska State Council of Defense and the Lutheran Churches, 1917–1918," *Concordia Historical Institute Quarterly*, XXXVII (April, 1964), 1–16; Frederick C. Luebke (ed.), "Superpatriotism in World War I: The Experience of a Lutheran Pastor," ibid., XLI (February, 1968), 3–11.

[2] Jack W. Rodgers, "The Foreign Language Issue in Nebraska, 1918–1923," *Nebraska History*, XXXIX (March, 1958), 1–22.

[3] Staatsverband Nebraska, *Gründung und Entwicklung des Staatsverbandes Nebraska. Jahres-Bericht der Beamten.* (December, 1915); Deutschamerikanischen Bürgerbundes von Nebraska, *Von unserer Arbeit und von unseren Zielen* (Omaha: December, 1929); Frederick C. Luebke, "The German-American Alliance in Nebraska, 1910–1917," *Nebraska History*, IL (Summer, 1968), 165–185.

[4] See Robert W. Cherny, "The 1940 Election in Nebraska with Special Attention to Isolationist Voting among Nonurban German Stock Voters of the State" (unpublished Master's thesis, Columbia University, 1967).

type of political behavior to persistent ethnoreligious factors.[5] That this should be so seems to conform to the findings of this study.

The German inhabitants of Nebraska, who had constituted a significant part of the population ever since territorial days, were largely lower-middle-class people, literate but not well educated. The majority were farmers, although craftsmen and merchants were numerous. They were concentrated in rural and frontier areas where land, which they valued highly, was readily available. Gradually, ethnoreligious communities developed in many parts of the state. Social pressure on members to conform to group norms was intense. Compared to native Americans, the German immigrants displayed a tendency to remain on the land they had acquired. In this, as in other aspects of their behavior, they seem to have been strongly influenced by traditional Old World attitudes and by the environmental pressures that accompanied immigrant status in American society.

In America the typical German immigrant, like other newcomers, developed a new sense of identity. In Europe neither his speech nor his clothes, his mannerisms nor his religion had particularly differentiated him from the mass of society. In America he found himself a member of an ethnic minority group. Inevitably he tended to seek out others of his own kind and to conform to the norms and attitudes of his ethnic group. The more closely the immigrant identified with his fellows the more likely was his behavior to conform to the group pattern. This was also true of his politics, which was but one aspect of the process of adjustment to American society.

In political affairs, as in other areas of life, considerable variation existed in assimilation of individuals. Length of residence in the United States, urban or rural residence, occupation, economic status, education, church affiliation, all are factors which had a bearing upon the level and degree of participation in the political process by the immigrant. The generational factor was also important, as was the reaction of the established society to the European newcomers. In general, the fewer interpersonal contacts that an immigrant had with members of the host society, the slower was his rate of conformance to its norms and standards. Conversely, if an immigrant had numerous contacts with native Americans, he could be expected to assimilate rapidly.

The degree to which the German-American identified with immigrant institutions and participated in their functions also had a bearing upon his rate of assimilation. If, for example, an immigrant's primary interpersonal contacts were within a rural German Lutheran community that maintained a

5 Samuel Lubell, *The Future of American Politics* (New York: Harper and Brothers, 1952), p. 133 and *passim*. See also John H. Fenton, *The Catholic Vote* (New Orleans: Hauser Press, 1960).

parochial school and a variety of auxiliary social organizations, his political behavior was likely to vary considerably from that of an immigrant merchant in a small town dominated by non-Lutheran protestant churches. In any individual case, however, electoral decisions were always the product of many complex forces, only a few of which may be identified. The possible combinations of influences are legion. In one instance group membership may have meant very little, while in another group membership may have been paramount.

In order to test hypotheses developed in connection with the relationships of social characteristics to the political behavior of Nebraska's Germans, the biographies of more than six hundred predominantly middle-class persons of German stock have been analyzed statistically. Generally, occupation and urban—or rural—residence (essentially socioeconomic characteristics) were discovered to be the least reliable indices of party identification. This finding was in substantial agreement with other parts of this study that also indicate that economic factors seemed to have had relatively little impact upon the political behavior of German immigrants.

Church membership was the most reliable guide to immigrant political behavior. For many of the newcomers the church provided primary group relationships, second in importance only to the family itself. The church was often the strongest pillar in the immigrant's crumbling house of culture. Inevitably, therefore, political attitudes and electoral decisions were conditioned by the ways in which the world of politics was perceived as impinging upon the interests of the immigrant church. Slow assimilators, often loyal to immigrant institutions and anxious to preserve German cultural patterns, tended to find the Democratic party more compatible with group goals and interests, whereas the Republican party was favored by Germans whose contacts with the native American society were more frequent and who were more often members of nonimmigrant churches and societies. These rapid assimilators accommodated themselves more readily to the norms of the host society, both in terms of partisan identification and in levels of political activity.

A special value of the multiple-biographies approach is that such biographies demonstrate the varied character of the German community. They reveal the tendency of Catholic Germans, for example, to vote Democratic in contrast to the Republican leanings of non-Lutheran protestants. Similarly, second-generation Germans are shown to have a slight tendency to identify with the rival of the party of the first generation.

While it is true that wide variations in political behavior existed within the German community, analyses of voting records show that as a group the Germans displayed distinctive characteristics when compared to the total

voting population. Composite patterns of their voting behavior were discovered through the use of statistical correlations between percentages of
German-American adult male population on a precinct basis as determined
by census manuscripts and percentages of votes cast in those precincts for
candidates for major political offices. When placed in time sequence, the
coefficients of correlation repeatedly conformed to the same general pattern
in the counties selected for special analysis. Like the analysis of the multiple
biographies, this analysis disclosed regional variations in partisan affiliation.
The tendency of Germans to vote Republican was stronger in counties with
histories of Republican dominance. Conversely, Democratic tendencies
were more pronounced in Democratic areas.

Coefficients of correlation calculated on the basis of census and election
records reveal the importance of ethnic origins in electoral decisions within
single counties. Voting statistics grouped by precincts according to concentration of German stock cut across county lines to give a composite
picture of German immigrant voting behavior. The latter method demonstrates that as early as the election of 1880—a contest that aroused only
slight interest—German voters displayed a noticeable preference for the
Democratic party.

Throughout the 1880's the tendency of the Germans to vote more heavily
Democratic than the rest of the population increased until it reached a climax
in the election of 1890. This trend is revealed both by aggregate voting
statistics and by coefficients of correlation for individual counties placed in
time sequence. Statistics, however, do not reveal causal relationships; these
may be inferred only from impressionistic evidence.[6]

Contemporary newspapers in the English and German languages reveal
that prohibition and woman suffrage, political symbols of the clash between
native and immigrant cultures, provided the substance of political debate
on the local level. The tariff and political and economic reforms (railroad
regulation in particular) were of secondary importance to most immigrants.
The rapid assimilators were often concerned about reform, but the slow
assimilators looked on the legislative proposals of moralistic reformers as
threats to their way of life.

The political phase of the cultural clash was a dominant theme throughout
the 1880's. In 1881 a high-cost liquor license law was enacted in Nebraska.
The following year the legislature submitted a woman suffrage amendment
to the electorate. In 1884 nativism and neo-Know-Nothingism, associated
with James G. Blaine, the Republican candidate for president, excited
immigrant fears. In each of the subsequent elections of the decade, debates

6 William O. Aydelotte, "Quantification in History," *American Historical Review*, LXXI
(April, 1966), 816 and *passim*.

raged over the submission of a prohibition amendment to a vote of the people. By 1890 intense antagonisms generated by the liquor question as well as by an attack on German-language schools fused the heterogeneous German community into a nearly solid bloc of support for the Democratic party as the political defender of German ethnocultural interests. At the same time, German rejection of the Republican party reached its highest level.

The decade of the 1890's was a period of unparalleled shifts in partisan alignments. Among Nebraska's Germans, the loyalties that had been built up during the 1880's were subject to radical changes. Though issues and candidates are transitory, it is impossible to divorce these violent shifts from the issues of the day and from the way in which Germans perceived them as impinging upon their interests.

While many Germans found many Populist reforms attractive (as evidenced by the extensive support they accorded Weaver's candidacy in 1892), the conservatism that characterized the immigrant outlook caused them to reject free silver nostrums for the economic ills of the day. While they responded politically to economic stimuli, they responded in ways conditioned by their cultural matrix and for reasons often very different from those of the native citizenry. The Germans retained their suspicions of the Populists as nativists. Noting predominantly Anglo-Saxon membership of the Populist movement and its historic antecedents in the Greenback and Anti-Monopoly movements, they feared the conversion of the movement into a moralistic crusade. Thus, in 1894, when the Democrats and Populists joined forces on a program which emphasized free silver, sufficient numbers of German voters moved into the Republican and Gold Democratic columns to eradicate their historic distinction as a Democratic group. In some localities Germans tended to vote more heavily Republican than their non-German fellows.

For the remainder of the decade the German vote was badly split. Aggregated voting data show that the political behavior of the German element, taken as a whole, lost all distinctiveness by comparison to the total voting population. Locally, however, wide variations existed in the electoral decisions made in the heavily German precincts. Small-town and rural differences were sometimes important, especially in the election of 1894. A small measure of distinctiveness returned to the German vote in 1900 when a slight over-all tendency toward the Democratic party was restored under the impact of imperialism. Although imperialism was a salient issue for the leaders of the German community, the rank-and-file German voters were not greatly aroused by it. The Republican attempt to woo German support through a German candidate for governor was a failure. Charles H. Dietrich had been structurally assimilated into American society, and his efforts to win the support of Germans lacked authenticity.

During the last few elections of the nineteenth century there was no intense ethnocultural issue to unite the Germans as opposition to prohibition and compulsory education legislation had a decade earlier. Under these conditions, as Lee Benson has predicted, a "multiplicity of 'localistic' factors" produced wide variations in German voting patterns.[7] Historic partisan attachments of the community, traditions based upon primary group relationships in the family and church, and the influences of local leadership appear to have been important as determinants of the voting decisions of Germans from 1896 to 1900.

This is not to say that there was a decrease in ethnic politics during those years. The evidence indicates the opposite to have been the case. Both major parties made overt appeals to the German vote through issues, candidates, and political practices. The Germans, in turn, had become increasingly aware of their identity as a minority group capable of exercising political power. German partisan attachments became progressively more unstable as cultural leaders upheld political independence as the ideal. At the same time, the German element, conscious of its political potential, demanded considerations from the major parties that normally were the rewards of steadfast loyalty, not arrogant nonpartisanship. Failure to receive the recognition they felt they deserved merely intensified their group frustrations and, no doubt, contributed to a retardation of their assimilation. As Milton Yinger has pointed out, a decline in the distinctiveness of ethnic group norms may be accompanied by a heightened sense of ethnicity.[8] The pride of membership in the German community, which was much more explicit in 1900 than in 1880, may have been a mask to cover the alienation and low morale common to the second generation, which, by the turn of the century, had come to dominate the German element in Nebraska.

The evidence suggests that by 1900 the German community was well assimilated in terms of political behavior. The Germans had learned to participate extensively and intelligently in the political process. Their rate of naturalization was one of the most favorable in the nation.[9] Their rate of voter turnout was high.[10] They had achieved significant levels of political

[7] Lee Benson, *The Concept of Jacksonian Democracy: New York as a Test Case* (Princeton: Princeton University Press, 1961), p. 292.

[8] J. Milton Yinger, "Social Forces Involved in Group Identification or Withdrawal," *Daedalus*, XC (Spring, 1961), 248.

[9] U.S. Census Office, *Eleventh Census: 1890. Population*, II, lxvi.

[10] A series of coefficients of correlation calculated on the basis of data from the state census of 1885 and the election of 1884 and 1886 indicate that generally the Germans were voting as frequently as the total voting population. If the proportion of Germans who had

activity, as the multiple-biographies study demonstrates. Individual political leaders like Paul Schminke and Henry Sprick functioned at a high level of sophistication; they played the game of politics as skillfully as their native-American peers.

Yet it is equally clear that the German element as a whole was far from being structurally assimilated into Nebraska politics by 1900. Except for "Per Hansa" types like Charles Dietrich, Fred Hedde, or Melchior Brugger, the voters of Nebraska who were of German ethnic origins continued to vote as Germans. That is to say, their electoral decisions appear to have been largely influenced by ethnic considerations even though the corporate decision lacked distinctiveness. Structural assimilation could come only when ethnic politics disappeared, when political appeals to the German element were fruitless, and when Germans in America ceased to identify themselves as German-Americans.

not yet taken out their first naturalization papers (roughly 15 to 20 per cent) is taken into consideration, it will be found that in some localities the German voter turnout rates actually exceeded those of the native population.

APPENDICES

Nebraska Counties Ranked According to Largest Numbers and Highest Percentages of German-Born Inhabitants, 1870–1900

TABLE A-1

Ten Counties with Largest Number and Highest Percentage of German-Born Inhabitants, 1870[a]

County	Total Population	Total Foreign-Born	Total German-Born	Per Cent German-Born
Counties with Largest Number of German-Born				
Douglas	19982	7537	1957	9.8
Otoe	12345	2736	1173	9.5
Dodge	4212	1656	854	20.3
Cuming	2964	1323	788	26.6
Richardson	9780	1527	737	7.5
Lancaster	7074	1737	558	7.9
Cass	8151	1308	497	6.1
Washington	4452	1010	494	11.1
Hall	1057	516	345	32.6
Cedar	1032	460	324	31.4
Counties with Highest Percentage of German-Born				
Pierce	152	108	108	71.1
Hall	1057	516	345	32.6
Cedar	1032	460	324	31.4
Stanton	636	237	180	28.3
Cuming	2964	1323	788	26.6
Madison	1138	361	263	23.1
Dodge	4212	1656	854	20.3
Platte	1899	911	322	17.0
Washington	4452	1010	494	11.1
Douglas	19982	7537	1957	9.8
State:	122,993	30,748	10,954	8.9

[a] In order to avoid the distortion that would be caused by including very thinly populated counties, only those counties which had a German-born population exceeding 100 are listed.

SOURCES: U.S. Census Office, *Ninth Census: 1870. Population*, I, 317, 363 f; *Nebraska's Population* (Nebraska State Planning Board, 1937), pp. 16–18.

TABLE A-2

Ten Counties with Largest Number and Highest Percentage of German-Born Inhabitants,
1880

County	Total Population	Total Foreign–Born	Total German–Born	Per Cent German–Born
Counties with Largest Number of German-Born				
Douglas	37645	12138	3616	9.6
Lancaster	28090	6051	2166	7.7
Dodge	11263	3514	1816	16.1
Otoe	15727	2913	1454	9.2
Cuming	5569	2199	1280	23.0
Platte	9511	3828	1203	12.6
Hall	8572	1886	1052	12.3
Seward	11147	1959	1035	9.3
Cass	16683	2539	983	5.9
Washington	8631	1770	925	10.7
Counties with Highest Percentage of German-Born				
Pierce	1202	432	288	24.0
Stanton	1813	682	420	23.2
Cuming	5569	2199	1280	23.0
Cedar	2899	885	561	19.4
Dodge	11263	3514	1816	16.1
Madison	5589	1453	839	15.0
Platte	9511	3828	1203	12.6
Hall	8572	1886	1052	12.3
Wayne	813	163	90	11.1
Washington	8631	1770	925	10.7
State:	452,402	97,414	31,125	6.9

SOURCES: U.S. Census Office, *Tenth Census: 1880. Population*, p. 519; *Nebraska's Population*, pp. 16–18.

TABLE A-3

Ten Counties with Largest Number and Highest Percentage of German-Born Inhabitants,
1890

County	Total Population	Total Foreign–Born	Total German–Born	Per Cent German–Born
Counties with Largest Number of German-Born				
Douglas	158008	40757	10771	6.8
Lancaster	76395	11104	3943	5.2
Dodge	19260	5388	2973	15.4
Otoe	25403	4595	2816	11.1
Cuming	12265	4479	2794	22.8
Gage	36344	4770	2722	7.5
Platte	15437	5397	2245	14.5
Hall	16512	3247	2110	12.8
Cass	24080	4249	1905	7.9
Seward	16140	2919	1788	11.1

Table A-3 continued

County	Total Population	Total Foreign-Born	Total German-Born	Per Cent German-Born
Counties with Highest Percentage of German-Born				
Cuming	12265	4479	2794	22.8
Stanton	4619	1183	805	17.4
Pierce	4864	1160	807	16.6
Dodge	19260	5388	2973	15.4
Platte	15437	5397	2245	14.5
Cedar	7028	1595	923	13.1
Hall	16512	3247	2110	12.8
Sarpy	6875	1476	869	12.6
Madison	13669	2957	1668	12.2
Wayne	6169	1478	741	12.0
State:	1,062,656	202,244	72,000	6.8

SOURCES: U.S. Census Office, *Compendium of the Eleventh Census: 1890. Part I. Population*, 650 f.; *Nebraska's Population*, pp. 16–18.

TABLE A-4

Ten Counties with Largest Number and Highest Percentage of German-Born Inhabitants, 1900

County	Total Population	Total Foreign-Born	Total German-Born	Per Cent German-Born
Counties with Largest Number of German-Born				
Douglas	140590	32244	8373	6.0
Lancaster	64835	9404	2987	4.6
Cuming	14584	4029	2571	17.6
Dodge	22298	4949	2540	11.4
Otoe	22288	3414	2259	10.1
Gage	30051	3557	2137	7.1
Platte	17747	4701	1949	11.0
Hall	17206	2788	1833	10.7
Madison	16976	3232	1776	10.5
Seward	15690	2476	1549	9.9
Counties with Highest Percentage of German-Born				
Cuming	14585	4029	2571	17.6
Stanton	6959	1688	952	13.7
Pierce	8445	1634	1048	12.4
Wayne	9862	2137	1212	12.3
Dodge	22298	4949	2540	11.4
Platte	17747	4701	1949	11.0
Hall	17206	2788	1833	10.7
Sarpy	9080	1659	965	10.6
Madison	16976	3232	1776	10.5
Otoe	22288	3414	2259	10.1
State:	1,066,300	177,117	66,810	6.3

SOURCES: U.S. Census Office, *Twelfth Census: 1900. Population*, I, 568 f.; *Nebraska's Population*, pp. 16–18.

TABLE A-5
German-Born Population of Nebraska Counties, 1880 and 1900

County	Total Population 1880	German-Born Population 1880	Per Cent German-Born 1880	Total Population 1900	German-Born Population 1900	Per Cent German-Born 1900
Adams	10235	639	6.2	18840	1363	7.2
Antelope	3953	91	2.3	11344	563	5.0
Banner	—	—	—	1114	13	1.2
Blaine	—	—	—	603	32	5.3
Boone	4170	61	1.5	11689	502	4.3
Boxbutte	—	—	—	5572	215	3.9
Boyd	—	—	—	7332	371	5.1
Brown	—	—	—	3470	136	3.9
Buffalo	7531	383	5.1	20254	908	4.5
Burt	6937	215	3.1	13040	299	2.3
Butler	9194	297	3.2	15703	772	4.9
Cass	16683	983	5.9	21330	1363	7.2
Cedar	2899	561	19.4	12467	1243	5.0
Chase	70	0	.0	2559	69	2.7
Cherry	—	—	—	6541	280	4.3
Cheyenne	1558	90	5.8	5570	261	4.7
Clay	11294	567	5.0	15735	720	4.6
Colfax	6588	528	8.0	11211	793	7.1
Cuming	5569	1280	23.0	14584	2571	17.6
Custer	2211	34	1.5	19758	448	2.3
Dakota	3213	94	2.9	6286	365	5.8
Dawes	—	—	—	6215	204	3.3
Dawson	2909	99	3.4	12214	516	4.2
Deuel	—	—	—	2630	103	3.9
Dixon	4177	178	4.2	10535	629	6.0
Dodge	11263	1816	16.1	22298	2540	11.4
Douglas	37645	3616	9.6	140590	8373	6.0
Dundy	37	2	5.4	2432	56	2.3
Fillmore	10204	436	4.3	15087	742	4.9
Franklin	5465	216	4.0	9455	737	7.8
Frontier	934	21	2.2	8781	466	5.3
Furnas	6407	263	4.1	12373	389	3.1
Gage	13164	891	6.8	30051	2137	7.1
Garfield	—	—	—	2127	49	2.3
Gosper	1673	53	3.2	5301	437	8.2
Grant	—	—	—	763	8	1.0
Greeley	1461	37	2.5	5691	208	3.7
Hall	8572	1052	12.3	17206	1833	10.7
Hamilton	8267	289	3.5	13330	478	3.6
Harlan	6086	302	3.3	9370	392	4.2
Hayes	119	4	3.4	2708	117	4.3
Hitchcock	1012	27	2.7	4409	137	3.1
Holt	3287	50	1.5	12224	513	4.2
Hooker	—	—	—	432	7	1.6
Howard	4391	217	4.9	10343	439	4.2
Jefferson	8096	552	6.8	15196	1276	8.4
Johnson	7595	403	5.3	11197	850	7.6
Kearney	4072	112	2.8	9866	289	2.9
Keith	194	11	5.7	1951	110	5.6
Keyapaha	—	—	—	3076	82	2.7
Kimball	—	—	—	758	16	2.1

Table A-5 continued

County	Total Population 1800	German-Born Population 1880	Per Cent German-Born 1880	Total Population 1900	German-Born Population 1900	Per Cent German-Born 1900
Knox	3666	223	6.1	14343	1015	7.1
Lancaster	28090	2166	7.7	64835	2987	4.6
Lincoln	3632	110	3.0	11416	446	3.9
Logan	—	—	—	960	19	2.0
Loup	—	—	—	1305	22	1.7
McPherson	—	—	—	517	11	2.1
Madison	5589	839	15.0	16976	1776	10.5
Merrick	5341	406	7.6	9255	623	6.7
Nance	1212	18	1.5	8222	144	1.8
Nemaha	10451	615	5.9	14952	697	4.7
Nuckolls	4235	127	3.0	12414	515	4.1
Otoe	15031	1454	9.2	22288	2259	10.5
Pawnee	6920	224	3.2	11770	314	2.7
Perkins	—	—	—	1702	76	4.5
Phelps	2447	35	1.4	10772	176	1.6
Pierce	1202	288	24.0	8445	1048	12.4
Platte	9511	1203	12.6	17747	1949	11.0
Polk	6846	176	2.6	10542	284	2.7
Redwillow	3044	95	3.1	9604	367	3.8
Richardson	15031	906	6.0	19614	1079	5.5
Rock	—	—	—	2809	131	4.7
Saline	14491	674	4.7	18252	846	4.6
Sarpy	4481	380	8.5	9080	965	10.6
Saunders	15810	720	4.6	22085	1117	5.1
Scotts Bluff	—	—	—	2552	39	1.5
Seward	11147	1035	9.3	15690	1549	9.9
Sheridan	—	—	—	6033	273	4.5
Sherman	2016	218	10.6	6550	510	7.8
Sioux	699	27	3.9	2055	158	7.7
Stanton	1813	420	23.2	6959	952	13.7
Thayer	6113	414	6.8	14325	1204	8.4
Thomas	—	—	—	628	30	4.8
Thurston[a]	109	1	.9	6517	363	5.6
Valley	2324	63	3.1	7339	198	2.7
Washington	8631	925	10.7	13086	1250	9.6
Wayne	813	90	11.1	9862	1212	12.3
Webster	7104	317	4.5	11619	590	5.1
Wheeler	644	19	3.0	1362	56	4.1
York	11170	475	4.3	18205	766	4.2
Unorganized territory	2913	91	3.1	—	—	—
State:	452,402	31,125	6.9	1,066,300	66,810	6.3

[a] In 1880 Thurston County was called Blackbird County.

SOURCES: U.S. Census Office, *Tenth Census: 1880. Population*, p. 519; *Twelfth Census: 1900. Population*, I, 768 f.; *Nebraska's Population*, pp. 86–89.

APPENDIX II

Some Comments on the Use of Coefficients of Correlation

THE USE OF CORRELATIONAL FORMULAS by historians is a comparatively recent development. Since few of Clio's devotees have been initiated into the mysteries of statistics, it is understandable that these devices have not received widespread use. The discoveries they make possible have not been accepted without suspicion. Yet other students of man in society, notably political scientists, have been employing coefficients of correlation with election data for several decades. Needless to say, historians may profit much from such studies.

There are, however, two basic criticisms that may be made concerning their use. First, the county has almost always been used as the basic unit in the correlations, even though it has been generally recognized that the county is an unsatisfactory unit by reason of its size and internal variations. Precinct returns, by contrast, are capable of establishing distinctions between voting groups, factions, and parties with much greater precision. The continued use of county data has been governed by the fact that published voting records, as well as social and economic statistics, are rarely available in units smaller than the county. Hence, if correlations are to be conducted on the ideal level of the precinct, unusual efforts must be made to acquire the necessary data from such sources as census manuscripts, from precinct voting records kept by county clerks, or from records that may have been preserved in county newspapers.

A second criticism that must be directed at many correlational studies is that they have used the Pearson product-moment correlation coefficient. Even though it is the standard index of correlation between two variables, the Pearson formula is not intended for use with voting statistics because it is based on the assumption that the data employed are both metric and linear. Metric data are acquired by measurement rather than by enumeration or frequency. An example of a metric statistic may be the score a person achieves on a test. The statistical object in this case is an individual, an indivisible unit. Voting data, by contrast, are enumerative, not metric, because they reveal how many voters cast their ballots for a candidate. In this case, the statistical unit is a county or a precinct, that is, a group of persons. In order for such units to be correlated, the variable must be expressed as a percentage. W. S. Robinson has demonstrated that such "ecological" correlations calculated from percentages of groups of persons tend to give an exaggerated picture of the relationship between the variables and that this inflating influence increases with the size of the group.[1] The formula assumes that the size of the units being correlated is uniform; voting data never satisfy that assumption. Moreover, Robinson's contention appears to be supported by assimilation theory, which assumes that, as a colony of immigrants increases in size and exclusiveness, the social pressure on individuals to conform to ethnic group norms is intensified. Hence, the assumption of the Pearson formula that the relationships of variables are linear is likewise not satisfied by voting statistics.[2] In fact, assimilation theory assumes a curvilinear relationship.

Despite these difficulties, the Pearson formula has been regularly used, presumably because (1) the divergence from linearity has often not been great, (2) the magnitude of coefficients of correlation that have been obtained in some cases seem to discount the objection, and (3) a suitable alternative formula is lacking, especially one that is appropriate for use with large numbers of units, as is usually the case when counties are used.[3]

The tool employed in this study is Charles Spearman's rank-difference coefficient of correlation:

$$\rho = 1 - \frac{6 \sum D^2}{N(N^2 - 1)},$$

in which D is the difference in rank orders between the two variables and N is the number of units ranked. The advantage of the Spearman formula over the Pearson for use with precinct data is that it is nonparametric, that is, it does not attempt to reveal actual relationships that take the size of intervals between the units into account. Since the concentration of German population in a given township was determined by the Nebraska state census of 1885, the same figures must be used in correlation with the voting data for every election from 1880 to 1900. Obviously, the quantitative relationship of the Germans to the total population of the county changed throughout

[1] W. S. Robinson, "Ecological Correlations and the Behavior of Individuals," *American Sociological Review*, XV (June, 1950), 351–357.

[2] Cf. Angus Campbell and Donald Stokes, "Partisan Attitudes and the Presidential Vote," in Eugene Burdick and Arthur J. Brodbeck (eds.), *American Voting Behavior* (Glencoe, The Free Press, 1959), p. 369.

[3] *Ibid.*

the twenty-year period. It would seem, however, that, if the data were kept on an ordinal scale rather than on an interval scale, the amount of distortion over time would be minimized. To illustrate, Grand Prairie Precinct in Platte County is likely to retain its rank through the years as the third most German township regardless of increases in the German population after 1885; on the other hand, the relative differences in German-ness between the several precincts (expressed as percentages) are likely to change significantly over the twenty-year period. Another advantage of the Spearman formula is that, when the number of units being correlated is less than thirty (as was the case in the typical Nebraska county), the Spearman coefficient is considered to be almost as reliable as the more sophisticated Pearson coefficient. Finally, the relative simplicity of the Spearman formula may also be considered an advantage.

Bibliography

Manuscripts and Collections

STUDIES OF POLITICAL BEHAVIOR are necessarily based on the attitudes, activities, and partisan preferences of thousands of unnamed voters rather than on the personal records of prominent leaders. Hence few manuscript collections exist to undergird this study. Indeed, of the few German-American political leaders in Nebraska at the end of the nineteenth century who attained a modicum of public stature, only Governor Charles H. Dietrich left any papers. Located in the archives of the Nebraska State Historical Society in Lincoln, the Dietrich collection contains a few letters and a scrapbook of newspaper clippings that are of special value to a study such as this.

The William H. Werkmeister collection, also located in the Nebraska State Historical Society, contains a wide variety of materials pertinent to a study of the German community in Nebraska. A professor of philosophy at the University of Nebraska for many years, Werkmeister was active in several German cultural and political organizations during the 1920's and 1930's. Intending to write a popular history of the Germans in his state, he collected pamphlets, booklets, newspaper clippings, and personal reminiscences of all kinds. He prepared a preliminary draft entitled "Die Deutschen in Nebraska: Ein historischer Bericht." Never published, the manuscript lacks continuous pagination; hence individual chapters only have been cited rather than the work as a whole: "Deutsche Zeitungen in Nebraska," "Die Deutschen Gruenden Norfolk," "Deutschen Katholiken in Nebraska," and "Weitere deutsche Siedlungen."

Another unpublished manuscript in the Nebraska State Historical Society collections—Victor Rosewater's "The Life and Times of Edward Rosewater"—also contained material pertinent to the subject of this volume.

Public Documents and Reports

PUBLISHED MATERIALS

Basic statistical information has been derived from reports of the U.S. Bureau of the Census and its predecessor, the U.S. Census Office, especially the volumes on population, from the Ninth Census (1870) through the Twelfth Census (1900). Tables of immigration in *Historical Statistics of the United States: Colonial Times to 1957* (1960) are also valuable. A comparable collection of data at the state level is *Nebraska's Population: A Preliminary Report*, published by the Nebraska State Planning Board, December 15, 1937. Some of the findings of the Nebraska state census of 1885 have been published in *Population, Farms, and Industries of Nebraska from the Census Returns of June 1, 1885* (Lincoln, 1885). *Nebraska Blue Book for 1901 and 1902* tabulates county election totals for all elections from statehood to 1900. Valuable information on churches may be obtained in two publications of the U.S. Bureau of the Census, *Report on Statistics of Churches in the United States at the Eleventh Census* (1894) and *Religious Bodies: 1906* (2 vols., 1910).

United States *Statutes at Large*, XII and XIII, were the sources for references to national legislation. *Laws of Nebraska, 1881* and *Compiled Statutes of the State of Nebraska, 1881* (3rd edition, with amendments to July 1, 1887) provided information on state legislation. Actions taken by the Nebraska legislature are recorded in *House Journals of the Legislature of the State of Nebraska, Sixteenth* [1881], *Eighteenth* [1883], and *Twenty-first* [1889] *Regular Sessions*.

MICROFILMED MATERIALS

All ethnic population data on the precinct level was obtained from *Schedules of the Nebraska State Census of 1885*, microfilmed from the original census manuscripts by the National Archives in 1961.

UNPUBLISHED MATERIALS

Election records of Clay, Cuming, Hall, Hitchcock, Jefferson, Madison, Otoe, Platte, Seward, Stanton, Thayer, Washington, and York counties. See Sources of Election Data, below.

General Index to Deeds, Seward County. Vol. I. Office of the County Clerk, Seward, Nebr.

Tax Lists for the Years 1885, 1886, 1888, 1890, 1892, 1894, 1896, 1898. Seward County, Nebraska. Office of the County Treasurer, Seward, Nebr.

Sources of Election Data

For the total votes cast by the state and the counties in the elections from 1880 to 1900, the *Nebraska Blue Book for 1901 and 1902* (see above) was used. For precinct returns, the election records of the several county clerks' offices served as sources. When these records were not extant, the newspaper sources listed below were employed.

CLAY COUNTY:
Election Book. Vols. I–III. Office of the County Clerk, Clay Center, Nebr.

CUMING COUNTY:
Abstracts of Election. Vols. I–III. Office of the County Clerk, West Point, Nebr.

HALL COUNTY:
Abstract of Votes Cast. Vols. A and B. Office of the County Clerk, Grand Island, Nebr.

HITCHCOCK COUNTY:
Abstracts of Election. Vols. I and II. Nebraska State Historical Society, Lincoln, Nebr.

JEFFERSON COUNTY:
Fairbury Gazette, 1880–1886.
Abstract of Votes. Vol. I. Office of the County Clerk, Fairbury, Nebr.

MADISON COUNTY:
Norfolk Journal, 1882–1886.
Norfolk Daily News, 1888–1890.
Election Book. Office of the County Clerk, Madison, Nebr.

OTOE COUNTY:
Nebraska City News, 1880–1890.
Syracuse Journal, 1884.
Abstracts of Election. Book 4. Office of the County Clerk, Nebraska City, Nebr.

PLATTE COUNTY:
Columbus Journal, 1880–1882.
Abstract of Votes Cast. Books B, C, and D. Office of the County Clerk, Columbus, Nebr.

SEWARD COUNTY:
Blue Valley Blade (Seward), 1880–1886.
Nebraska Reporter (Seward), 1884.
Abstract of Votes. Vol. I. Office of the County Clerk, Seward, Nebr.

STANTON COUNTY:
Election Record. Office of the County Clerk, Stanton, Nebr.

THAYER COUNTY:
   Abstract of Election. 3 vols. Office of the County Clerk, Hebron, Nebr.
WASHINGTON COUNTY:
   The Pilot (Blair), 1880, 1898.
   Blair Courier, 1890–1896.
   Nebraska Blue Book for 1901 and 1902 (see above), used for the election
      of 1900.
YORK COUNTY:
   York Republican, 1880–1884.
   Abstract of Votes. Vol. II. Office of the County Clerk, York, Nebr.

Newspapers

All newspapers listed below are in the Nebraska State Historical Society,
Lincoln, Nebraska. All were published in Nebraska unless otherwise indicated.

   Adams County Democrat (Hastings), 1900.
   Advertiser News (Sutton), 1896.
   The American (Omaha), 1892–1896.
   Die Beatrice Post, 1896–1900.
   Blair Courier, 1889–1900.
   Blue Valley Blade (Seward), 1880–1900.
   Columbus Era, 1880.
   Columbus Journal, 1878.
   Columbus Telegram, 1890.
   Cuming County Advertiser (West Point), 1892, 1898.
   The Democrat (Columbus), 1884, 1888.
   Fairbury Gazette, 1880–1900.
   Grand Island Anzeiger, 1892.
   Grand Island Anzeiger und Herold, 1894–1900.
   Grand Island Daily Independent, 1892–1900.
   Grand Island Herald, 1886 (English-language newspaper published by the
      editor of *Der Herold*).
   Grand Island Independent, 1886–1890.
   Hamilton County Register (Aurora), 1889.
   Hastings Tribune, 1900.
   Hebron Journal, 1880.
   Der Herold (Grand Island), 1886, 1887 (later merged with *Grand Island
      Anzeiger*).
   Hitchcock County Republican (Culbertson), 1892.
   Humphrey Democrat, 1896.

Lincoln Daily Call, 1890.
Lincoln Evening News, 1890.
Lincoln Freie Presse, 1892–1900.
Lincoln Weekly Herald, 1890.
Milford Nebraskan, 1886.
Milford Ozone, 1884.
Nebraska Biene (Columbus), 1898–1900.
Nebraska City News, 1882–1900.
Nebraska Reporter (Seward), 1884.
Nebraska Staats Anzeiger (Lincoln), 1893–1900.
Nebraska State Journal (Lincoln), 1890.
Nebraska Tribüne (Omaha), 1900 (throughout most of its existence called
   the *Omaha Tribüne*).
Nebraska Volksblatt (West Point), 1885–1898.
Nebraska Vorwaerts (Omaha), 1894–1896.
Norfolk Times, 1880.
Norfolk Times Tribune, 1900.
Omaha Daily Bee, 1890–1900.
Omaha Herald (weekly edition), 1882–1888.
Omaha Tribüne, 1892–1894.
Personal Rights Advocate (Chicago, Ill.), 1890.
The Progress (West Point), 1884, 1896 (later called *West Point Progress*).
Seward County Democrat (Seward), 1896.
Seward Independent-Democrat, 1897–1900.
Syracuse Journal, 1882.
World Herald (Omaha), 1890–1900.

Maps, Atlases, and Plat Books

The basic source for the township boundaries of the county maps included
in this study was the *Official State Atlas of Nebraska* (see below), published
in the same year that the Nebraska State Census of 1885 was taken. The
other maps and plat books listed below were of supplementary use; in some
instances they provided information that was not available elsewhere.

Atlas and Plat Book of Seward County, Nebraska. Beaver Crossing, Nebr.:
   E. A. McNeil, 1921.
Atlas of Cuming County, Nebraska. Mason City, Iowa: Anderson Publishing
   Co., 1918.
Atlas of Washintgon County, Nebraska. Chicago: Gillen and Davey, 1884.
Munn's Atlas of Otoe County, Nebraska. Chicago: Rand McNally and Co.,
   1902.

Nebraska State Railway Commission. *Map of Nebraska.* 1953.

Official State Atlas of Nebraska. Compiled from Government Surveys, County Records, and Personal Investigations. Philadelphia: Everts and Kirk, 1885.

Plat Book of Jefferson County, Nebraska. N.p.: Northwest Publishing Co., 1900.

Plat Book of Madison County, Nebraska. N.p.: Northwest Publishing Co., 1899.

Plat Book of Platte County, Nebraska, 1914. (Title page missing.)

Rand McNally Sectional Map of Nebraska. 1887.

Searcy, N. D. and A. R. Longwell. *Nebraska Atlas.* Kearney, Nebr.: Nebraska Atlas Publishing Co., 1964.

Shepherd, William R. *Historical Atlas.* 7th ed., rev. New York: Henry Holt and Co., 1929.

Standard Atlas of Hall County, Nebraska. Chicago: Geo. A. Ogle and Co., 1904.

Books and Pamphlets

[Andreas, A. T.] *History of the State of Nebraska.* Chicago: Western Historical Co., 1882.

Arndt, Karl J. R., and May E. Olson. *German-American Newspapers and Periodicals, 1732–1955: History and Bibliography.* Heidelberg: Quelle and Meyer, 1961.

Ayer, N. W. *American Newspaper Annual* [1883]. Philadelphia: N. W. Ayer and Son, 1883.

Baltzell, E. Digby. *The Protestant Establishment: Aristocracy and Caste in America.* New York: Random House, 1964.

Bartlett, [Maurice] and [P. F.] O'Sullivan. *History of Cuming County, Nebraska with Complete Directory.* Fremont, Nebr.: Fremont Tribune, 1884.

Beck, Walter H. *Lutheran Elementary Schools in the United States: A History of the Development of Parochial Schools and Synodical Educational Policies and Programs.* St. Louis: Concordia Publishing House, 1939.

Benson, Lee, *The Concept of Jacksonian Democracy: New York as a Test Case.* Princeton: Princeton University Press, 1961.

Blegen, Theodore C., ed. *The Land of Their Choice: The Immigrants Write Home.* Minneapolis: University of Minnesota Press, 1955.

Boynton, Percy. *The Rediscovery of the Frontier.* Chicago: University of Chicago Press, 1931.

Brown, Francis J., and Joseph S. Roucek, eds. *One America: The History Contributions, and Present Problems of Our Racial and National Minorities.* New York: Prentice-Hall, 1945.

Brunner, Edmund de S. *Immigrant Farmers and Their Children.* Garden City, N.Y.: Doubleday, Doran and Co., 1929.

Buechler, A. F., R. J. Barr, and Dale P. Stough. *History of Hall County, Nebraska.* Lincoln: Western Publishing and Engraving Co., 1920.

Burdick, Eugene, and Arthur J. Brodbeck, eds. *American Voting Behavior.* Glencoe: The Free Press, 1959.

Burns, J. A. *The Growth and Development of the Catholic School System in the United States.* New York: Benziger Brothers, 1912.

Buss, William H., and Thomas T. Osterman, eds. *History of Dodge and Washington Counties, Nebraska, and Their People.* 2 vols. Chicago: American Historical Society, 1921.

Campbell, Angus, Philip E. Converse, Warren E. Miller, and Donald E. Stokes. *The American Voter.* New York: John Wiley and Sons, 1960.

Carr, Daniel M., ed. *Men and Women of Nebraska. A Book of Portraits. Washington County Edition.* Fremont, Nebr.: Progress Publishing Co., 1903.

Casper, Henry W. *History of the Catholic Church in Nebraska: The Church of the Northern Plains, 1838–1874.* Milwaukee: Bruce Press, 1960.

Cather, Willa. *O Pioneers!* Boston: Houghton Mifflin Co., 1913.

Child, Irvin L. *Italian or American? The Second Generation Conflict.* New Haven: Yale University Press, 1943.

Coletta, Paolo E. *William Jennings Bryan: I. Political Evangelist, 1860–1908.* Lincoln: University of Nebraska Press, 1964.

Commager, Henry Steele, ed. *Immigration and American History: Essays in Honor of Theodore C. Blegen.* Minneapolis: University of Minnesota Press, 1961.

Cox, W. W. *History of Seward County, Nebraska Together with a Chapter of Reminiscences of the Early Settlement of Lancaster County.* Lincoln: State Journal Co., 1888.

————. *History of Seward County, Nebraska, and Reminiscences of Territorial History.* 2nd ed. University Place, Nebr.: Jason L. Claflin, 1905.

Curry, Margaret. *The History of Platte County, Nebraska.* Culver City, Calif.: Murray and Gee, 1950.

Curti, Merle *et al. The Making of an American Community: A Case Study of Democracy in a Frontier County.* Stanford, Calif.: Stanford University Press, 1959.

Degler, Carl N. *The Age of Economic Revolution.* Glenview, Ill.: Scott, Foresman and Co., 1967.

Deindoerfer, Johannes. *Geschichte der Evangel.-Luth. Synode von Iowa und anderen Staaten*. Chicago: Wartburg Publishing House, 1897.

Deutschamerikanischen Bürgerbundes von Nebraska. *Von unserer Arbeit und von unseren Zielen*. Erster Bericht. Omaha: December, 1929. (Werkmeister Collection, Nebraska State Historical Society.)

Diller, Robert. *Farm Ownership, Tenancy, and Land Use in a Nebraska Community*. Chicago: University of Chicago Press, 1941.

Directory of our Lutheran Churches of America. Missouri and Wisconsin Synods. Madison County, 1918. N.p.: n.d. (Werkmeister Collection, Nebraska State Historical Society.)

Eckhardt, E. *Geschichte des Nebraskadistriktes*. Battle Creek, Nebr.: E. Eckhardt, n.d. (Werkmeister Collection, Nebraska State Historical Society.)

Eisenach, George J. *A History of the German Congregational Churches in the United States*. Yankton, S.D.: Pioneer Press, 1938.

Eisenstadt, S. N. *The Absorption of Immigrants*. Glencoe: The Free Press, 1955.

Faust, Albert Bernhard. *The German Element in the United States*. 2 vols. Boston: Houghton Mifflin Co., 1909.

Fenton, John H. *The Catholic Vote*. New Orleans: Hauser Press, 1960.

Fishman, Joshua, *et al. Language Loyalty in the United States: The Maintenance and Perpetuation of Non-English Mother Tongues by American Ethnic and Religious Groups*. The Hague: Mouton and Co., 1966.

Gingerich, Melvin. *The Mennonites of Iowa*. Iowa City: The State Historical Society of Iowa, 1939.

Glad, Paul. *McKinley, Bryan, and the People*. Philadelphia: J. B. Lippincott Co., 1964.

Goebel, Julius. *Der Kampf um deutsche Kultur in America*. Leipzig: Verlag der Dürr'schen Buchhandlung, 1914.

Gordon, Milton M. *Assimilation in Amerian Life: The Role of Race, Religion, and National Origins*. New York: Oxford University Press, 1964.

Grimes, Alan P. *The Puritan Ethnic and Woman Suffrage*. New York: Oxford University Press, 1967.

Gusfield, Joseph R. *Symbolic Crusade: Status Politics and the American Temperance Movement*. Urbana: University of Illinois Press, 1963.

Hagedorn, Eugene. *The Franciscans in Nebraska*. Prefaced by Historical Sketches of Mid-Nebraska by Francis Dischner. Humphrey and Norfolk, Nebr.: Humphrey Democrat, Norfolk News, 1931.

Handlin, Oscar, ed. *Children of the Uprooted*. New York: George Braziller, 1966.

――――. *The Uprooted: The Epic Story of the Great Migrations that Made the American People*. New York: Grosset's Universal Library, 1951.

Hansen, Marcus Lee. *The Atlantic Migration, 1607–1860*. New York: Harper Torchbooks, 1961.

——. *The Immigrant in American History*. New York: Harper Torchbooks, 1964.

Hawgood, John A. *The Tragedy of German-America: The Germans in the United States of America during the Nineteenth Century—and After*. New York: G. P. Putnam's Sons, 1940.

Hicks, John D. *The Populist Revolt: A History of the Farmers' Alliance and the People's Party*. Lincoln: University of Nebraska Press, 1959.

Higham, John. *Strangers in the Land: Patterns of American Nativism, 1860–1925*. New Brunswick, N.J.: Rutgers University Press, 1955.

Kinzer, Donald L. *Episode in Anti-Catholicism: The American Protective Association*. Seattle: University of Washington Press, 1964.

Kraditor, Aileen S. *The Ideas of the Woman Suffrage Movement, 1890–1920*. New York: Columbia University Press, 1965.

Kriege, Otto, Gustav Becker, Mathäus Hermann, and C. L. Körner. *Souvenir der West Deutschen Konferenz der Bischöflichen Methodistenkirche*. Cincinnati: Jennings and Graham, 1906.

Eine kurze Geschichte der Ev.-Luth. St. Pauls-Gemeinde zu Norfolk, Nebraska. Zur Erinnerung an das fünfzigjährige Jubiläum. Zusammengestellt 1866–1916. Milwaukee: Northwestern Publishing House, 1916. (Werkmeister Collection, Nebraska State Historical Society.)

Lazarsfeld, Paul F., Bernard Berelson, and Hazel Gaudet. *The People's Choice*. New York: Columbia University Press, 1948.

Lentz, A. B., *et al. Story of the Midwest Synod. ULCA. 1890–1950*. N.p.: n.d.

Lipset, Seymour Martin. *The First Nation: The United States in Historical and Comparative Perspective*. New York: Basic Books, 1963.

——. *Political Man: The Social Bases of Politics*. Garden City, N.Y.: Doubleday and Co., 1963.

Lubell, Samuel. *The Future of American Politics*. New York: Harper and Brothers, 1952.

[Lutheran Church—Missouri Synod.] *Statistisches Jahrbuch der deutschen evang.-lutherischen Synode von Missouri, Ohio, und anderen Staaten für das Jahr 1885*. St. Louis: Luth. Concordia-Verlag, 1886.

——. *Synodal Bericht. Statistisches Jahrbuch der deutschen evang.-lutherischen Synode von Missouri, Ohio und anderen Staaten für das Jahr 1900*. St. Louis: Concordia Publishing House, 1901.

——. [Nebraska District.] *Synodal-Bericht des Nebraska-Distrikts der deutschen evang.-luth. Synod von Missouri, Ohio, und anderen Staaten*. 1st, 3rd, and 6th reports, 1882, 1885, 1889. St. Louis: Luth. Concordia Verlag, 1882–1890.

Malin, James C. *The Grassland of North America : Prolegomena to its History with Addenda.* Lawrence, Kan.: published by the author, 1961.

Martin, Sister M. Aquinata. *The Catholic Church on the Nebraska Frontier (1854–1885).* Washington: Catholic University of America, 1937.

McAvoy, Thomas T., ed. *Roman Catholicism and the American Way of Life.* Notre Dame, Ind.: University of Notre Dame Press, 1960.

Memorial and Biographical Record and Illustrated Compendium of Biography . . . of Butler, Polk, Seward, York, and Fillmore Counties, Nebraska. Chicago: Geo. A. Ogle and Co., 1899.

Merrill, Horace Samuel. *Bourbon Democracy of the Middle West, 1865–1896.* Baton Rouge: Louisiana State University Press, 1953.

[Methodist Episcopal Church. West German Conference]. *Deutscher Kalender für das Jahr 1901. Verhandlungen und Berichte der 22sten jahrlichen Sitzung der West Deutschen Konferenz der Bischöflichen Methodistenkirche . . . 1900.* Cincinnati: Jennings and Pye, n.d.

Meyer, Carl S., ed. *Moving Frontiers : Readings in the History of the Lutheran Church–Missouri Synod.* St. Louis: Concordia Publishing House, 1964.

Morton, J. Sterling, Albert Watkins, and George L. Miller. *Illustrated History of Nebraska.* 2 vols. Lincoln: Jacob North and Co., 1907. vol. 3. Lincoln: Western Publishing and Engraving Co., 1913.

Nebraska State Gazetteer and Business Directory for 1882–1883. Compiled and published by J. M. Wolfe. Omaha: Herald Book Printing House, 1882.

Niebuhr, Helmut Richard. *The Social Sources of Denominationalism.* New York: Meridian Books, 1960.

Nugent, Walter T. K. *The Tolerant Populists : Kansas Populism and Nativism.* Chicago: University of Chicago Press, 1963.

Olson, James C. *History of Nebraska.* Lincoln: University of Nebraska Press, 1955.

——. *J. Sterling Morton.* Lincoln: University of Nebraska Press, 1942.

Outhouse, Meroe J. *A History of Stanton County, Nebraska.* (Submitted as a Master's thesis, Colorado State Teachers College, 1944.) N.p.: n.d.

Overton, Richard C. *Burlington West : A Colonization History of the Burlington Railroad.* Cambridge: Harvard University Press, 1941.

Park, Robert E., and Herbert Miller. *Old World Traits Transplanted.* New York: Harper and Brothers, 1921.

Phillips, G. W., ed. *Past and Present of Platte County, Nebraska.* 2 vols. Chicago: S. J. Clarke Publishing Co., 1915.

Portrait and Biographical Album of Otoe and Cass Counties, Nebraska. Chicago: Chapman Brothers, 1889.

Reilly, Daniel F. *The School Controversy (1891–1893)*. Washington: Catholic University of America Press, 1943.

Rölvaag, Ole E. *Giants in the Earth: A Saga of the Prairie*. New York: Harper and Brothers, 1927.

———. *Peder Victorious*. New York: Harper and Brothers, 1929.

Roseboom, Eugene H. *A History of Presidential Elections*. New York: Macmillan Co., 1957.

Rossiter, Clinton. *Parties and Politics in America*. Ithaca: Cornell University Press, 1960.

Rowell, George P. *American Newspaper Directory* [1889, 1901]. New York: Geo. P. Rowell Co., 1889, 1901.

Sandoz, Mari. *Old Jules*. Boston: Little, Brown, and Co., 1935.

Schock, Adolph. *In Quest of Free Land*. San Jose, Calif.: San Jose State College, 1964.

Scoville, C. H., compiler. *History of the Elkhorn Valley, Nebraska*. Chicago: National Publishing Co., 1892.

Sheldon, Addison E. *Nebraska: The Land and the People*. 3 vols. Chicago: Lewis Publishing Co., 1931.

Shrader, Forrest B. *A History of Washington County, Nebraska*. N.p.: 1937.

Sinclair, Andrew. *The Better Half: The Emancipation of the American Woman*. New York: Harper and Row, 1965.

Smith, William C. *Americans in the Making: The Natural History of the Assimilation of Immigrants*. New York: Appleton-Century-Crofts, 1939.

Solomon, Barbara Miller. *Ancestors and Immigrants: A Changing New England Tradition*. New York: John Wiley and Sons, 1956.

Staatsverband Nebraska. *Gründung und Entwicklung des Staatsverband Nebraska. Jahres-Bericht der Beamten*. N.p.: Dec. 1915. (Werkmeister Collection, Nebraska State Historical Society.)

Story of Peace Lutheran Church, Deshler, Nebraska, 1883–1933. 50th anniversary pamphlet. N.p.: n.d.

Thomas, William I. and Florian Znaniecki. *The Polish Peasant in Europe and America*. 2 vols. Boston: Richard G. Badger, 1918.

U.S. Bureau of the Census. *Immigrants and Their Children. 1920*. Prepared by Niles Carpenter. Census Monographs VII. Washington: Government Printing Office, 1927.

[U.S. Work Projects Administration]. *Nebraska Party Platforms, 1858–1940*. Sponsored by the University of Nebraska. March, 1940.

Vander Zanden, James W. *American Minority Relations: The Sociology of Race and Ethnic Groups*. New York: Ronald Press, 1963.

Walker, Mack. *Germany and the Emigration, 1816–1885*. Cambridge: Harvard University Press, 1964.

Warner, W. Lloyd and Leo Srole. *The Social Systems of American Ethnic Groups*. New Haven: Yale University Press, 1945.

[Wegener, A. F.] *A Brief History of the Southern Nebraska District of the Lutheran Church–Missouri Synod, 1922–1947*. N.p.: Southern Nebraska District, 1947.

Wiebe, Robert H. *The Search for Order, 1877–1920*. New York: Hill and Wang, 1967.

Winther, Sophus Keith. *Mortgage Your Heart*. New York: Macmillan Co., 1937.

Wittke, Carl. *The German-Language Press in America*. Lexington: University of Kentucky Press, 1957.

———. *We Who Built America: The Saga of the Immigrant*. Rev. ed. Cleveland: Press of Western Reserve University, 1964.

Yinger, J. Milton. *A Minority Group in American Society*. New York: McGraw-Hill, 1965.

Articles

Ander, O. Fritiof. "The Immigrant Church and the Patrons of Husbandry," *Agricultural History*, VIII (October, 1934), 155–168.

Aydelotte, William O. "Quantification in History," *American Historical Review*, LXXI (April, 1966), 803–825.

Bargen, Peter F. "Mennonite Land Settlement Policies," *Mennonite Life*, XV (October, 1960), 187–190.

Benson, Lee. "Research Problems in American Political Historiography," in Mirra Komarovsky, ed. *Common Frontiers of the Social Sciences*. Glencoe: The Free Press, 1957, pp. 113–183.

Boeck, George A. "A Historical Note on the Uses of Census Returns," *Mid-America*, XLIV (January, 1962), 46–50.

Buchanan, J. R. "The Great Railroad Migration into Northern Nebraska," *Proceedings and Collections of the Nebraska State Historical Society*, (2nd series, vol. X), XV (1907), 25–34.

Burnham, Walter Dean. "The Changing Shape of the American Political Universe," *American Political Science Review*, LIX (March, 1965), 7–28.

Cochrane, Thomas C. "The 'Presidential Synthesis' in American History," *American Historical Review*, LIII (July, 1948), 748–759.

Coletta, Paolo E. "The Morning Star of the Reformation: William Jennings Bryan's First Congressional Campaign," *Nebraska History*, XXXVII (June, 1956), 102–119.

———. "The Nebraska Democratic State Convention of April 13–14, 1892," *Nebraska History*, XXXIX (December, 1958), 317–333.

————. "William Jennings Bryan's First Nebraska Years," *Nebraska History*, XXXIII (June, 1952), 71–94.

Daniels, George H. "Immigrant Vote in the 1860 Election: The Case of Iowa," *Mid-America*, XLIV (July, 1962), 146–162.

Degler, Carl N. "American Political Parties and the Rise of the City," *Journal of American History*, LI (June, 1964), 41–59.

Diamond, William. "Urban and Rural Voting in 1896," *American Historical Review*, XLVI (January, 1941), 281–305.

Dobbert, G. A. "German-Americans Between New and Old Fatherland, 1870–1914," *American Quarterly*, XIX (Winter, 1967), 663–680.

Dorpalen, Andreas. "The German Element and the Issues of the Civil War," *Mississippi Valley Historical Review*, XXIX (June, 1942), 55–76.

Eisenstadt, S. N. "The Place of Elites and Primary Groups in the Absorption of New Immigrants in Israel," *American Journal of Sociology*, LVII (November, 1951), 222–231.

Eldersveld, Samuel J. "Theory and Method in Voting Behavior Research," *Journal of Politics*, XIII (February, 1951), 70–87.

Fuchs, Lawrence. "Some Political Aspects of Immigration," *Law and Contemporary Problems*, XXI (Spring, 1956), 270–283.

"Geschichte des Nebraska-Distrikts," *Ev.-Luth. Gemeinde-Blatt*, Organ der Allgemeine Evang.-Luth. Synode von Wisconsin und anderen Staaten, LXI (August 15, 1926), 257–265.

Gingerich, Melvin, "Russian Mennonites React to Their New Environment," *Mennonite Life*, XV (October, 1960), 175–180.

Gordon, Milton M. "Assimilation in America: Theory and Reality," *Daedalus*, XC (Spring, 1961), 263–285.

Handlin, Oscar. "Historical Perspectives on the American Ethnic Group," *Daedalus*, XC (Spring, 1961), 220–232.

Hays, Samuel P. "History as Human Behavior," *Iowa Journal of History*, LVIII (July, 1960), 193–206.

————. "Political Parties and the Community-Society Continuum," in William N. Chambers and Walter D. Burnham, eds. *The American Party System: Stages of Political Development*. New York: Oxford University Press, 1967, pp. 152–187.

————. "The Social Analysis of American Political History, 1880–1920," *Political Science Quarterly*, LXXX (September, 1965), 373–394.

Hollingshead, August de Belmont. "Changes in Land Ownership as an Index of Succession in Rural Communities," *American Journal of Sociology* XLIII (March, 1938), 764–777.

————. "The Life Cycle of Nebraska Rural Churches," *Rural Sociology*, II (June, 1937), 180–191.

Johnson, Hildegard Binder. "The Location of German Immigrants in the Middle West," *Annals of the Association of American Geographers*, XLI (March, 1951), 1–41.

Kennedy, Ruby Jo Reeves. "Single or Triple Melting Pot? Intermarriage Trends in New Haven, 1870–1940," *American Journal of Sociology*, XLIX (January, 1944), 331–339.

Kleppner, Paul J. "Lincoln and the Immigrant Vote: A Case of Religious Polarization," *Mid-America*, XLVIII (July, 1966), 176–195.

Luebke, Frederick C. "The German-American Alliance in Nebraska, 1910–1917," *Nebraska History*, IL (Summer, 1968), 165–168.

———. "German Immigrants and the Churches in Nebraska, 1889–1915," *Mid-America*, L (April, 1968), 116–130.

———. "The Immigrant Condition as a Factor Contributing to the Conservatism of the Lutheran Church—Missouri Synod," *Concordia Historical Institute Quarterly*, XXXVIII (April, 1965), 19–28.

———, ed. "Superpatriotism in World War I: The Experience of a Lutheran Pastor," *Concordia Historical Institute Quarterly*, XLI (February, 1968) 3–11.

Manley, Robert N. "Language, Loyalty, and Liberty: The Nebraska State Council of Defense and the Lutheran Churches, 1917–1918," *Concordia Historical Institute Quarterly*, XXXVII (April, 1964), 1–16.

Miller, D. Paul. "Jansen, Nebraska: A Story of Community Adjustment," *Nebraska History*, XXXV (June, 1954), 127–136.

———. "The Story of the Jansen Churches," *Mennonite Life*, X (January, 1955), 38–40.

Mills, C. Wright. "The American Business Elite: A Collective Portrait," *Journal of Economic History*, V (Supplemental issue, 1945), 20–44.

"Nebraska Newspapers," *Nebraska History Magazine*, XV (April–June, 1934), 67–75.

Parsons, Stanley B., Jr. "Who Were the Nebraska Populists?" *Nebraska History*, XLIV (June, 1963), 83–99.

Renner, Frederick. "Reminiscences of Territorial Days," *Proceedings and Collections of the Nebraska State Historical Society*, 2nd series, V (1902), 60–68.

Robinson, W. S. "Ecological Correlations and the Behavior of Individuals," *American Sociological Review*, XV (June, 1950), 351–357.

Rodgers, Jack W. "The Foreign Language Issue in Nebraska, 1918–1923," *Nebraska History*, XXXIX (March, 1958), 1–22.

Sallet, Richard. "Russlanddeutsche Siedlungen in den Vereinigten Staaten von Amerika," *Jahrbuch der Deutsch-Amerikanischen Historischen Gesellschaft von Illinois*, XXXI (1931), 5–126.

Schafer, Joseph. "Who Elected Lincoln?" *American Historical Review*, XLVII (October, 1941), 51–63.

Trask, David F. "A Note on the Politics of Populism," *Nebraska History*, XLVI (June, 1965), 157–161.

Unruh, John D., Jr. "The Burlington and Missouri River Railroad Brings the Mennonites to Nebraska, 1873–1878," *Nebraska History*, XLV (March and June, 1964), 3–30, 177–206.

Wilhite, Ann Wiegman. "Sixty-Five Years Till Victory: A History of Woman Suffrage in Nebraska," *Nebraska History*, IL (Summer, 1968), 149–164.

Yinger, J. Milton. "Social Forces Involved in Group Identification or Withdrawal," *Daedalus*, XC (Spring, 1961), 247–262.

Unpublished Theses and Dissertations

Anderson, Helen Marie. "The Influence of Railway Advertising upon the Settlement of Nebraska." Unpublished Master's thesis, University of Nebraska, 1926.

Bienhoff, Esther Alma. "The Original German Settlement at Grand Island, Nebraska (1857–1866)." Unpublished Master's thesis, University of Nebraska, 1929.

Boell, Jesse E. "William Jennings Bryan Before 1896." Unpublished Master's thesis, University of Nebraska, 1929.

Carlson, Martin E. "A History of the American Protective Association in Nebraska." Unpublished Master's thesis, Colorado State College of Education, 1947.

Cherny, Robert W. "The 1940 Election in Nebraska with Special Attention to Isolationist Voting Among Non-Urban German Stock Voters of the State." Unpublished Master's thesis, Columbia University, 1967.

Fuhlrodt, Verne C. "The Pioneer History of Fontenelle, Nebraska." Unpublished Master's thesis, University of Nebraska, 1930.

Hollingshead, August de Belmont. "Trends in Community Development, A Study of Ecological and Institutional Processes in Thirty-Four Southeastern Nebraska Communities, 1854–1934." Unpublished Ph.D. dissertation, University of Nebraska, 1935.

Jakl, Mary Ann. "The Immigration and Population of Nebraska to 1870." Unpublished Master's thesis, University of Nebraska, 1936.

Murphy, Francis Allen. "The Foundation and Expansion of the Catholic Church in Nebraska, 1850–1900." Unpublished Master's thesis, University of Nebraska, 1933.

Parsons, Stanley B., Jr. "The Populist Context: Nebraska Farmers and Their Antagonists, 1882–1895." Unpublished Ph.D. dissertation, State University of Iowa, 1964.

Schmidt, Theodore. "The Mennonites of Nebraska." Unpublished Master's thesis, University of Nebraska, 1933.

Sellin, Lloyd Bernard. "The Settlement of Nebraska to 1880." Unpublished Master's thesis, University of Southern California, 1940.

Siekmann, Louis H. "The German Element and Its Part in the Early Development of Otoe County, Nebraska," Unpublished Master's thesis, University of Nebraska, 1930.

Spencer, Morris N. "The Union Pacific's Utilization of Its Land Grant with Emphasis on Its Colonization Program." Unpublished Ph.D. dissertation, University of Nebraska, 1950.

Storms, Helen Elizabeth. "A Study of the Nebraska State Election of 1890." Unpublished Master's thesis, University of Nebraska, 1924.

Stough, Ruth Knox. "The American Protective Association." Unpublished Master's thesis, University of Nebraska, 1931.

Stubenhaus, Kieve. "Origins and Growth of the Nebraska Population, 1870–1900." Unpublished Master's thesis, University of Nebraska, 1935.

Trask, David Stephens. "Anti-Populism in Nebraska." Unpublished Master's thesis, University of Nebraska, 1968.

Wegener, Wilfried William. "A Historical Study of the Parochial Schools of Trinity, Immanuel, St. Peter's, and St. Mark's Lutheran Churches of the Missouri Synod in Thayer County, Nebraska." Unpublished Bachelor's thesis, Concordia Teachers College, 1941.

Zimmerman, William F. "Legislative History of Nebraska Populism, 1890–1895." Unpublished Master's thesis, University of Nebraska, 1926.

Index

Absorption. *See* Assimilation

Acculturation. *See* Assimilation

Advertising, by immigrants, 45

Agricultural data: correlated with election data, 118–119

Albion, Nebr., 50

Alien land ownership, 140

Allen, William V., 168

"American letters," 29

American Protective Association, 44, 154, 155, 157, 161, 162, 167

Amish Mennonites, 29, 86

Andres, Philip, 176

Anglo-Americans. *See* Native Americans

Anglo-conformity, 43

Anti-Catholicism, 43. *See also* American Protective Association

Anti-Monopoly party, 127, 131, 132, 135, 139, 183; attraction of, for Germans, 90, 130

Anti-Saloon League, 175

Assimilation: attitudes of native Americans toward, 42–44; characteristics of rapid, 36–37, 70, 124, 137; characteristics of slow, 37–40, 70, 143, 181; and ethnic institutions, 44–48; related to reference groups, 49–51; theories of, 34 n, 59–60, 70 n, 195; types of described, 33–34; variables influencing rates of, 35–36

Association of German Agricultural Societies of Nebraska, 147

Aughey, Samuel, 26

Australian ballot, 72 n, 144, 155

Baptists, 66, 101, 113, 145, 175 n; German conferences of 28, 57

Beatrice Post, Die, 41, 170

Beckman, Andrew, 155

Bellevue, Nebr., 16

Beneke, Gustav, 136

Benson, Lee, 6–8, 15, 184

Berge, George, 172

Bernecker, Oscar E., 135

Bimetallism. *See* Free silver

Bismarck, Otto von, 161

Bittenbender, Ada M., 128

Blaine, James G., 134, 135, 136, 182

Blegen, Theodore, 29, 54

Blue Valley Blade (Seward), 123, 134, 136

Boer War, 170

Bohemians, 6, 35, 85, 89, 106, 108, 110, 132, 133

Boyd, James E., 144, 145, 146, 147, 153

Brede, Adam, 173

Bruechert, F. H. W., 145

Brugger, Melchior, 137, 185

Brunner, Edmund de S., 42

Bryan, William Jennings, 79, 103, 115, 140, 152, 155, 156, 158, 159, 160, 161, 162, 170, 171, 172

Businessman and Bankers Association, 142

Catholics, 6, 44, 51, 56, 57, 175; in Cuming County, 108; in Madison County, 106; in Otoe County, 76; in Platte County, 99, 102; and political party identification, 65–66, 69; settlements of German, 18, 27, 50, 57 n; in Seward County, 85; voting behavior of, from 1880 to 1890, 149–150

213